BASIC
COMPUTING

A COMPLETE COURSE

BASIC
COMPUTING

A COMPLETE COURSE

Tim Crawford, B.A., B.Ed., C.D.P.
Director of Business Education
Eastview Secondary School
Barrie, Ontario

McGraw-Hill Ryerson Limited
Toronto, Montreal, New York, St. Louis, San Francisco, Auckland, Bogotá,
Guatemala, Hamburg, Johannesburg, Lisbon, London, Madrid, Mexico, New
Delhi, Panama, Paris, San Juan, São Paulo, Singapore, Sydney, Tokyo

BASIC Computing: A Complete Course

Copyright © McGraw-Hill Ryerson Limited, 1981.

3 4 5 6 7 8 9 10   D   10 9 8 7 6 5 4 3 2

Printed and bound in Canada

Canadian Cataloguing in Publication Data

Crawford, Tim, date
BASIC computing

For use in schools.
Includes index.
ISBN 0-07-548076-X

1. Electronic digital computers. 2. Electronic
digital computers—Programming. 3. Electronic
data processing. I. Title.

QA76.C72   001.64   C81-094519-3

Acknowledgements

Bill Waddell, Randy Arthur, Anthony Scian, Commodore Canada Ltd., Dave Hook, Bertram Kelso, Leslie Smith, Frances DeWilde, Sylvia Fuchs, Bev Crawford, and all the suppliers of hardware who so generously consented to provide photos and information to make the text a better learning tool.

To four people
who were
at
the right place
at
the right time
with a hand
to provide
a boost
or a shove—,

Wishart Campbell
W. Allen Fisher
Harold J. Johnson
Bob Mitchell

TABLE
OF
CONTENTS

TO THE STUDENT

You do not have to be told that the era of computers is upon us. Computers make the present most interesting and will make the future fascinating. An introductory course in computers should provide you with the following:

1) a general understanding of what computers are and how they work
2) a general understanding of how computers can be used to solve certain problems in many diverse sectors of our society to provide a better economy, more exciting scientific progress, better health care and in general a better way of life.
3) a basis of information which would aid you in your chosen career whether or not it directly involves computers
4) an appreciation of the discipline of computer science and an opportunity to judge whether or not you should pursue some aspect of computing as a career
5) sufficient understanding of computers so that you would feel comfortable with a computer either in your career, at home using the computer as a household appliance, or using the computer as a recreational device

Obviously the benefit you receive from this course will at least in part be proportional to the effort you put into the course.

There are many different topics in the text. Some you will find to be routine, but others should stimulate considerable curiosity and interest. Perhaps unlike any other subject, this course will provide you with academic highs and lows as you struggle with a problem until you obtain a solution. With that solution comes satisfaction and in some cases the exhilaration of making the computer work correctly.

CAREERS

There are literally hundreds of computer related jobs. Programming is only one small (but important) part of the computer scene. If you find that you do not enjoy programming, as some students do, do not become discouraged. The material and concepts you will learn in the balance of the course will be invaluable in non-programming computer careers. Key people are needed in many different positions which are available in information processing. Clever and/or hard working people who just do not have the programming knack will feel very comfortable working with computers. In other words, DO NOT "TURN OFF" COMPUTERS SHOULD PROGRAMMING NOT BE PART OF YOUR GAME!

So get involved, learn, enjoy. Build a broad basis for your future career or careers (for you will likely have 5 to 10 careers if the current trend continues). Your teacher or instructor will be glad to work with you to help discover your interests and aptitudes and help you develop along the lines most useful to you. Good luck!

POSSIBLE ORGANIZATION OF COURSES

Survey Course (core)	Additional Units (for open-ended study, or for advanced and/or technology students)

LEVEL I MODULES	**LEVEL II MODULES**

PART I COMPUTERS, PROBLEM SOLVING AND PROGRAMMING

PART II A LOGICAL APPROACH

PART III INFORMATION PROCESSING

PART IV EXPANDING USES AND THE FUTURE

APPENDIX Programming Code of Ethics

---

* Alternate starting points

** There is a high level of student interest in these topics. Consider covering them earlier in the course—perhaps after chapter 7 or 12.

*** De-emphasize this section with students who are taking a general interest course. Put extra emphasis on the core of this section with streamed students preparing for a career in vocational programming on a small business system.

Part I: COMPUTERS, PROBLEM SOLVING AND PROGRAMMING

CHAPTER 1

WHERE DID COMPUTERS COME FROM?

Level 1

MICRO COMPUTERS AND ROBOTS

A robot, whether it is R2D2 from the movie *Star Wars,* or whether it is an automated machine in a factory, is controlled by some sort of guiding mechanism. Modern airplanes are, in a sense, robots, in that many of them are able to take off, fly and land by themselves—a remarkable achievement! Machines are able to act as if they are intelligent.

The micro computer directs the robot-like action of most modern devices. It enables these devices to operate in a 'thinking' fashion. The micro computer has caused a dramatic acceleration in the development of automated machines. A brief overview of major stages in the development of computers should bring you up to date.

Figure 1.1

EARLY COMPUTING

The very first computer was the human brain. All of us are able to *compute*. The computing might be some type of arithmetic or some other kind of processing. We are able to store in our brain both data and instructions. Of course we are able to *follow* most of those stored instructions. Our brain can:

RECEIVE INFORMATION
GIVE OUT INFORMATION
STORE DATA
STORE INSTRUCTIONS
FOLLOW THOSE STORED INSTRUCTIONS
MAKE CALCULATIONS

Perhaps the first human computing which could be demonstrated was counting. Shepherds kept track of sheep as they went out to pasture by putting stones in a circle drawn on the ground with a stick. Each stone would represent one sheep. As the sheep came into the fold in the evening the shepherd would remove the stones. If, when all the sheep appeared to be in, there were one or more stones left in the circle the shepherd would know that some sheep were lost.

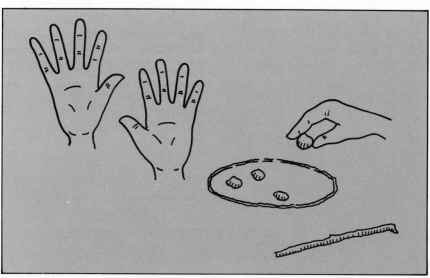

Figure 1.2

Number systems were developed to make easier the various calculations which had to be done. Perhaps as a direct result of us having 10 fingers, the **decimal number system** was developed using 10 as its base. (More about base numbers later.) Certainly many of us first learned to calculate or count by using our fingers.

THE ABACUS

The Chinese are given credit for the development of the **abacus**. This simple device enables difficult calculations to be made quite rapidly. Different values are assigned to the various beads. By moving the beads complex calculations are performed by this ingenious device.

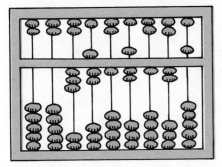

Figure 1.3

DEVELOPING A CALCULATOR

In the early 17th century **Napier** took the next step up from the abacus to make difficult computations easier. He developed a series of rods or 'bones' as they were called on which numbers were printed. Calculations involving large numbers were made by shifting the rods. Napier's principles were the foundation of logarithm tables which were used for many years by mathematicians and engineers for complex calculating. Of course the modern calculator and computer have replaced the log tables.

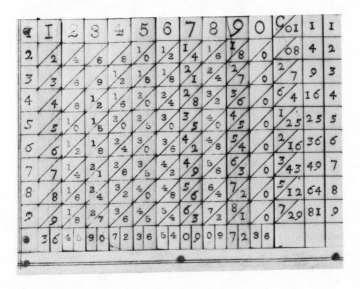

Pascal developed a device much like the distance indicator on an automobile. Calculating was done by rotating wheels. A complete rotation of the right-most wheel caused the wheel to its left to rotate one notch or one-tenth of a rotation.

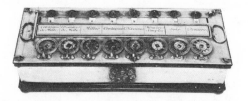

BABBAGE'S ENGINE

An inventor, **Charles Babbage**, developed a **differential engine** which could do complex calculation. The design was valid, but technology was not sufficiently refined at the time to make an accurate device. Society, by the way, was not able to really understand nor accept the principle involved. Babbage was considered to be a fool! It was many years after the death of Babbage that his idea was dusted off and its potential fully appreciated.

Figure 1.4

LEIBNIZ'S STEP WHEELS

The mechanical calculator and devices such as meters to measure electricity usage and automobile odometers find their roots in a **step wheel machine** invented by Pascal and developed by **Wilhelm Leibniz**. Leibniz's machine could multiply by repeated additions.

JACQUARD'S LOOM

A weaver called **Jacquard** found it difficult to accurately produce various patterns. He developed the idea of punching holes in a certain pattern in thin boards. Rods, which control the weaving process, would push through the board wherever there was a hole. By placing a number of these boards in a type of chain, complex patterns could be woven. (By the way, a certain type of fabric with an intricately woven pattern is called Jacquard.)

Figure 1.5

A MAJOR STEP FORWARD RESULTING FROM A SERIOUS NEED

In the late 1800s a problem was developing for those who were responsible for taking and making reports on the census. Massive amounts of data about a nation's population is collected every 10 years. In the United States the tabulation of the census data was taking longer each time around. For example, it took up to 7 years to complete reports of the 1881 census. It was estimated that it would take about 12 years to complete the same report on the 1891 census. In other words, the final report would come out well after the raw data for the *next* census had been collected.

HOLLERITH'S TABULATING MACHINES

Herman Hollerith worked for the census board and experimented with Jacquard's idea of the punched board. Hollerith developed a system of punching holes in cards. The holes represented census data. These cards were run through, what was then, high speed **tabulation devices** developed by Hollerith. Various reports could be produced by running the cards through the devices, tabulating different types of data each time. As a result of the development of this system, the 1891 census was taken and the reports tabulated within a couple of years. Hollerith's unit record devices were widely used at least into the 1970s.

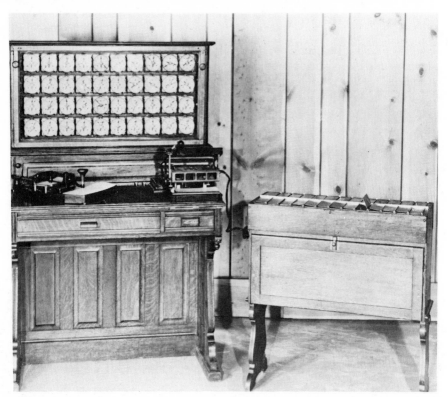

Figure 1.6

THE DEVELOPMENT OF THE ELECTRONIC COMPUTER

Move ahead in time from 1891 to about 1944. **Dr. Howard Aiken** of Harvard University wanted to use modern electronics to produce a machine which would do complex computations much in the same way that Babbage had hoped his machine would perform. Unlike Babbage, Aiken had modern technology working for him rather than against him. Dr. Aiken put together over 3000 switches which would perform the function of 'moving the beads on this electronic abacus.' His five tonne machine was able to calculate very rapidly—for that time!

A few years later **Eckert** and **Mauchly** used vacuum tubes to replace most of the switches found in Aiken's device, resulting in computations

1000 times faster. A number of models were produced, each better than the former.

The electronic development of the 1940s and 1950s had a parallel development in the application of mathematical principles to the new computers. A mathematician called **Von Neumann** realized that numbers and even stored programs could be coded in the computer using the binary number system. (More about that system later.) Storing both data and instructions electronically was a major link in making the developing computer much more diversified.

THE FIRST COMMERCIALLY AVAILABLE COMPUTER

Univac and International Business Machines saw the potential of this invention and invested considerable money to develop a machine that could be widely used in the business world. In a sense IBM combined the punched card system as developed by Hollerith, which it had been selling, with the electronics similar to those used by Aiken. These computers used data on cards as input and a high speed printer. They became widely used in business and industry. The mass produced, electronic computer was born.

Figure 1.7

Since then, there have been many refinements and changes *inside* the computer. The main principles, however, remain the same—high speed data entry, high speed processing or calculating and high speed printing. Devices for storing data electronically made the electronic computer even more useful.

ADVANCING TECHNOLOGY

As technology advanced the inside of the computer changed. The switches used by Aiken became vacuum tubes, which in turn became transistors. It was found that the function of the transistor could be carried out using miniature circuitry. Ultimately, complete complex circuits could be created on a small 'chip' the size of a finger nail. At this stage the computer became so small it was considered to be 'micro.' The inside of the computer shrank, and the speed and power of the computer increased.

Level 2

EVOLVING TECHNOLOGY

The heart of IBM's early computers were a series of **mechanical registers**, similar in nature to the mechanical calculator of Leibniz. A series of cog wheels were used to add or subtract. Part of the programmer's task was to hook up wires to run from certain areas on the read station (where the data cards were read) into the appropriate calculator. The same information might also be sent to the printer. The programmer planned where wires were required. This task was called **panel wiring**.

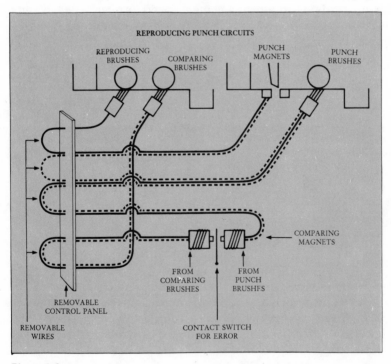

Figure 1.8

In producing an invoice, for example, each card relating to a purchase was read. Signals would be sent to the tabulators or calculators. After the final results were calculated a series of wires would carry the results to the printer.

CORE STORAGE

With the development of technology, it was found that instead of storing data in cog wheels, data could be represented electronically. The first electronic medium used was **core storage**. Very tiny iron rings could be magnetized or de-magnetized on command. By running a weak current

Figure 1.9

impulse along each of two wires intersecting inside the ring, a magnetic field around the wires was created causing the ring to become magnetized. A magnetized ring was considered to be 'on' and a ring not magnetized was considered to be 'off.'

Figure 1.9(a)

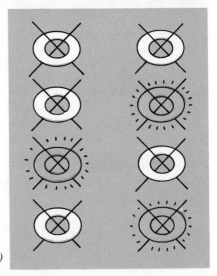

Figure 1.9(b)

Various patterns of *on* or *off* rings represent data. Data from cards was converted to electrical impulses which passed through electronic circuits to be stored in core. Core was used to store the results of calculations. Core effectively replaced the mechanical registers or calculators of the earlier computers. Later it was found that with additional core a *program* could be loaded into core and executed by the computer. This eliminated the need for panel wiring as a programming technique. This one electronic development opened the door to much more convenient and more sophisticated programming!

Although better methods of electronic storage have been developed, core still is used in certain special applications, namely in some space craft applications.

THE TRANSISTOR

Modern science enabled the next dramatic breakthrough in computer technology. The vacuum tubes which replaced the switches of Aiken's computer generated considerable heat and required that the computer room have powerful air-conditioning.

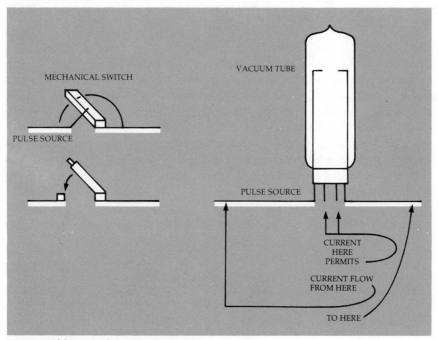

Figure 1.9(c)

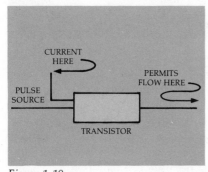

Figure 1.10

The tubes were also somewhat unreliable because they would burn out and have to be replaced. This resulted in considerable 'down-time.' Bell laboratories were working with a type of material that was a semi-conductor. It was neither a good conductor nor a bad one. Under certain conditions it would conduct electricity, whereas under other conditions it would not. A small electrical current applied to this "transfer resistor" or *transistor* as it became known, would cause it to conduct electricity or switch 'on.'

This tiny Nobel Prize winning development could replace the vacuum tube in computers. In fact, over 200 of these electronic switches could fit in the space of one vacuum tube! Electrical impulses no longer had to go through the vacuumed space of the tube but could now go through solid circuits. **Solid state circuitry** was born.

INTEGRATING CIRCUITS

Instead of relatively thick wires forming the circuits inside the computer, a circuit of thin wires and transistors could be made on a thin board. Wires from either end of the transistor could be pushed through holes in a **circuit board.** Parts of one side of the board were treated with a compound in a circuit pattern. In other words, paths to carry currents were drawn on the board with special 'ink.' The board was then floated in molten solder. Lines of solder formed where there was 'ink' making up the circuits. Although this was an important breakthrough this process was far too slow for the fantastic demand for circuit boards. Prices of computer equipment, therefore, remained high.

Figure 1.11

THE SILICON CHIP

A firm called Intel was experimenting with some material called **silicon.** A silicon rod is made from the same material as ordinary sand. It is cut into thin wafers about the size of a large silver coin. Silicon itself is neutral with respect to electricity, being neither positive nor negative, so chemicals are added. Certain chemicals make the silicon positive, whereas other chemicals make it negative. It was found that by a chemical process, very tiny parts of silicon could be made into an electronic switch. The switch could be turned on or off many times in a second and appeared not to wear out. In fact, the switch could turn on and off a billion times in one second.

If that does not boggle the mind consider this. Up to 5000 of these high speed, durable switches could be created in the space inside this small letter 'o.'

Figure 1.12

LARGE SCALE INTEGRATION

It was found that design engineers could plan very complex circuits on very large sheets of paper—paper which would cover a large section of a wall.

Once designed, the pattern is reduced photographically and **etched** on one of these **silicon wafers**. After applying a chemical process, the pathways for currents are created. Each line on the original design becomes a tiny conductor. The chemical process also creates the micro switches.

Many of the same patterns of this circuit can be micro-engraved on one wafer. This process is called *large scale integration* or LSI. The wafer is then cut into sections about 0.5 cm^2. The small section called a **chip** is hooked up electrically to its host device with fine gold wires and prongs which form part of this host block.

Figure 1.13

THE MICRO PROCESSOR

Putting many complex circuits together as a unit is called **large scale integration**. The resulting chip should really be called a **micro-processor**. It is the micro-processor which enabled development of the digital watch,

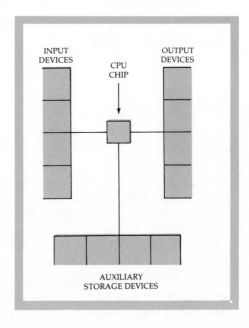

Figure 1.14

pocket calculator, and the very popular video games. More importantly the micro-processor gave birth to the micro-computer.

As you will find out later the micro-processor, the heart of the computer, must be able to do some specific functions. Certainly it must be able to calculate, that is, to do arithmetic. But the computer must be able to control the various devices which make up the whole computer. For example, the computer must be able to monitor and send signals to its output, either the video display tube or a printer.

These are specialized tasks that require a considerable amount of circuitry. Large scale integration of circuits has enabled computer designers to put onto one chip *all* the necessary circuits to do the processing, as well as control and monitor the various devices which form the rest of the computer system. Technology had produced a 'computer on a chip.'

Certainly two of the problems of the earlier computers were reliability and relatively slow speed. For example, at one time, computer designers could not build a computer which could operate at the speed they wanted because the wires inside were too long! They wanted to design a computer which would have no wires longer than 1 m, for it took too long for an electrical impulse to go from one end to the other! And just how fast does an electrical impulse move in a wire? About 27×10^7 m/sec! Recently the processing speed was almost doubled when technologists limited the length of any circuit to about 12 cm.

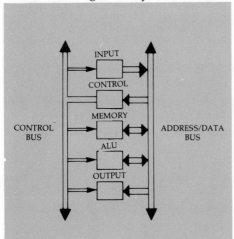

Figure 1.15

With the advent of the silicon chip, thousands of metres of wire in the old-fashioned sense were now etched on a chip about one-half the size of your thumb nail. And remember the circuits and 'switches' on the chip were almost indestructible. Now the technologists had the speed they wanted, the necessary reliability and compactness almost to an extreme.

COMPUTING FOR THE MASSES

Prior to the perfecting of Intel's magic chip, the computer language

BASIC was developed. It is an extremely simple but useful language. The humble tape cassette had also been developed. The language BASIC, the micro-processor and the cassette tape brought computer power to the average person who might have an interest in this field. No longer were computers expensive devices which rented for literally thousands of dollars per month. No longer could just big businesses, universities and government afford to rent a computer. Now the little guy had his own pet computer to play with!

CHECKING YOUR READING—LEVEL 1

1. What logical approach did the early shepherds have to keep track of their sheep?
2. What is the name given to the number system most commonly used by the general public? What is its base?
3. Perhaps the first calculating device was developed by the Chinese. What is this device called?
4. What did each of the following contribute to the development of the computer: Napier, Pascal, Liebniz, Babbage?
5. A weaver named Jacquard had something to do with modern data processing. What was his contribution?
6. What serious problem was developing in tabulating the census in the United States near the end of the last century? What was the name of the person who helped solve the problem?
7. What was the name of the person who developed the first electronic computer?
8. What contribution was made by Eckert and Maulchy and by Von Neumann?
9. What combination or 'mix' was performed by Univac or IBM to produce the first commercial, or business-oriented computer?
10. List in sequence, the devices which replaced the switches of the first electronic computer?

VOCABULARY ASSIGNMENT

Extract from this section words and phrases in **bold type**. Write a short, simple definition for each.

CHECKING YOUR READING—LEVEL 2

1. How was the early, commercial computer programmed?
2. How is core turned 'on'?
3. What was the major technological change which took place with the development of the transistor?
4. What is meant by the integration of circuits?
5. Compare and contrast the technology of the soldered transistorized circuit board and the silicon chip.

6. What is large scale integration or LSI?

VOCABULARY ASSIGNMENT

Continue building a vocabulary list by selecting key words and phrases in bold type from this section. Write a short, simple definition for each.

PROJECTS

1. Prepare a time line on which you may record the significant development of data processing up to the current time.
2. Establish a special notebook in which you may make certain special notes, or paste in news articles about information processing. On one of the inner pages set up a table of contents which you can keep up to date. Make your first entry in your scrapbook to get a start.
3. Begin a search for actual computer related material such as computer tape, punch paper tape, old circuit boards, discarded chips, old disc packs, old mechanical calculators, etc. If enough material becomes available not only will it be used in the classroom for illustrative purposes, but could also be used to set up a display case.
4. Begin a short research project into some aspect of early computers. For example, you might prepare a report on the workings of the Jacquard loom, the abacus or Napier's bones.
5. Establish a section in your scrapbook for computer applications. If you read or hear about an interesting computer application, make a brief write-up of it in this section of your scrapbook.

CHAPTER 2

WHAT IS A COMPUTER?

Level 1

JUST WHAT IS A COMPUTER?

As stated earlier, the human brain was the first computer. By studying it, one can identify certain functions which manufactured computers should have. The brain receives its information from a variety of senses, particularly those of sight and hearing. These senses are the brain's **input**.

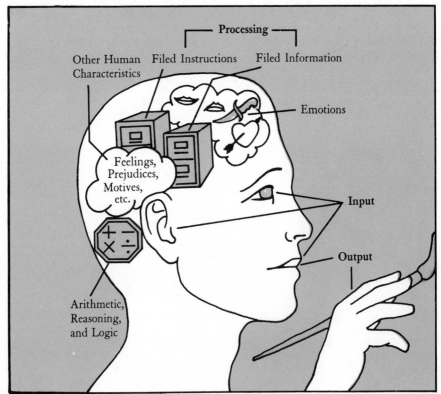

Figure 2.1

The brain is able to store information and combine information into a unique or creative pattern. The brain controls the movement of data as it moves in and out of the brain. The eyes and ears provide input. The most common form of **output** is speaking. Writing is another form. The brain also controls movement of information within the brain. It is able to store instructions and is able to follow instructions which have been stored.

The key functions of the brain's computer system, therefore, are:
1) input
2) storage and manipulation of data
3) storing instructions
4) following instructions
5) controlling the flow of data
6) output

WHAT MAKES THE COMPUTER DIFFERENT?

Many devices in existence today have input, some type of processing, and output. For example, a telephone has a microphone, speaker and electronics to transmit and receive signals. But what makes the computer unique is its ability to be programmed. It can carry out a wide variety of functions depending on certain conditions. Certainly the computer is helpless without a program. The program changes it from a useless pile of electronics into an amazing tool.

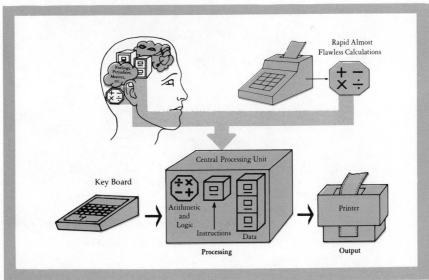

Figure 2.2

INPUT

The computer has three main parts: input, a processing unit, and output. At one time, the most common form of input was from computer cards.

Programs were punched into cards and read into memory. Similarly, data was key punched into cards or keyed onto magnetic tape. Large groups of data were then fed in through a **card reader** or **tape drive** for processing. This is called **batch processing**. **Direct entry** of data has become more popular. Direct entry means that the data is keyed directly into the computer by the operator or data entry clerks. This eliminates the two step process of punching data into cards or encoding it onto magnetic tape.

Figure 2.3

OUTPUT

The two most common forms of output are display and printing. In some business applications a 'hard copy' of output is required. In cases such as this the data is outputted on paper by a **printer.** Data on paper is available

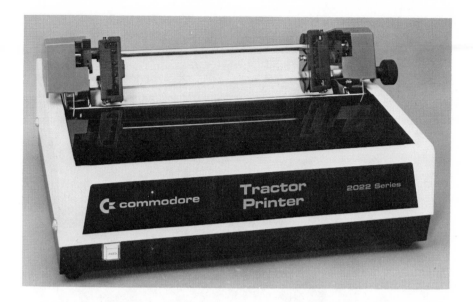

Figure 2.4

for filing, mailing, or studying. Payroll cheques, of course, would be produced by the printer.

If only a small amount of data is required from the computer to make an instant decision it is usually more convenient to have the data displayed on the video screen. This 'soft copy' of data is very convenient in applications such as airline reservation inquiry systems.

DATA VS. INSTRUCTIONS

Before discussing the central processor it is helpful to understand that there are different types of information handled by a computer. Data is processed, manipulated and stored. In order for the computer to do these tasks it must have a program in its memory. A program is made up of a

Figure 2.5

series of instructions. The instructions cause the computer to do some function. For example,

1 STEPHANIE BROWN   18   (Data)
2 ADD OVERTIME HOURS TO REGULAR HOURS
   (Instruction)

In example 1 above you will note that data is a statement of fact. In example 2 the instruction causes some action.

THE CPU

The heart of the computer is the **central processing unit** or CPU. This unit carries out all the **program instructions** which have been loaded in by the programmer. These instructions might include functions or actions such as:

Computer Functions	Type of Instruction
INPUT	INPUT or READ . . .
PROCESSING	ADD or SUBTRACT or DIVIDE or MULTIPLY . . .
OUTPUT	DISPLAY or PRINT or OUTPUT

Very simply, the computer could, for example, be programmed to *read* in some numeric data, *add* it all up and *print* the sum.

The CPU is composed of 3 main parts. One is called the **control**. All programmed instructions are moved into control, one at a time, to be analysed and carried out. Some instructions require arithmetic to be done on data.

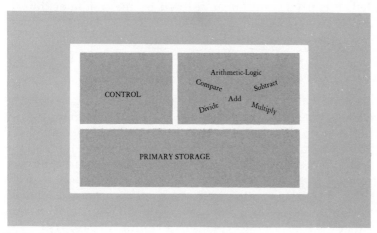

Figure 2.6

This arithmetic is done in a separate unit called the **arithmetic-logic unit** or ALU. The third main part of the CPU is **storage**. Stored in the storage section are *both instructions* put into the computer by the programmer, and *data*. The instructions are moved from storage to control to be carried out.

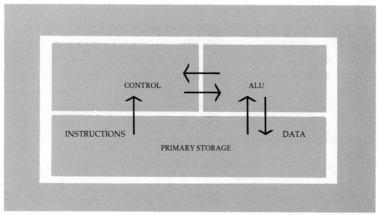

Figure 2.7

Data is moved from storage to the ALU for arithmetic to be carried out on it, or from storage to an output device.

STORAGE ADDRESSES

Storage can be thought of as many cells, each of which can hold a character. Digits or letters of the alphabet are examples of characters which can be stored. Groups of related characters are stored under an identifying system. Obviously stored data (and instructions) have to be found when needed. When they are initially stored by the computer the address of the cells used is recorded by the computer. To locate the information the computer looks up the **data address**.

REVIEW

Just to make sure that you are not too confused by all the new terms which have been presented in this section a short review is in order. The computer is made up of three main components. They are called the input, such as a keyboard; output, such as a video display tube; and the CPU. The central processing unit is itself made up of three parts: the control, the arithmetic-logic unit, or ALU, and storage. Programmed instructions and data are stored in addressable storage. Instructions are moved to the control section to be carried out or executed. Data is moved from storage to either the ALU for calculations or an output device.

THE CPU CONTROLS THE WHOLE COMPUTER

The CPU also has the task of monitoring the various devices hooked up to it. It sends and receives signals to and from the input and output devices. Much like a traffic officer it directs the total operation of the computer.

TYPES OF COMPUTERS

The most commonly used computer is the **digital** computer. Another type is the **analog**. The digital computer handles numbers and alphabetic information. It adds and subtracts. The analog computer *measures*. It measures speed and changes in speed. It measures output of refineries and steel mills directing adjustments should the output not be exactly as required.

A computer which is a combination of both the digital and analog computer is called a **hybrid** computer. This type of computer is used for special applications rather than as a general purpose machine.

Level 2

REGISTERS

The control section of the CPU is made up of 5 main parts called **registers**. Each register has a special series of circuitry which enables it to carry out the task assigned to it.

CONTROL

INSTRUCTION REGISTER

INSTRUCTION ADDRESS REGISTER

OPERATION REGISTER
A-ADDRESS REGISTER
B-ADDRESS REGISTER

Figure 2.8

Each part can be thought of as having cells, each of which is able to electronically contain a digit or special character. One can think of a register as being somewhat like the odometer on an automobile. Instead of the contents of the register increasing in steps of 1 (as does the odometer), the registers receive coded instructions from storage. Their special circuitry causes the instructions to be carried out.

To illustrate, assume that in storage is an instruction to add two numbers. The numbers are contained in memory addresses, number 60 and 61.

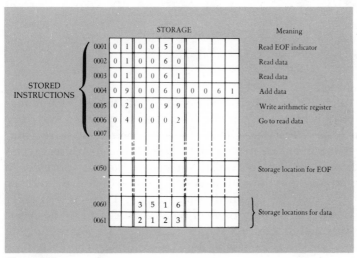

			STORAGE								Meaning
0001	0	1	0	0	5	0					Read EOF indicator
0002	0	1	0	0	6	0					Read data
0003	0	1	0	0	6	1					Read data
0004	0	9	0	0	6	0	0	0	6	1	Add data
0005	0	2	0	0	9	9					Write arithmetic register
0006	0	4	0	0	0	2					Go to read data
0007											
0050											Storage location for EOF
0060			3	5	1	6					Storage locations for data
0061			2	1	2	3					

STORED INSTRUCTIONS {

Figure 2.9

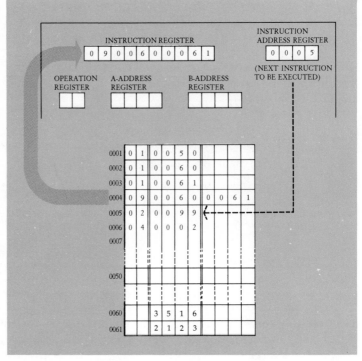

Figure 2.10

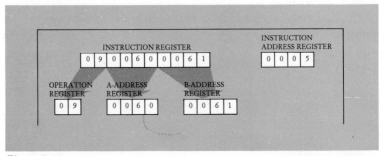

Figure 2.11

The first instruction is moved up to the control, into the **instruction register**. From there it is broken down into three parts and moved into three other registers. The operation ADD is moved to the **operation register**. The two address numbers are moved to **A-Address** and **B-Address** registers. The circuitry in the registers causes the data in the two addresses to be copied from storage into the arithmetic-logic unit to be added. Another instruction would then be obtained from storage. There is a register which is responsible for keeping track of what instruction is to be called up next. The **Instruction Address Register** contains the address of the *next* instruction to be called from storage. This next instruction might be to "output the result."

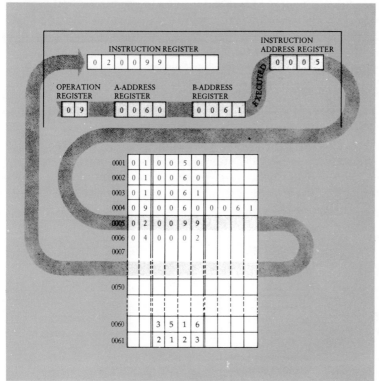

Figure 2.12

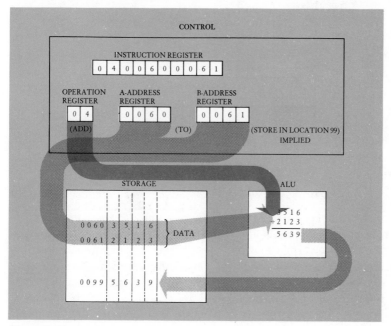

Figure 2.13

This instruction as well is found and moved to the instruction register. There it would be analysed and the circuitry would cause the previously calculated sum to be located in its storage address and displayed or printed on the computer's output device.

√TYPICAL MICROCOMPUTER ORGANIZATION

When the control RUN is given, the 'next instruction' pointer is set to point at the beginning of the program. The BASIC interpreter searches for a reserved word in the instruction. When one is found, control is transferred to the appropriate BASIC subroutine. The subroutine checks the instruction for other information and performs the required tasks. When the subroutine is finished, the instruction pointer points to the next instruction and the process is repeated.

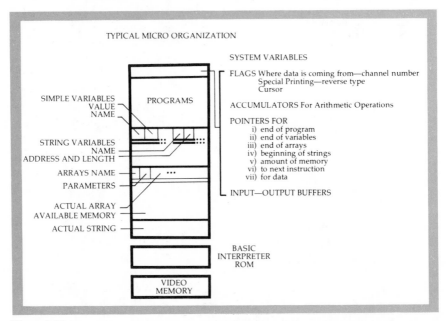

Figure 2.14

THE CONTROL CONTROLS

In addition to carrying out programmed instructions, the control of the computer is also responsible for making sure that 'pathways' for the movement of data are clear and are operational. For example, control is used by a special series of programs called the **operating system**. The operating system is written by the manufacturer. Part of it is designed to make sure the input and output devices are working properly. If one of these devices is not working, an instruction would cause the computer to produce an error or fault message of some sort.

Although it will be easier to understand just what the registers do after you learn more about programming, it is sufficient at this time that you understand that:

1) the registers are used to receive instructions from storage,
2) the registers decode and analyse the instructions, and
3) the registers are able to direct electrical impulses to carry out the instructions.

IS IT THE COMPUTER OR THE PROGRAM . . .?

Perhaps you have noticed that the words *instruction* and *program* have been used frequently, rather than 'the computer does this' or 'the computer does that.' This is done on purpose, for the computer really cannot do anything on its own—it is just a bunch of circuits on a chip of sand. The computer requires a series of instructions to function. These instructions called a **program** are prepared by the manufacturer or by the user of the computer. The instructions cause thousands of electronic switches to be turned on or off, routing electrical impulses through a maze, causing them to activate the equipment in the desired fashion.

In summary, the control part of the CPU is made up of components which are used to analyse and carry out instructions which have been loaded into the storage section. These components are made up of groups of electronic circuitry which route signals throughout the computer. Processed information is then stored and/or outputted. Of course if the instructions were incorrect, the wrong result would occur. Remember the computer is a bunch of circuits, and circuits do not have good judgement!

CHECKING YOUR READING—LEVEL 1

1. Write a brief outline of how the brain receives and processes and outputs information.
2. What are the key functions of the brain's computer system?
3. What unique feature has the computer which makes it different from any former calculating machine?
4. What is meant by 'direct entry' input?
5. Explain the difference between a 'hard copy' output and a 'soft copy' output?
6. The CPU is composed of what three main parts?
7. What two types of information are stored in storage?
8. What is the function of the ALU?
9. Copies of data in storage could be sent to what two parts of the computer?
10. What is addressing of storage and why is it necessary?
11. In addition to carrying out programmed instructions, what other function is performed by the central processing unit?
12. What is the key characteristic of a digital, analog and hybrid computer?

VOCABULARY ASSIGNMENT

Continue developing your vocabulary list by writing a short definition of the words and phrases in bold type in this section.

CHECKING YOUR READING—LEVEL 2

1. What are the names and functions of the 5 registers in control?
2. What must take place to execute an instruction stored in storage?
3. An instruction is broken up into how many parts in the control?
4. If two amounts are to be computed, how does the computer locate those amounts?
5. Where are the amounts taken for computing?
6. Summarize the movement that takes place in the CPU if an instruction in storage is to be executed. That instruction requires that two amounts in addresses in storage are to be multiplied and the results stored in another address in storage.

VOCABULARY ASSIGNMENT

Continue developing your vocabulary list by writing a short definition of the words and phrases in **bold type** in this section.

PROJECTS—LEVEL 1

1. Make a sketch of the three parts of the computer, and a sketch of a human head. Label the input, output, and processing unit of each.
2. In the sketch you have just completed, section the CPU into three parts and label each of those three parts.
3. Prepare a project on how the brain functions. If possible include the electro-chemical processes. As an alternative do your project on the eye or ear.

How is your scrapbook project coming? Have you a number of entries made in it? Is it time to fix it up a bit more, perhaps doing a design for the cover? If you put a little time and effort on it, not only will you have something worthwhile at the end of the course, but you might like to put it aside for a number of years to look back at and to enjoy.

PROJECTS—LEVEL 2

1. Sketch and label the 5 main parts of the control section of the CPU.
2. To the above diagram add an area to represent the storage. Use arrows to represent how data is moved from storage into the control section and how the instruction is further broken down in control.
3. Add to your diagram a section which you can label ALU and indicate using arrows the flow of information into and out of the ALU.

CHAPTER 3

THE COMPUTER'S LANGUAGE

THE NEED FOR LANGUAGES

Those who developed the early computers had to put into them special number codes. These were the instructions the computer was to carry out. The writing of the instructions in code was a very tricky procedure. Many errors were made even though this coding was being done by those who designed the computer! One would think the experts should not make errors! It soon became evident that there had to be a better way of instructing the computers if they were to be widely used by those other than the experts.

It was found that the computer could be programmed to read instructions in modified English or mathematical symbols. The instructions were then translated into code by a special computer program. In other words the computer was programmed to translate other programs! The group of special English words and mathematical symbols and the rules on how they were to be used was called a **computer language**. In other words *a computer language is composed of English words, mathematical symbols and the rules on how these are to be combined.*

TYPES OF LANGUAGES

Soon many languages were developed. It has been estimated that there now exist between 300 and 500 languages which could be used to instruct the computer. It became necessary for international conferences to be held to standardize some of the more popular languages. The military particularly was concerned about being able to use a program developed on one computer on other computers. When computers were replaced with newer models, programs had to be re-written. This was a great waste of time. Some languages were standardized and the manufacturers made sure each new general purpose computer could handle these languages.

COBOL LANGUAGE

Two languages receive most of the attention at these conferences. The one called COBOL which stands for *CO*mmon *B*usiness *O*rientated *L*anguage. You will note from the illustration that you are able to understand almost all the approximately 250 words and code used in COBOL. The trick of course is to make sure that the words are in the correct sequence with the correct punctuation.

COBOL was especially designed to manage massive amounts of data stored on tape or disc.

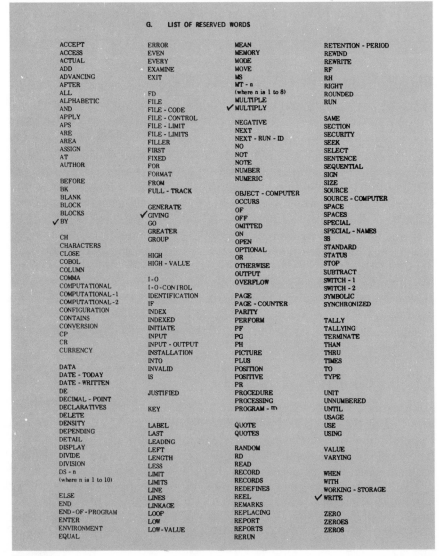

Figure 3.1

FORTRAN LANGUAGE

Another language called FORTRAN evolved. This language was designed primarily for high speed calculating. Engineers and mathematicians used FORTRAN to do literally hundreds of thousands of computations in a few minutes. The language itself looks very much like a series of algebraic formulae. These formulae are translated by the computer and used in the execution of the program. The word FORTRAN was formed by putting together the parts of the phrase FORmula TRANslation.

FORTRAN uses fewer words than COBOL. Its main feature, you will recall, is to enable the computer to execute mathematical functions, very similar to algebraic equations. Of course COBOL can calculate and FORTRAN can handle massive data. Each does its own task very efficiently.

OTHER LANGUAGES

Other popular languages include those that lie somewhere in between COBOL and FORTRAN in concept. COBOL contains many (English) words and is considered to be a *wordy* language. FORTRAN causes many computations to be done with as few symbols and instructions as possible. The language APL is considered by many programmers to use the best features of COBOL and FORTRAN. It was designed to eliminate most of the unfavourable features of each.

Some brands of computers are so widely used they have their own language. For example, there is a special language for the IBM 360/370 series called 360 Assembler. Of course these powerful computers also have the capability to translate programs written in the other commonly used languages. The special Assembler language, however, runs very efficiently on these computers.

BASIC

If there was a breakthrough in programming languages which made programming as simple as possible, it was the development at Dartmouth University of a language called BASIC. Compared to other languages, BASIC is very easy to learn. (It should be pointed out, however, that computer programming is not a snap for everyone.) Its name is formed from the phrase *Beginners' All-purpose Symbolic Instruction Code.* Most of the illustrations in this text are in BASIC.

COMPILERS

A language is stored in the computer as a complex computer program called a **compiler**. This program, written by the manufacturer, is designed to read in instructions and to analyse those instructions. If the compiler is able to understand the instruction, it translates or interprets it into the

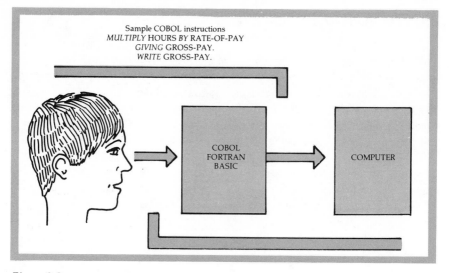

Figure 3.2

special code that the computer can understand and carry out.

If for some reason the programmer has made a mistake and not followed all the rules of the language, the compiler will reject the instruction and indicate to the programmer that an error has been made. The designers of the language established the various rules for the language. The compiler is programmed to 'understand' the instructions if the rules are followed. Most compilers, for example, are programmed to look for certain punctuation in certain places in the instruction. Should a programmer forget to use the punctuation correctly, the compiler would be unable to understand the instruction, and therefore would be unable to translate it.

TRANSLATORS

In the case of most micro computers the language BASIC is in the form of a **translator**, rather than a compiler. Compilers convert all instructions to machine code before any instructions are executed. Translators on the other hand, convert instructions to machine code, one at a time during the execution of the program. Each time a particular instruction must be executed, it must first be translated. Even if an instruction is within a loop in a program the translation is made each time, just before execution.

REVIEW

A short summary is in order. A computer language is the series of words, symbols and rules which make up the language. The compiler of a language translates instructions written in the language into machine code. If the rules of the language are not followed, an error message is produced.

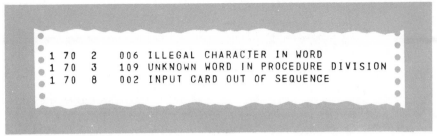

```
1 70  2    006 ILLEGAL CHARACTER IN WORD
1 70  3    109 UNKNOWN WORD IN PROCEDURE DIVISION
1 70  8    002 INPUT CARD OUT OF SEQUENCE
```

Figure 3.3

CONTROL INSTRUCTIONS

After a series of instructions has been translated, special instructions or commands called **control instructions** are given to the computer. Control instructions direct the computer to begin following the programmed instructions now that they are in machine code. More later about control instructions.

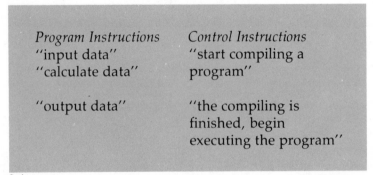

Program Instructions	*Control Instructions*
"input data"	"start compiling a
"calculate data"	program"
"output data"	"the compiling is
	finished, begin
	executing the program"

Figure 3.4

ADDRESSING

As you will recall, computers are able to store data electronically. This data is of two types. The first is numeric data on which calculations are carried. The second is alphabetic data. Each character or digit of data stored requires one memory cell. Although it does not seem obvious at first, it is very important that the location of each piece of data is known.

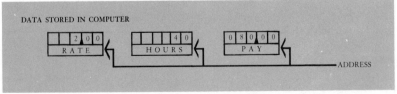

Figure 3.5

It would not make much sense to put data randomly in the thousands of available memory cells and not be able to find it. Certainly there could be some type of search for data made by the computer. It would obviously find data, but would it know where the data began or ended? Would it know that it had the right data even if it did identify the boundaries?

ADDRESS TABLES

All this difficulty is solved by using addressing. Much in the same way that families in houses have addresses, data items are stored in the computer's memory under an address. If you wanted to locate the J. F. K. Jones family, all you would have to do is to obtain their address, go to that place, and there would be the family. Similarly a group of characters forming a piece of data is stored in an address (group of memory cells). The address is noted and put in a type of *address table* in the computer's memory. If that piece of data is required, the address is looked up in the address table. The computer then goes to that address (electronically) and locates the group of characters.

ADDRESS	TABLE
PROGRAMMER'S ADDRESS NAME	ACTUAL MEMORY ADDRESS
RATE	3995
HOURS	3990
PAY	3985

Figure 3.6

In order to make addressing easier for a programmer, the computer permits the programmer to make up names for any given piece of data. The name or a short form of the name is stored in the computer's memory. When required, the name is used to locate the actual address of a group of memory cells in which the computer will store the data. Each time the programmer uses that name, the computer will be able to identify in which cells the data is stored. It is the job of the compiler to assign actual address locations to the address names or **symbolic addresses** made up for each type of data by the programmer.

COMPILERS ORGANIZE STORAGE

After a program has been compiled into machine code, it is placed in storage in the low order numbered addresses. The compiler usually assigns the data locations to high order numbered addresses, working backwards as each additional address is required.

In some micros, data addresses are assigned immediately following the program. Alphabetic data which varies during the execution of the program is assigned addresses at the 'bottom' of memory. Of course the important thing to remember is that the program is stored in memory and data addresses are assigned automatically by the computer.

Level 2

INSTRUCTIONS—PROGRAM AND CONTROL

When using a computer language such as BASIC, instructions written in that language are called program instructions. With the very odd exception, all program instructions written in BASIC will be understood and followed by any make of computer which can process that language. The instructions are universal.

Computers require types of instruction other than program instructions in order to operate. For example, an instruction must be given to the computer to start working, once it has the power turned on. Or an instruction must be given to the computer that it should begin doing or executing a program written in BASIC. The computer must also be told that a new program is about to be put into its storage. These instructions are not a language instruction but control instructions. Each make of computer has its own series of control instructions or signals. A computer manufacturer might use a special control word or a special key on the computer's keyboard for a control signal.

TYPES OF CONTROL INSTRUCTIONS

'wake up and get to work—your power has been turned on and there is work to be done'

'get ready to take in a new program in BASIC'

'erase from your memory a program which is no longer of any use'

'save for future use the program now in your memory'

'pardon the interruption, you may not know it but you are having trouble with the program you are now processing; there appears to be an error in it—stop working on it for a moment and wait for a further (control) instruction'

'everything appears to be okay now, continue with that program on which you were working'

'everything is a mess; erase that program you were working on and get ready to receive another (control) instruction'

It is important that you understand that:

a *program instruction* is written in BASIC or some other language, and causes the computer to process information

a *control instruction* is a signal to the computer to take some action pertaining to itself and its own operation

USING TIMESHARING TERMINALS

You may be using a **timesharing terminal** to process your programs or a micro computer. If it is a terminal you will have to know the principles of programming in BASIC using timesharing equipment. (If you are using a micro it is useful to acquire a general understanding of how timesharing works.)

[The timesharing computer has a large number of terminals hooked up to it. It also has massive storage, likely disc storage. Each authorized user is assigned a permanent space for storage. A code number identifies to the computer each user. The user's code also identifies the particular storage area assigned to the user. There is also a common temporary work space in which new programs may be developed. After a new program is developed it may be saved in the user's permanent space.]

CONTROL INSTRUCTIONS

Refer to the user manual for the special control instructions which have to be used with your terminal. You will likely find control instructions similar to the following:

> SAVE (save in my permanent storage the program currently located in the temporary work space)
>
> REPLACE or RESAVE (the old program now in my permanent storage locations with its revised version now in the temporary work space)
>
> RENAME
>
> NEW FILE NAME—_____(change the name of the program in the temporary work area to a new name: useful for saving other versions of a program already saved under another name)
>
> PURGE (*name of Program*) (remove from permanent storage the program which has been named)
>
> CATALOG (list all the programs or files which have been saved in permanent storage)
>
> BYE (a control statement which indicates that you are signing off)

TO USE A TIMESHARING COMPUTER

To access a timesharing computer, dial up the computer on your terminal. The computer responds with a message to say that you have its attention. For example, it might give its name and the current date, followed by a request for your **identification code**:

> TIMESHARING COMPUTER SERVICE YY/MM/DD
> ID—_____

It is then necessary for you to respond with the identification code you have been assigned. Suppose your name was Yogi Issac and your Code is composed of your two initials and some digits. After inputting this code, the computer would verify that you were a legitimate user and come back with a 'go ahead' message. If you were not a legitimate user it might give you one or two more chances to input the correct code then shut you off if the correct code was not finally inputted.

The 'go ahead' signal might be the word SYSTEM—, outputted on your terminal. The computer is really asking what language you are going to use. In this case it will be BASIC.

```
TIMESHARING COMPUTER SERVICE YY/MM/DD
ID—YI-12321
SYSTEM—BASIC
OLD OR NEW—NEW
NEW FILE NAME—TEST I
```

The computer, once told the language which will be used, responds with a request. 'Are you going to work on an old program or a new program?' Assuming that it is a new program, you would key in the word NEW.

USING A BATCH COMPUTER

If you have access to a card-orientated batch computer, you will likely prepare your program on computer cards. Perhaps you will be key punching the instructions and data into cards. More likely you will be marking boxes on the cards with a pencil so that the cards can be read by an optical mark reader. Instructions are rapidly loaded into the computer one right after another. This grouping of instructions before loading them into a computer is called **batching**.

You will have to learn the control instructions for the computer you are using. These instructions would be coded onto cards and these **control cards** would then be submitted to the computer with your program **instruction deck**. Refer to the user manual for your computer for the correct control card layout.

USING AN INTERACTIVE MICRO COMPUTER

If you have access to a stand alone micro computer you will learn the routine to turn on the computer and 'get it up and running.' Instructions are loaded one at a time. An almost instant response is made by the computer to the programmer. This *dialogue* between computer and programmer is considered to be **interactive**. Most of the micro computers have the same or similar control instructions. For example, if you wish to begin a new program after the computer signals READY, key in the word NEW. The computer then again signals READY. It has reorganized its memory, erasing any old programs which may have been in it.

You may wish to save a program on cassette. Most types of micros carry out this control function after the instruction SAVE is keyed in. In timesharing, the name of the program must be given before inputting the instructions. Most micros require that the name of the program be assigned just before saving. In fact it is assigned during the SAVE instruction. The computer then writes the *name* of your program on the cassette or disc, followed by *all the instructions*.

RE-RUNNING A PROGRAM

In order to reload a saved program, the control instruction CLOAD or just LOAD can be given. (Some makes of computers use CLOAD whereas others use just LOAD.) If you know that the program you want is the next available one on the tape, just the instruction LOAD is required. If the tape must be searched for a particular program then the program name must follow the load comment (usually in quotation marks):

> CLOAD "TEST1" or LOAD "TEST1"

Again, you will have to refer to the user manual of the computer you are using for special control instructions.

Once the control instructions have been learned, all other BASIC instructions illustrated in this text should work on your computer. Good luck!

CHECKING YOUR READING—LEVEL 1

1. What was the difficulty with the early form of programming a computer?
2. What were the names of the first two languages which were developed and widely used?
3. What was the main function of each of these two languages?
4. What is a compiler? What is a translator?
5. What is a control instruction?
6. In what way is an address inside the computer similar to the street address of a house?
7. How is a type of table or index used to hold address, names, and actual addresses? Illustrate your answer.
8. Sketch and label the two areas inside the computer storage where the program is stored, and where addresses are stored.

VOCABULARY ASSIGNMENT

Continue developing your vocabulary list by writing a brief definition for the words and phrases in this section which are in bold type.

CHECKING YOUR READING—LEVEL 2

1. Compare and contrast control instructions and program instructions.
2. Give an example of at least one control instruction.
3. What is the main characteristic of a timesharing computer?

4. What is the function of the user code?
5. What is batching?
6. What is an important feature of an interactive computer?
7. List and provide a brief description of the control words in this section.

VOCABULARY ASSIGNMENT

Continue developing your vocabulary list by writing a brief definition for the words and phrases in this section which are in bold type.

PROJECTS—LEVEL 1

1. Make a sketch to represent the compiler as either a dictionary or as a translator. Make the title the "COMPILER IN ACTION." Show instructions going into the compiler in one form and coming out of the compiler in some sort of machine code. You might show the compiler rejecting certain instructions which it is unable to understand.
2. Make a sketch of some memory cells with some type of address labelled on them. You might also show data represented in those cells.
3. Make a sketch of a box which could represent storage. Divide storage into two sections. Label the upper part as an area to store instructions. The other part is used to store data.

PROJECTS—LEVEL 2

1. Some students have difficulty distinguishing between a programmed instruction and a control instruction. Write a short note or prepare a sketch of some type to illustrate the difference between the two.
2. Make a sketch of a time-sharing computer with terminals attached to it. If you wish you could make the computer look like an octopus with the terminals at the ends of each of its arms.
3. Write a note or make a sketch, or a series of sketches, to contrast the difference between batch programming and interactive programming.

CHAPTER 4

PROGRAMMING THE COMPUTER

Level 1

Although it is possible to learn something of programming without access to a computer, it is highly desirable that you have computer access before attempting the next four chapters. The examples given are in BASIC. It is preferable, therefore, that the computer have a BASIC compiler.

THE APPROACH MUST BE LOGICAL

The computer is a passive combination of circuitry. This *machine* is unable to do any task without first being programmed. A program is a series of instructions, which when followed by the computer in the correct order, would bring about the desired result.

Programming the computer is very much like preparing a series of instructions for someone to put together a new bicycle. A person would write out the first step, then the second step, and so on, until the task would be complete. Obviously, it would be foolish to place Step #4 before Steps #2 or #3. The person making up the instructions does so knowing where each part should go and in what order they should be assembled.

The person who makes up the assembling instructions for the bicycle has them printed and included along with the unassembled bicycle. The person assembling the bicycle follows the directions which have been printed.

Similarly, in programming the computer one must first know what the desired end result should be. Instructions to bring about this result would then be planned. The instructions are then loaded into the computer's memory. Only after the program is completely loaded is the computer directed to follow the instructions, beginning with the very first one.

1. Decide what is wanted from the computer.
2. *Plan* how to instruct or order the computer to do what is required.
3. Instruct or program the computer.
4. Have the computer follow the instructions.
5. Check the result to see if it is what is required.

Figure 4.1

USING A COMPUTER LANGUAGE

It was pointed out earlier that a computer program, called a compiler, was designed to 'understand' English-like instructions. Once an instruction is 'understood' by the compiler it translates the instruction into the machine code. The computer is then able to understand and **execute** or carry out the instruction.

The person designing the language has decided to use certain words or algebraic phrases called **reserved words**. These words and phrases are built right into the compiler program. They are then available to be matched up with the same words and phrases which would be fed into the computer by a programmer. The choice of the words and rules by those who designed the compiler is arbitrary. But once these are settled on, *all other programmers using the compiler must use the words and follow exactly the rules of the language.*

Figure 4.2

For example, one compiler has both the words DISPLAY and WRITE. Another compiler has the word PRINT. If you asked the one compiler to understand PRINT it would not, nor would the other compiler understand DISPLAY or WRITE. If you tried to use a word not in the vocabulary of the computer language, an error message would result.

DIAGNOSTIC MESSAGES

Many beginning programmers have tried various words and become upset by the "stupid computer" because it did not understand the word. First of all, it is really not the computer which does not understand the word—it is the compiler. And technically, it was not the compiler's fault either. Its designer did not pre-store or 'teach' that word to it! Messages produced by the compiler when it does not understand an instruction are called **diagnostic messages**.

So as you begin programming, DO follow the rules which *have* been built into the language. DON'T blame the computer or compiler if it does not understand something because you did not follow the rules. Fair enough?

AN IMPORTANT REVIEW

It is agreed that instructions for the computer have to be in a logical sequence if the desired result is to be obtained. It is also agreed that the instructions would have to follow the rules established by the designers of the language. It has also been pointed out that all the instructions must be fed into the computer before a signal is given to the computer to begin following those instructions. So let us get started.

YOUR FIRST PROGRAM

One of the easiest and shortest tasks to program the computer to do is to output some words. For example, you could have the computer output any word or combination of words, such as "Look Mom, I programmed the computer." To do this, simply direct the computer to print it with an instruction or statement like this:

100 PRINT "LOOK MOM, I PROGRAMMED THE COMPUTER"

Notice that the instruction has the number 100 in front of it called, appropriately, the **instruction number**. Each instruction must have a unique number assigned to it. The numbers could be 1, 2, 3 . . . but by convention the numbers begin at 100 and go up in steps of ten. More about this later. Each instruction also has some **operation** or action which the computer is to do. Finally, there is some indication of what the computer is to *operate* on. This is formally called the **operand**.

CONTROL INSTRUCTIONS

A considerable amount has been said to this point about program instructions. A series of program instructions designed by the programmer will cause the computer to do a task, sometimes a very complex task. As indicated earlier there is another type of instruction called a control instruction or signal.

CONTROL INSTRUCTIONS YOU WILL SOON BE GIVING TO THE COMPUTER

1) begin working when the power is turned on (This could be the command CLEAR or NEW.)
2) stop memorizing program instructions and begin executing those instructions
3) erase a program from memory
4) stop executing a program even though it has not yet logically finished.

The first two control signals you need to know at this point are the control instructions NEW and RUN. The control instruction NEW causes the computer to prepare to receive program instructions. The control instruction RUN causes the computer to stop attempting to memorize instructions and to begin executing the instructions which have been memorized.

DO IT

Now you are ready to have the computer execute your first program:

> NEW (control instruction)
> 100 PRINT "LOOK MOM, I PROGRAMMED THE COMPUTER"
> (program instruction)⏎
> RUN (control instruction)

The computer would now obey the control signal and carry out the program instruction and output the required line. For those using video screen perhaps you might like to insert an extra instruction as instruction #90. (Now, already we have found out why instructions are numbered in such large steps. Additional instructions may be inserted almost anywhere while keeping the instructions in the correct sequence.)

> (READY) (status signal the computer gives back to the operator)
> NEW
> (READY)
> 90 CLS (Clear the video screen or instruction to skip to top of page.)

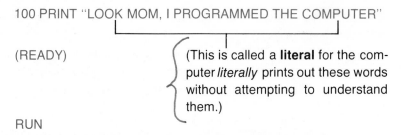

100 PRINT "LOOK MOM, I PROGRAMMED THE COMPUTER"

(READY)

(This is called a **literal** for the computer *literally* prints out these words without attempting to understand them.)

RUN

Are you obtaining a feeling of *power* over this machine?

Now that you are able to make the computer print what you command, proceed to program it to print out anything you want. Perhaps you want it to produce your name, your address and your telephone number. Go ahead, boss it around!

You may wish to cause the computer to produce a paragraph by using a number of print statements:

```
(READY)
NEW
(READY)
100 clear screen or top of page instruction
110 PRINT "THIS COMPUTER IS ABLE TO PRODUCE A"
120 PRINT "PARAGRAPH OF INFORMATION IF YOU KNOW"
130 PRINT "HOW TO MAKE IT DO IT. I HAVE LEARNED
HOW"
140 PRINT "AND AM NOW DEMONSTRATING . . .          "
150 PRINT "                                        "
160 PRINT "                                        "
RUN
```

How impressive! In such a short time, you have been able to put words into the computer's mouth so to speak. (Ooooops!)

THE COMPUTER AS A CALCULATOR

There is something else you can do which is equally as impressive. Using some of the principles of algebra, create an unknown and cause the computer to solve for that unknown. For example, find the area of a field, perhaps a football field, so that you will know how much sod or artificial turf will be required to cover it. To find area, the length and width are multiplied.

In BASIC the equal sign is used in an instruction but it has a slightly different meaning in arithmetic. In BASIC it means *give or assign the value of everything which is to the right of the equal sign to the unknown or variable on*

the left. So the statement which would give us the product of the length and width would be:

120 LET X = 110 * 55 (Let the content of the address
labelled X now be assigned
130 PRINT X   the value of 110 multiplied by 55)
RUN

Hmmm, what is that * doing in that instruction? It is the BASIC symbol for multiplication. The mathematical operations for BASIC are:

Operation	BASIC Operation Code
add	+
subtract	−
multiply	*
divide	/
raise to the power	↑

VARIABLES

The X in the instruction is called a **variable**. It is the name given to the address which is to hold the calculation. It could be represented graphically this way.

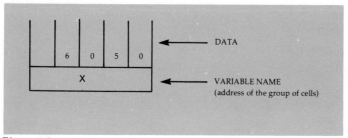

Figure 4.3

Note that the PRINT instruction had to be present. If it were omitted, the computer would calculate the result and keep it in its memory. It would not give you the answer, in fact, you would not be sure that the computer even did the calculation! It is important, therefore, to instruct the computer to print out or display the information you want it to produce for you. A computer is not a mind reader. In executing this PRINT statement, the computer notes that it is to PRINT *the content of the vaor address called X. It then locates X in its memory and takes a copy of its content to output.*

It is also possible to do arithmetic right in a PRINT statement.

Example

130 PRINT A = 25 + 30

This really causes two instructions to be executed. The first instruction adds the 25 and 30. The second outputs the result.

MORE ARITHMETIC

One of the features of the language BASIC is its ability to be programmed to carry out a wide variety of arithmetic very quickly and very efficiently. Study the illustration below. Notice how much the instructions look like mathematics you have done in the past.

Example

```
120 LET X = 30
130 LET Y = 40
140 LET Z = 65
150 LET A = X + Y − Z
160 PRINT A
```

You could calculate the answer faster than you could program the computer to compute it. But consider this example.

```
120 LET X = 25.1789
130 LET Y = 123.4567
140 LET Z = 65432.987
150 LET A = Y * Z / X
160 PRINT A
```

In a calculating race maybe we will *let* the computer win that one. We would not want to give it an inferiority complex.

OUTPUT IN E NOTATION

Sometimes computed output will have a rather unusual answer. For example the result might look like 2.23454678E + 12, or 4.45678E − 8. Very large or very small numbers are outputted in E notation. There is one digit (and only one) in front of the decimal. A number of digits follow. Then comes the E notation. This function is designed to output in a reasonably brief form very large or small numbers.

In the case of an E+, the number following the plus is the number of places to the right you have to move the decimal to obtain the proper decimal number. In the case of E−, the decimal has to be moved to the left the number of places indicated by the number following the minus sign. It is confusing at first but stop to think about it for a minute. The number following the E tells you how many places to move the decimal to obtain the correct number in ordinary decimal notation.

E Notation	Decimal Notation
3.456654567E + 12	3 456 654 567 000.
1.2345E − 10	.000 000 000 123 45

TEACHING THE COMPUTER TO COUNT

A very common feature used in programming requires that a count be maintained of the number of times that something is done. The computer can be taught to count relatively simply:

```
120 LET X = 0
130 LET X = X + 1
140 PRINT X
150 LET X = X + 1
160 PRINT X
170 LET X = X + 1
180 PRINT X
190 PRINT "JUST CALL ME DRRRACULA!. . . GET IT?"
```

The output of this program would be the counting numbers 1, 2, 3. Notice that the address of X is initially given the value 0. The content of X (the value of 0) is then added to 1 and the result is stored back into the address X. A copy of the contents is then outputted.

DESTRUCTIVE MOVE IN; NON-DESTRUCTIVE MOVE OUT

Now is as good time as any to explain an interesting feature of the moving of information inside storage. If data is moved into an address, the old content of that address would be erased and replaced by the data being moved in—destructive move in. If you record music on a tape, what was on the tape is erased and replaced by the music just recorded. The same idea holds for recording or moving data in computer storage. Old data is erased as new data is recorded.

Taking the tape recorder idea one step further, if you had two tape recorders and copied one tape onto another, the original tape would still be intact, unless something was wrong with your machine. The original tape would still have the music on it. Similarly, in computer storage, if a *copy* of data is moved from one area into another, the original data still remains in the 'sending address.' This is considered to be non-destructive move out, or non-destructive read.

When the statement 130 LET X = X + 1 is executed, the old value of X is copied out of its address, taken to the ALU, added to 1, and the sum is copied back into the address X, erasing the old value. Conversely, the instruction 140 PRINT X causes the computer to obtain a copy of the data in the address X and move it to the output device. X still retains its current value.

STILL MORE ARITHMETIC

The BASIC language was designed so that the computer would be able to follow the mathematical rules of the 'order of operation' used in reducing an expression.

Example 1

      130 LET A = 25 + 60 / 2

Example 2

      160 LET B = (3 + X) (Y − 5) + 50./3.14

In both of the above illustrations the dividing would be done first. In Example 1 the 60 would be divided by 2 and the 25 would then be added to the 20. In the second example, the contents of what was in the brackets would be calculated, then multiplied together. The result would then be added to the result of the 50 divided by the 3.14. If an expression contained only multiplication and division operations, the computer would execute them working from left to right. One micro computer manual makes a point of stressing the MDAS rule. If there are no brackets, the computer works from left to right first doing exponentials then Multiplication. On the next pass it does Division. It then does Addition, then Subtraction. When in doubt as to the order of operations use brackets to make sure the computer calculates in the exact order you require.

ORDER OF OPERATIONS
Generally, work from left to right (in doing so) compute what is in the inner-most brackets first, using the following order of operations:
    calculation of exponential expressions, then
    multiplication and division, then
    addition and subtraction

Figure 4.4

So now you are able to have the computer do your mathematics homework. As long as you know the rules of order of operation and program the computer accordingly, the computer will follow those same rules to give you correct answers every time! The catch is, of course, you must program the computer correctly in the first place.

REPLACING THE POCKET CALCULATOR?

If you do happen to have the ready use of a micro computer and wish to use it as a calculator, a short form for the operation PRINT is the *question mark*. To have the micro do and output a series of mathematical operations you would enter an instruction number, the question mark, the variable name which will contain the final result, and the mathematical expression, as complicated as you wish to make it. Of course, you must give the control signal to RUN before the output is given.

```
100 ? A = (2(5 + 3) ) + 4 − 5 (9/3 − 2) /7
     ↑Replaces PRINT
RUN
```

Some micros function as a calculator with even fewer instructions. The instruction number may be omitted. When the 'enter' or 'return' key is pressed the instruction runs automatically.

FINISHING TOUCHES

If you wish to use the computer strictly as a calculator the BASIC instructions above would be sufficient for the problem at hand. If a program is to be saved and used repeatedly, it should be fixed up a little. For example, an instruction or two could be printed to tell what the program is able to do.

```
90 REM     THIS PROGRAM CALCULATES THE AREA OF
92 REM     A FOOTBALL FIELD
100 LET A = 110 * 55
110 PRINT A
```

Instruction 90 is a REMARKS instruction. The REM is the short form for remark. Everything which follows REM is ignored by the computer. It is only used to communicate the purpose of the program, or, if used part way through the program, to explain what is going on. In other words, the REM instruction is used to inform people, not to instruct the computer.

Even instruction number 110 could be improved. For example, we could combine the printing of the value of A with a literal, in this way:

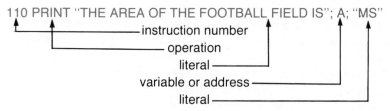

```
110 PRINT "THE AREA OF THE FOOTBALL FIELD IS"; A; "MS"
```
instruction number
operation
literal
variable or address
literal

The program could be improved even further. In addition to the REMARKS statements, literals describing the output could be included:

```
90  REM     THIS PROGRAM CALCULATES THE
91  REM     AREA OF A FOOTBALL FIELD
95  clear screen or slew to top of page
```

```
96 PRINT "***BELOW IS THE AREA OF A FOOTBALL
   FIELD***"
97 PRINT
98 PRINT
100 LET A = 110 * 55
110 PRINT "THE AREA OF THE FIELD IS"; A;"METERS
    SQUARED"
```

In this example there appears to be some duplication of the REM statements in the PRINT instructions. When the program is run, the REMs do not show up on the screen or page. They are simply to identify the program. The print instructions do form part of the output. In time the separate functions of the REM and PRINT "literal" will become a little clearer.

Notice that there are two print instructions which appear not to have any output associated with them. These simply cause blank lines to be outputted to make the output a little better spaced. By the way, the two print instructions could have been combined into one:

    97 PRINT:PRINT

Although this is not encouraged at this time, more than one instruction may be included beside an instruction number or line number if separated by a colon.

ERROR AND ERROR MESSAGES

In instruction number 110, the computer was instructed to output three different things. These three things were clearly identified for the computer by separating them with the semi-colon. If these semi-colons were missing the computer would have difficulty identifying just what it was expected to print. The compiler would give an error message or diagnostic message informing you that it was having difficulty understanding your instructions. The message might be syntax error which means the compiler is looking for some punctuation which is not there. You may, if you wish, try this program without the necessary punctuation to see what happens. If you are like most other students, however, you either have already experienced error messages or soon will.

So you are off and running as a programmer. You understand why you have to follow the programming rules of the language; you know how to cause the computer to print out literals or words; you know how to make the computer do mathematical calculations; and, you know how to print out the results of those calculations using a literal to make output easier to identify.

Level 2

NUMBER SYSTEMS

One of the principles which makes the computer function is that almost all instructions and other information can be reduced to code. The code activates certain circuits, which are in one of two states—'on' or 'off.' In effect, the computer is based on the **binary number system**. A review of the binary number system is in order. But first it is helpful to have some understanding of number systems in general. Study the following series of numbers:

octal (handwritten annotation) *binary* (handwritten annotation)

A	B	C	D	E	F	G	H	I
						100		
						33*		
						32		
						31		
12				20		30		
11	12			15*		23*		
10	11	12	13	14	20	22	101	
9	10	11	12	13	14*	21	100	
8	8*	10	11	12	13	20	22*	
7	7	7*	10	11	12	13*	21	
6	6	6	6*	10	11	12	20	110
5	5	5	5	5*	10	11	12*	101
4	4	4	4	4	4*	10	11	100
3	3	3	3	3	3	3*	10	11
2	2	2	2	2	2	2	2*	10
1	1	1	1	1	1	1	1	1
0	0	0	0	0	0	0	0	0
A	B	C	D	E	F	G	H	I

There is a definite pattern to each column of numbers. Column A is the very familiar decimal number series. Decimal stands for 10. The digits 1 to 9, and 0 make up the system. The values from zero to nine are represented by one digit. The value 10 has to be represented by two digits. Column A is based on the number 10 and is said to be **base 10**. The value of each digit position from right to left is the value of the powers of 10.

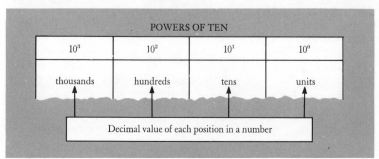

POWERS OF TEN

10^3	10^2	10^1	10^0
thousands	hundreds	tens	units

Decimal value of each position in a number

Figure 4.5

Column B is composed of 9 digits. Note that only the values 0 to 8 can be represented by one digit in this system. The decimal value '9' is represented by the two digits 10! The value of each digit position of a number in base 9 is the same as the powers of base 9

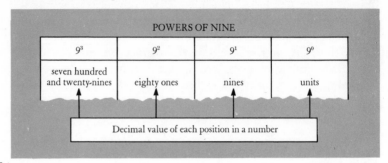

Figure 4.6

The base 9 number 372 would be represented in decimal as 306.

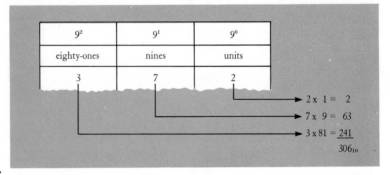

Figure 4.7

Column C is composed of values of base 8 or **octal**. Only the numbers 0 to 7 can be represented by one digit. The value decimal 8 must be represented by the two digits 10. The value of each digit position is the same value as the powers of 8.

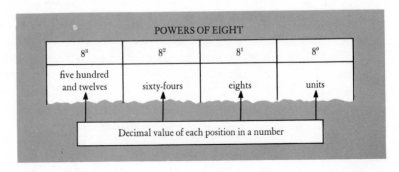

Figure 4.8

The base 8 number 263 would be represented in decimal as 179.

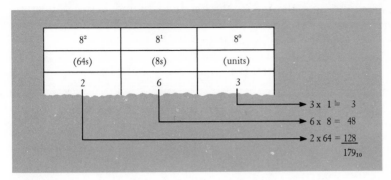

$$3 \times 1 = 3$$
$$6 \times 8 = 48$$
$$2 \times 64 = \underline{128}$$
$$179_{10}$$

Figure 4.9

The same explanation can be made for each of the other number systems.

Study the last column, column I. What base is this number system? Following the previous rule, it must be base 2 or binary because only the values 0 and 1 can be represented by a single digit. The decimal number 2 is represented by a 1 and a 0. As this number builds from right to left, the value of each position is the same as the powers of 2.

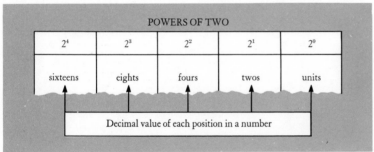

Figure 4.10

The binary number 10101 would be the number 21 in the decimal system.

ADDING AND SUBTRACTING IN BINARY

To add in binary, one must remember that only 0s and 1s may be used. To add $1_2 + 0$, the result, of course, is 1_2. But $1_2 + 1_2 = 10_2$! In the same way that a 'carry' takes place in the decimal system when the units value is more than 9, so a carry takes place in binary when the unit position values goes over 1. There are considerably more 'carries' in binary. Examine the following examples:

Example A
$$10_2$$
$$\underline{11_2}$$
$$101_2$$

Example B
$$11_2$$
$$101_2$$
$$\underline{110_2}$$
$$1110_2$$

In the units column of example A, $1 + 0 = 1$ with no carrying. In the next column (twos column) is the $1 + 1$ which is 10 in binary. The '0' is written in the sum area and the '1' is carried.

In the units column of example B, the sum results in a 10 ($0 + 1 + 1 = 10_2$). The '0' is written and the '1' is carried. The twos column is $1 + 1 + 1$ which is 11 ($1 + 1 = 10_2$; $10_2 + 1 = 11_2$).

SUBTRACTING IN BINARY

The 'adding the complement' method of subtraction is sometimes used in a computer. To subtract a number in binary, change all the 1s to 0s in the subtrahend, and the 0s to 1s and add.

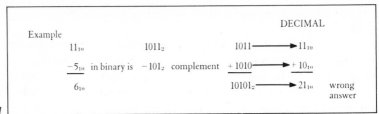

Figure 4.11

At first the answer does not appear correct. But if the extra leftmost '1' is added to the units column of the sum, the correct answer is obtained.

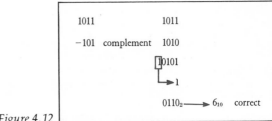

Figure 4.12

If the extra leftmost digit in the sum is '0,' simply attach a minus sign and re-complement the answer by changing 0s to 1s , and 1s to 0s.

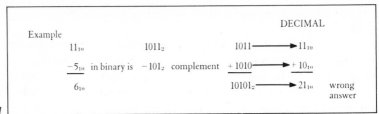

Figure 4.13

CHECKING YOUR READING—LEVEL 1

1. In addition to electricity, what must be present in order for a computer to function?
2. In what way is the sequence of instructions important?
3. In what way are the rules of a compiler arbitrary when first developed, but compulsory after the compiler has been fully developed?
4. If a programmer does not follow exactly the rules for the compiler, resulting in an error, to whom or what should 'blame' be assigned— the computer, the programmer, the compiler, the designer of the compiler? Give a reason for your answer.
5. What are diagnostic messages?
6. What BASIC word causes the computer to output information?
7. Give an example of an instruction which outputs a phrase or sentence.
8. What is the difference between a programming instruction and a control instruction? Give an example of each.
9. How is the equals sign (=) used differently in a BASIC instruction than in mathematics.
10. What are the BASIC symbols for the 4 mathematical operations?
11. What is a variable?
12. What is the difference between destructive move in, and, non-destructive move out?
13. In what order does the computer do the operations reducing an expression such as: 110 LET D = 2 (5 + 6)/(8*4) − 9/3

VOCABULARY ASSIGNMENT

Continue compiling your vocabulary list by writing brief definitions for the words and phrases in bold print in this section.

CHECKING YOUR READING—LEVEL 2

1. What general rule could you make up to determine the number of digits in any particular number system? (Remember that zero is considered to be a digit.)
2. What is meant by position value in determining a number greater than the largest *unit* value?
3. If the computer operates by using on or off circuits, or on or off memory units, in what way is the binary number system suitable for computer use?
4. Why are there so many 'carries' when performing addition in binary?
5. Write a clear statement on how one subtracts in binary by the complement and add method.

VOCABULARY ASSIGNMENT

Continue with the task of compiling your vocabulary list by writing brief definitions of the words and phrases in bold print in this section.

PROJECTS

Checking For Errors

Most, but not necessarily all the following BASIC *program* instructions contain an error or have bad form. Rewrite the instructions making the necessary corrections.

1. PRINT "I HAVE PROGRAMMED THE COMPUTER"
2. PRINT "THIS PROGRAM IS EASY"
3. 120 PRINT "ONE HAS TO BE CAREFUL WHEN PROGRAM-MING".
   130 RUN
4. 120 LET X = 25
   130 PRINT "THE VALUE OF X IS X"
5. 120 LET X = 30
   130 PRINT "THE VALUE OF X IS": X
6. 110 LET X = X + 1 (the very first instruction in the program)
   120 PRINT X
7. 160 LET X − ((34 + 10) * 23 ÷ 5
8. 130 LET R = 20
   140 LET A = 3.14 × R × R
   150 PRINT "THE AREA OF THE CIRCLE WITH RADIUS 20 IS"; R

PROGRAMMING ASSIGNMENTS

For the following arithmetic calculations, prepare a BASIC program to output the answer:

The Computer as a Calculator

1. $(4 + 5) \times (3 + 6)$

2. $(4(5 - 2) + 1) \div (2 + 3(6 + 10))$

3. X = 3
   $(6 + X) + (12 \div X) \times ((X + 4)2)$

4. X = 8
   $7 (X^2 + 1) \div 5$

5. *Discounting*

   P = 25   Where P = price, D = discount and N = net price
   D = .15
   N = P − (P × D)

Note: It is strongly recommended that if your computer can handle variable words longer than two characters, full variable names should be used in the program.

6. *Payroll*

   H = 40   Where H = hours worked, R = rate of pay,
   R = 5   I = insurance premium, T = tax rate (on gross pay
   I = 2   less insurance premium) N = net pay
   T = .22
   N = (H × R − I) − T(H × R − I)

7. *Interest*

   P = 5000   Where P = principal, R = interest rate, T = time,
   R = .12   in years, and, I = simple interest over 5 years
   T = 5
   I = P × R × T

8. *Area*

   L = 8.5   Where L = length of room in metres, W = width,
   W = 6   P = price per square metre and, C = cost of
   P = 12   broadloom
   C = ?

9. *Decorating*

   L = 6.25   Where L = length of room in metres, W = width
   W = 5.5   of room, H = height of room, R = cost of
   H = 2.5   broadloom per square metre, W1 = cost of
   R = 10   wallpaper per square metre, P = cost of paint per
   W1 = 12   square metre for ceiling, and C = cost of materials
   P = 3   to refinish a room.
   C = L × W × R + (2(L × H) + 2(W × H))W1 + L × W × P

10. *Shingling*

    R1 = 14   Where R1 = ridge on main roof, R2 = ridge on
    R2 = 10   secondary roof, S1 = is the length of the slope
    S1 = 8   on the main roof, S2 = the length of the slope
    S2 = 6   on the secondary roof, and, C = the cost of the
    C = 20   shingles per square metre.
    P = (2(R1 × S1) + 2(R2 × S2)) × C

11. *Siding*

S1 to S8 values as shown on diagram
H1 = 3   Where S1 to S8 = lengths of sections of a
H2 = 2   house, H = height of wall, H1 and H2 =
H3 = 1.5   height of the two gables, and P = price of
P = 20   siding per square metre
C = (H(S1 + S2 + S3 + S4 + S5 + S6 + S7 + S8) + 2(.5 × S1 ×
H1) + (.5 × S4 × H2)) × P

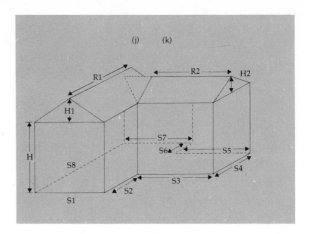

ADDITIONAL PROGRAMMING ASSIGNMENTS

1. Have the computer print out the following statements:
   a) programming a computer is easy
   b) my name is _____
   c) John F. Kennedy was the 35th President of the United States
   d) the government of John Diefenbaker earned the largest majority in modern Canadian history
   e) defenseman Bobby Orr of the Boston Bruins earned the scoring title in the NHL in 1970
2. Have the computer print out a short paragraph about how you feel about computers in this stage of your career.
3. Have the computer produce a short paragraph insulting itself.
4. Have the computer print out a short note explaining your absence from school. Take it home and have your parents sign it and date it. Then present it to your home room teacher.
5. Prepare a program of your choice which is formally completed with a REMARKS statement as well as any outputted words or phrases which give meaning to the output.

CHAPTER 5

REPEATED INSTRUCTIONS

Level 1

Up to now you have been able to do relatively simple operations on the computer such as printing out words and doing simple mathematics. Now it is time to show you some of the power of the computer. So get ready to be impressed, perhaps even dazzled!

A MATTER OF EFFICIENCY

Assume we require the printing of the counting numbers from 1 to 1000. If one had the time and patience the computer could be programmed in this way to do the task:

```
110 LET X = 0
120 LET X = X + 1
130 PRINT X
140 LET X = X + 1
150 PRINT X
160 LET X = X + 1
170 PRINT X
```
etc. until the number 1000 would be outputted!

Some task. There must be an easier way.

FOR . . . NEXT

One of the super features of a computer is that it can repeat instructions many times, very fast and very accurately. In programming jargon there is a very *powerful* instruction which causes the computer to execute a series of instructions many times in a fraction of a second. It is called the FOR . . . NEXT instruction. In simple terms it sets up a beginning and an ending point for a series of instructions. There is a built-in counter which keeps track of how many times the series of instructions is repeated. The programmer sets the limit or number of repeats, and the counter does just as implied—it *counts* the repeats until the pre-set count is reached. Study this example:

```
130 LET X = 0
140 FOR C = 1 TO 1000
150 LET X = X + 1
160 PRINT X
170 NEXT C
180 . . .
```

In English the FOR . . . NEXT instructions, say, *perform or do the series of instruction between FOR and NEXT using C as a counter, beginning the count at 1 and ending the repeating after the count is 1000.*

Instruction 140 sets up the counter C with an initial value of 1 and a final limit of 1000. In other words the series of instructions between the FOR and the NEXT instructions is to be repeated 1000 times. These instructions cause the computer to add to an address or variable, and to print out the content of that variable. Each time that this is done, the computer adds 1 to C and checks to see if the C is now greater than 1000. If it is not (as it will not be for 1000 repeats) the FOR . . . NEXT statements will cause the enclosed series of instructions to be repeated again. Finally C will equal 1001 (*after* the series has been done 1000 times) and the computer will branch to instruction 180.

INITIALIZATION

The assigning X = the value 0 is called **initializing.** Initializing means setting the content of an address, to some value. Do not get the idea that initialization is always assigning an address a zero value. There will be times when you will initialize an address with an amount other than zero, but more about that later.

Notice that both C and X are increased by 1. This program could be made more efficient by using C for both tasks.

```
130 FOR C = 1 TO 1000
140 PRINT C
150 NEXT C
160 . . .
```

If you try this, you will note that the program works just as well. In fact it will work slightly faster, although you will likely not notice the difference. The computer has fewer instructions to follow to obtain the same output. One should always be on the lookout for ways to make programs more efficient. Do not seek efficiency to the degree that you begin to cause errors nor should you make the instructions so sophisticated that they are almost impossible for your colleagues (perhaps even your instructor) to follow. [At one time efficient programming was extremely important. Recently, mainly due to the very high speed of computers, it is more important to write programs which are easy for others to follow than to save the computer 0.000 005 of a second!]

FINISHING TOUCHES

Let us assume that you want to keep this program for future use. It should be finished with appropriate modifications and additions such as:

```
110 REM    COUNTING NUMBERS FROM 1 TO 1000
120 PRINT "THIS PROGRAM PRINTS OUT THE COUNTING
NUMBERS"
130 FOR C = 1 TO 1000 (If your output is on paper, modify the
                        number of repeats from 1000 to 10)
140 PRINT C
150 NEXT C
```

It could be improved even further by clearly identifying the end of the program. An END statement is included to indicate that there are no more instructions in the program. This statement is optional for some BASIC compilers but compulsory for others. When the computer reaches the END instruction, it is informed that there are no more instructions and comes to a logical halt.

This instruction is traditionally given a very high number. If the program is enlarged and additional instructions inserted these instructions must have a lower number than the END instruction. (Later you will be shown an exception to this rule.)

Example
```
9999 END
```

END-OF-JOB INDICATOR

To have the computer signal the end of processing, or the end of output, another instruction is traditionally used. That instruction is the 'end of job' signal. The last thing the computer should be programmed to do before it stops executing a program is to display the letters EOJ or the phrase END-OF-JOB. This instruction could be numbered 1 *less than the END instruction.*

```
170 NEXT C
9998 PRINT "EOJ"
9999 END
```

If for any reason the program was unable to be completely run, the operator would know it did not come to a logical end if EOJ was not outputted.

From now on, as you 'fix up' (later a more formal term will be used) a program to be saved or to be turned into your instructor, add the END and EOJ instructions to 'finish off' your programming with a little class!

TIME TO GET REALLY INVOLVED

Remember that the FOR . . . NEXT is a powerful programming function? The program you have just finished caused a series of instructions to be carried out 1000 times. It is time to run a more challenging program. Program the computer to add up all the numbers 1 to 1000, and print out the sum.

```
130 LET X = 0
140 FOR C = 1 TO 1000
150 LET X = X + C
160 NEXT C
170 PRINT X
```

X is initialized at 0. The lower limit of C is given the value 1 and the upper limit of 1000. Each new value of X is calculated by adding the current value of C to the old value of X. A '1' is added to the count C and the computer loops back to instruction 140 to see if C now is greater than 1000. It is not, so the series is repeated. In a few seconds, all the instructions have been carried out as required and the sum is printed as directed by statement 170. If you wished to see just how fast this works, and you have access to a video display output, insert the instruction:

```
155 PRINT C
```

This causes an output for each loop—all 1000 of them. Do not try this without special permission if your only form of output is a printer. The output will use up 1001 lines of paper!

STEPPING UP AND DOWN

From the above illustration it would appear as if the FOR . . . NEXT statement always does a simple count. It may be altered slightly to cause it to add *other than* a 1 to its counter. To accomplish this, the word STEP is added to that instruction.

```
140 FOR C = 1 TO 999 STEP 2
```

In this case the counter would be initialized at 1 and be incremented or increased by 2 for each repeat (1, 3, 5, 7, etc.,). Note that the upper limit was not 1000, for the counter would never be equal to 1000.

Assume that a programmer was a little careless and intended to have the computer write out the 'count by twos' series using the FOR . . . NEXT statement:

```
130 FOR C = 1 TO 100 STEP 2
140 PRINT C
150 NEXT C
```

First of all the programmer would not get the output expected. The output would be 1, 3, 5, etc., whereby the series 2, 4, 6, . . . was desired. Furthermore, as counter C approached 100 it would hold the values 97, 99, 101, . . . and would never equal 100. Some computers would go on forever, the condition C = 100 never being reached. Other compilers are designed to stop the computer if the value C *goes over* the upper limit.

The counter is also able to be incremented by a fraction of an amount or by a negative. Study the following:

```
100 (clear screen or top page)
110 PRINT "FAHRENHEIT TO CELSIUS"
120 LET C = 0
130 FOR F = 32 TO 39.2 STEP 1.8
140 PRINT " ";F;"      ";C
150 LET C = C + 1
160 NEXT F
```

or:

```
110 PRINT "CELSIUS TO FAHRENHEIT"
120 LET C = 0
130 FOR F = 32 to − 14 STEP − 1.8
140 LET C = C − 1
150 PRINT " ";C;"      ";F
160 NEXT F
```

In both examples, the initial value of F was not 1 but 32. In the first example the step was a positive decimal fraction. In the second example the step was a negative value which also included a decimal fraction.

NESTED STRUCTURES

It is possible in fact it is *easy*, to have a series of instructions performed many times inside a 'larger' series of instructions. In the example below instructions 150 to 170 are executed 15 times *each time* instructions 130 to 180 are executed. This 'larger' series is executed 25 times. This is called a **nested loop** or **nested structure**.

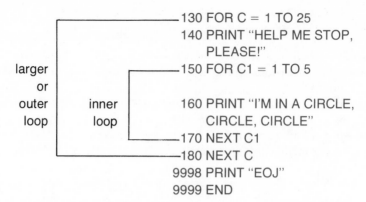

```
larger       130 FOR C = 1 TO 25
or           140 PRINT "HELP ME STOP,
outer              PLEASE!"
loop         150 FOR C1 = 1 TO 5

      inner  160 PRINT "I'M IN A CIRCLE,
      loop         CIRCLE, CIRCLE"
             170 NEXT C1
             180 NEXT C
9998 PRINT "EOJ"
9999 END
```

Notice that for every time the instructions in the larger structure are executed the instructions in the inner structure are executed 5 times.

```
HELP ME STOP, PLEASE
I'M IN A CIRCLE, CIRCLE, CIRCLE
I'M IN A CIRCLE, CIRCLE, CIRCLE
I'M IN A CIRCLE, CIRCLE, CIRCLE
I'M IN A CIRCLE, CIRCLE, CIRCLE
I'M IN A CIRCLE, CIRCLE, CIRCLE
HELP ME STOP, PLEASE
I'M IN A CIRCLE, CIRCLE, CIRCLE . . .
```

Isn't that fun?

Now if you are having trouble following what has been going on think of it this way: direct someone to run around the building you are now in 25 times; each time they pass the front door they are to spin around or pirouette 5 times. If this is done, what would be the total number of times the person would pirouette? If your answer is 125 times you are correct (25 times around the building with 5 spins each time is $25 \times 5 = 125$ spins). Now you should be getting the idea.

It is extremely important that you keep the complete structure within another structure. For example the following would be wrong:

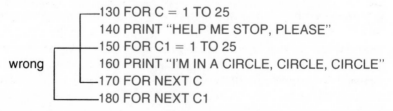

```
        130 FOR C = 1 TO 25
        140 PRINT "HELP ME STOP, PLEASE"
        150 FOR C1 = 1 TO 25
wrong   160 PRINT "I'M IN A CIRCLE, CIRCLE, CIRCLE"
        170 FOR NEXT C
        180 FOR NEXT C1
```

Always make sure that each structure is completely nested inside the other loop.

OFF-SETTING NESTED STRUCTURES

Could we go further and nest a structure, inside a structure, inside a structure? Certainly. For ease of keeping track, programmers sometimes offset each structure as follows:

120 X = 0	120 X = 0
130 FOR C = 1 TO 10	130 FOR C = 1 TO 10
140 FOR C1 = 1 TO 5	140 FOR C1 = 1 TO 5
150 FOR D = 1 TO 15	150 FOR D = 1 TO 15
160 LET X = X + D	160 LET X = X + D
170 NEXT D	170 NEXT D
180 LET Y = Y + (X * .25)	180 LET Y = Y + (X * C1)
190 NEXT C1	190 NEXT C1
200 LET Z = Z + (Y/3)	200 LET Z = Z + (Y/3)
210 NEXT C	210 NEXT C
220 PRINT Z	220 PRINT Z

Working from the inside out, the numbers from 1 to 15 are added up and assigned to the address X. Moving out to the next loop, the value of X is now multiplied by 1 and the result added to Y. In subsequent loops the value X will be multiplied by 2, 3, 4, and 5. Now moving to the outside loop, the content of Y will be divided by 3 and added to the address Z. This will be done 10 times. The final result of Z will be printed out. Now, to test your understanding, how many times will the instructions listed below be executed:

Instructions	Times Executed
160?	750 (15 x 5 x 10)
180?	50 (5 x 10)
200?	10

Go ahead and figure them out. The answer will show up below.

You have discovered the power of the FOR . . . NEXT function in BASIC. A series of instructions can be performed a set number of times or a number of times which is computed using steps other than 1. The programmer does not have to count how many times the loop must be performed. The conditions under which the computer is to stop performing the loop are stated and the computer carries on doing the loop until that condition occurs. You have also learned that a structure can exist inside another structure as long as it is completely within that other structure. (Answers to questions above: 750, 50, 10, respectively.)

Level 2

In an earlier section it was pointed out that computers work in an 'on or off' state. Either a circuit is forwarding an impulse (on) or it is not (off). This feature requires that the data and instructions be coded using this on or off concept. The binary number system has digits 0 and 1 making up the system and is suited to computer circuitry.

HEXADECIMAL NUMBER SYSTEM

In addition to the binary number system being used in a computer, another number system is frequently used. This system is called **hexadecimal** and is base 16.

Hexadecimal	Decimal
.	.
12	18
11	17
10	16
F	15
E	14
D	13
C	12
B	11
A	10
9	9
8	8
7	7
6	6
5	5
4	4
3	3
2	2
1	1
0	0

The decimal number ten is represented by a *digit* A! The decimal number eleven is represented by the digit B; and the decimal number fifteen is represented by F. Note that A, B, . . . F are technically *not* alphabetic letters but digits!

The position value of hexadecimal is the same value as the powers of base 16.

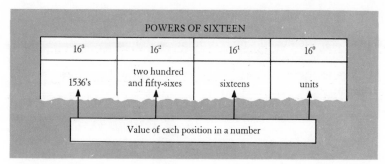

Figure 5.1

The hexadecimal number 13F in decimal is 318.

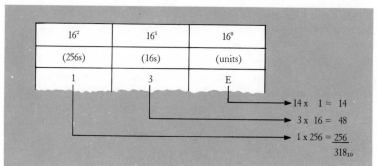

Figure 5.2

To add up a hexadecimal number the same carrying rules apply.

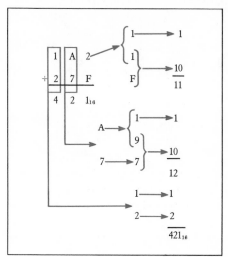

Figure 5.3

HEXADECIMAL ADDRESSING

In some computers, the hexadecimal number system is used to designate addresses of stored information.

In the illustration the literal "REPORT" is stored in hexadecimal address ending at $10B0_{16}$ which is 1712_{10}.

R	E	P	O	R	T
					10B0

Figure 5.4

Now that you have an idea as to how decimal numbers are coded in binary, it is a relatively easy step to understand the coding of hexadecimal numbers in storage. The binary positions of 1, 2, 4, and 8 are used, but instead of having a top value of 9, (an 8 and 1 bit turned on), hexadecimal digits are recorded by continuing the pattern right up to F (the decimal value 15). For example the value A (decimal 10) would be recorded by turning on bit positions 8 and 2. Similarly the value B could be recorded by turning on bit positions 8, 2 and 1. The value F would be recorded by turning on all four bit positions.

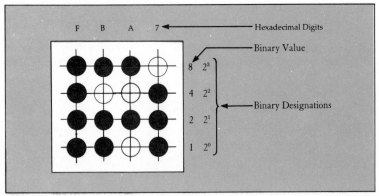

Figure 5.5

BINARY CODED DECIMAL

Some computers use a combination of binary and decimal. Decimal numbers are stored and operated on in binary. Each group of 4 binary digits, sometimes called an **octet**, represent a decimal digit. Groups of octets hold related decimal digits forming decimal numbers.

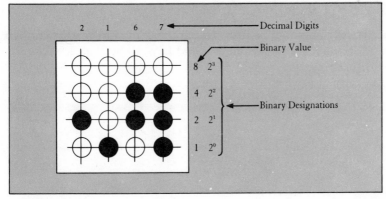

Figure 5.6

APPLYING NUMBER SYSTEMS TO COMPUTER CIRCUITRY

In the last few chapters you have been exploring various number systems. "Why" you are asking, "have these systems been included in a book on computers?" Now is the time to relate these number series to computers, particularly to the circuitry of the computer. First, look at the basics of computer circuitry.

COMPUTER LOGIC

If it were said that each person in your classroom was either strong or wise or both, the status of each person could be determined. Any one student would be one of:
- wise but not strong
- strong but not wise
- wise and strong

All possible conditions are given. Similarly, when it comes to combinations of electrical impulses in a pair of wires, computer circuits determine an 'either' or 'both' combination.

TYPES OF CIRCUITS

There are two main types of computer circuits. The one type creates a path for electrical impulses. These are called **combinational circuits**. The path is either open or closed. This 'go' or 'no go' situation is created by certain combinations of circuits called **gates**. (If the gate is open, the impulse goes through, but if the gate is closed, the impulse is blocked off.)

Another type of circuit is called a **sequential circuit**. Sequential circuits hold data in binary code. The circuit is either on or off—a 1 or a 0.

TYPES OF COMBINATIONAL CIRCUITS

The circuit board shown on Figure 5.6(a) is considered to be a *series* or an AND circuit. Switch 1 and Switch 2 would have to be closed before the light would come on.

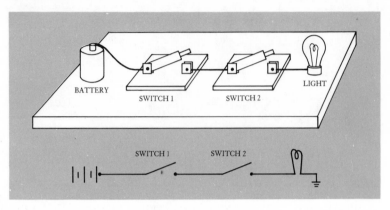

Figure 5.6(a)

The circuit board shown in Figure 5.7 is considered a *parallel* or an OR circuit. In this case the closing of only one switch would be all that is required for the light to come on. A truth table shows all the combinations.

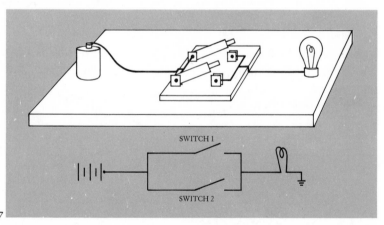

Figure 5.7

SWITCH		SERIES CIRCUIT "AND"	PARALLEL CIRCUIT "OR"
I	2	CURRENT TO LIGHT?	
OFF	OFF	NO	NO
ON	OFF	NO	YES
OFF	ON	NO	YES
ON	ON	YES	YES

Figure 5.8

Computer circuits are represented by diagrams.

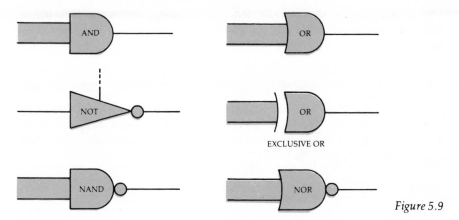

Figure 5.9

Note the difference between the diagram for the AND and the OR circuit.

Although this might sound unusual at first, a very important circuit is called a NOT circuit. If no impulse comes into the circuit, the NOT circuit generates an impulse. If an impulse does come into it, the NOT circuit prevents the impulse from leaving. Sounds strange doesn't it?

The NOT circuit is often linked with an AND or OR circuit making them NAND and NOR circuits respectively.

MAKING UP COMBINATIONS

In order to add impulses in binary, a combination of circuits is put together. If only one impulse goes into the half-adder in the illustration

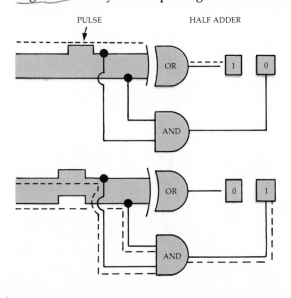

Figure 5.10

the value 01 comes out. If two impulses go in then the value 10 comes out.

By combining more circuits to the **half-adder** one gets the **full-adder**. This circuit is able to handle the 'carrying' of a 1.

✳ THE FLIP-FLOP

The sequential circuit called the **flip-flop** holds binary data. The 0 and 1 shown on the right are being held there for a period of time. In fact that information is able to be sensed by the computer. Combinations of flip-flops could hold any combination of 0s and 1s. Numbers and characters are therefore able to be 'held' in the circuits, coded in 0s and 1s.

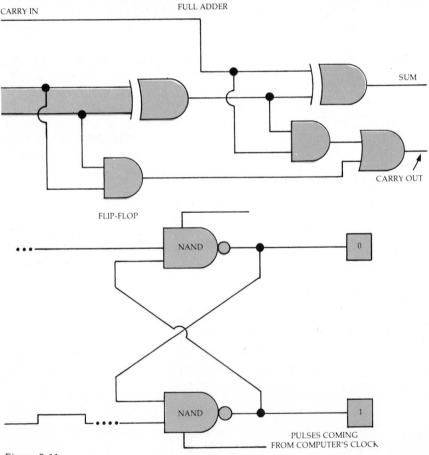

Figure 5.11

The flip-flop can be made to change its status by sending an electrical impulse into one of its wires on the left. That impulse combines with the 1 or 0 which is constantly being generated within itself to cause it to reverse its values. In other words it flips to the opposite combination of values.

WHAT TIME IS IT?

The computer has a clock which continually sends out impulses. These impulses activate certain circuits. For example if no other impulse is going into a NOT circuit, the clock impulse is re-routed out the NOT, thus creating the necessary impulse. An extra wire, not usually shown in the circuit diagrams, goes to most circuits. The clock keeps the value of the flip-flops continually generated. Should the power be turned off, the value of the flip-flop would be lost.

ONE-WAY VALVES

In some pressurized water systems there are stop valves which permit the water to go only the one way. Should something happen to the system and the water was forced back the other way the stop valve would stop it. A circuit called a **diode** permits electrical impulses to go only one way. If the impulse wants to go the 'wrong way' in a circuit the diode would stop it. In micro circuitry, transistors are used as diodes.

READ ONLY MEMORY

ROMs are combinations of circuits. A ROM is 'programmed' by creating certain combinations of 0s and 1s in it. To accomplish this originally all flip-flops have a 1 in them. In processing the ROM during manufacturing a mask is put over the circuit layout, such that certain paths are broken making some flip-flops a 0. Once the mask has been 'burned in' the ROM is permanently programmed.

CHECKING YOUR READING—LEVEL 1

1. Explain in simple terms the function of the FOR . . . NEXT.
2. Write out in simple English the meaning of the statement FOR D = 1 TO 50.
3. For what purpose is the D in the above statement used?
4. What does it mean when an address is initialized?
5. What finishing touches does one put at the beginning and end of a program in BASIC?
6. What function has the end-of-job indicator?
7. What is meant by stepping in the FOR . . . NEXT statement? (In your answer use the word **increment**).
8. Explain how or why initialization does not always mean to set an address in the computer memory to 0.

9. What is meant by a nested structure?
10. In BASIC why is it a tradition that nested structures be off-set?

VOCABULARY ASSIGNMENT

Continue developing your own vocabulary list by writing brief definitions of words and phrases in bold type in this section.

CHECKING YOUR READING—LEVEL 2

1. List the digits in hexadecimal.
2. What base is the hexadecimal number system?
3. Contrast how 4 bit positions can be used in binary and hexadecimal.
4. Illustrate electronic storage of binary coded decimal.
5. Sketch or describe the function of each of the following computer circuit terms:
   (a) combinational circuit or gate
   (b) sequential circuit
   (c) AND and OR circuit
   (d) NOT, NAND and NOR
   (e) half-adder
   (f) full-adder
   (g) flip-flop
   (h) clock
   (i) read-only circuits

VOCABULARY ASSIGNMENT

Continue developing your own vocabulary list by writing brief definitions of words and phrases in bold type in this section.

PROJECTS

Checking for Errors

Most but not necessarily all of the following BASIC statements contain an error. Rewrite the statements correcting, where necessary.

```
1. 120 LET X = 0
   130 FOR C = 1 TO 50
   140 PRINT X
   150 PRINT "THE SUM OF THE NUMBERS FROM 1 TO 50
   IS" X
   160 END
2. 120 FOR C = 1 TO 90
   130 LET C = 0
   140 LET X = X + 1
```

```
      150 PRINT C;X
      160 NEXT X
  3.  120 LET X = 25
      130 FOR C = 1 TO 30
      140 LET X = X − 1
      150 PRINT X
      160 NEXT C
      170 PRINT "X NOW EQUALS O"
  4.  120 LET X = 0
      130 FOR C = 1 TO 20 STEP 2
      140 PRINT X
      150 NEXT C
      160 PRINT "THE ABOVE IS A COLUMN OF COUNT-BY-
      TWOS"
      170 PRINT "FROM 2 TO 20"
  5.  120 LET X = 1
      130 FOR C = 25 TO 50 STEP − 1
      140 LET C = C + X
      150 PRINT C
      160 NEXT C
  6.  120 FOR C = 50 TO 0 STEP − 3
      130 PRINT C
      140 NEXT C
  7.  120 FOR C1 = 1 TO 25
      130 FOR C2 = 1 TO 5
      130 FOR C = 1 TO 10
      140 PRINT D = C1 + C2 + C
      150 NEXT C1
      160 NEXT C2
      170 NEXT C
  8.  120 FOR C = 1 TO 25
      130 FOR C1 = 1 TO C + 1
      140 FOR C2 = 1 TO C1
      150 PRINT C;C1;C2
      160 LET C = C + 1
      170 NEXT C1
      180 NEXT C2
  9.  110 X = 4
      120 Y = 6
      130 Z = 104
      140 FOR C = X TO Z STEP X + Y
      150 PRINT C AND X
      160 NEXT X
```

Checking for Errors Review

1. PRINT "I SURE CAN SPOT ERRORS"
   RUN
2. 120 LET X = 0
   130 PRINT "THE VALUE OF X IS" 0
   140 RUN
3. 110 PRINT X
   120 PRINT "IS THIS GARBAGE?"
   130 RUN

PROGRAMMING ASSIGNMENTS

1. Compound Interest

Using the supplied partial program as a basis for a compound interest project, write a complete program to calculate the interest at the end of each year if the interest is compounded N times a year for T years.

```
P =                          :REM P = PRINCIPAL
R =                          :REM R = ANNUAL RATE
N =                          :REM N = NUMBER OF TIMES
                               COMPOUNDED
T =                          :REM T = NUMBER OF YEARS
I2 = 0                       :REM I2 = TOTAL INTEREST
                               ACCUMULATOR
FOR C = 1 TO T
I1 = 0                       :REM I1 = CURRENT YEAR'S
                               INTEREST
FOR C1 = 1 TO N
I = P * R / N                :REM I = INTEREST PER PERIOD
I1 = I1 + I                  :REM ACCUMULATE YEAR'S
                               INTEREST
P = P + I                    :REM ADD INTEREST TO PRINCIPAL
I2 = I2 + I                  :REM ACCUMULATE TOTAL
                               INTEREST
NEXT C1
PRINT "INTEREST AT END OF YEAR";T;" = ";I2
PRINT "INTEREST FOR YEAR";T;" = ";I1
     :
```

2. Run the program a number of times to compare the effect of altering the number of times a year the interest is compounded.

3. Process Control Simulation

In mixing a certain chemical, the ratio of the mix of the three elements if 3:15:30 units respectively. Using the partial program which is supplied write a complete program to mix 480 units of the product.

```
FOR C = 1 TO _____ (hint: not 480)
    FOR C1 = 1 TO 3
        FOR C2 = 1 TO 5
            FOR C3 = 1 TO _____ (not 30)
            PRINT "SEND IMPULSE TO VALVE #3"
            NEXT C3
            PRINT "SEND IMPULSE TO VALVE .... #2"
        NEXT C2
        PRINT "SEND IMPULSE TO VALVE ....... #1"
    NEXT C1
NEXT C
```

4. Now alter the ratio to: i) 2:10:40
                               ii) 20:30:45

Simulating Measuring and Timing Devices

5(a) Write a program which could, if requested, print out the time of day, each and every second of the day, with output in the format similar to the following:
HOURS: MINUTES: SECONDS (use the 24 hour representation)
Also output a suitable heading for the time.
 (b) Some micros do about 500 empty FOR . . . NEXT loops in 1 second. For example, FOR I = 1 TO 500: NEXT I takes about 1 second. If you have access to a micro (not time-sharing) create a clock. Reduce the 500 indicated above to speed up the clock to test the minutes and hours routine.
 (c) Are you able to add tenths of seconds?
6. Write a program to simulate the workings of the odometer of an automobile.
7. Write a program to simulate the type of odometer which functions on the base 8 number system.

ADDITIONAL ASSIGNMENTS

1. Write a program, using 4 nested loops to output the count in binary up to 15.
2. Three gear wheels are interlocked. The smallest wheel has 25 teeth on it. Each time a tooth goes past a timing light an impulse is sent into a machine. The gear next to the smallest has 50 teeth in it and the larg-

est wheel has 200 teeth. The faster the larger gear goes, the faster the small generates the impulse. Write a program to simulate the impulses sent by the small gear as the larger gear rotates 1000 times. Before you begin, determine how many times the middle gear rotates for each rotation of the largest gear, and how many teeth of the smallest gear flash past the timing mechanism for each rotation of the middle gear.

ADDITIONAL PROJECTS

3.(a) Add the following:

i) 521	ii) 633	iii) 434	iv) 267
127_8	116_8	346_8	157_8

(b) Add the following:

i) 101_2	ii) 011_2	iii) 110_2	iv) 111_2
010_2	001_2	100_2	101_2

4. Main storage in the computer is usually made up of units of '1000' memory positions. These are usually represented by the character 'K.' For example a 12K memory would be considered to have 12 000 memory positions. If one K is really 2^{10}, how many memory positions are there in 12K?

CHAPTER 6

INPUTTING DATA

Level 1

There are a number of ways to put data into the computer to have it processed. One of the ways, as you have discovered, is to initialize certain addresses with data (20 LET X = 250). This technique works well in very specialized programs written to work on certain specific data. It does have some limitations, however. Many other programming applications handle variable data. The data varies from one execution of the program to the next. It would be a nuisance to have to alter the program each time to initialize new values of the data.

THE INPUT STATEMENT

One solution is to use the INPUT statement. This instruction causes a frequently run program to pause at the appropriate place. The operator of the computer then keys in the current data. Once this is done, the computer continues following the instructions of the program, processing the current data. Notice that a literal output may be combined with the INPUT statement:

```
130 INPUT "KEY IN THE HOURS WORKED";H
140 LET P = H*5
150 PRINT "THE PAY IS";P
```

Remember that the computer memorizes or stores all the instructions before it attempts to execute the program. After a control instruction is given to run or execute the program, the computer would begin with the first instruction and execute each in order down to and including instruction 130. The words "KEY IN THE HOURS WORKED" would be displayed and the INPUT instruction causes the computer to pause in its execution. It would wait for the operator to key in the data. Once done, the computer continues with instruction 140.)

READ . . . DATA

Another technique used to input data, is to use the READ instruction. This statement is usually used when there are a considerable number of data items. It causes the computer to look for data either on tape or disc, or somewhere else in the program. Examine the following:

```
130 FOR C = 1 TO 4
140 READ H
150 LET P = H*6.00
160 PRINT "THE PAY IS";P
170 NEXT C
9990 DATA 40, 44, 42, 35
9998 PRINT "EOJ"
9999 END
```

In this illustration, the READ statement will be done 4 times within the FOR . . . NEXT series. The first time when statement 140 is executed the computer looks for a statement beginning with the word DATA. Once found, the first piece of data in statement 9990, the value '40,' is obtained and assigned to H. The computer 'makes a note' that the first data item has been used and continues to instruction 150. The 40 in H is multiplied by 6.00 and the result is assigned to P.

The next time the statement 140 is executed, again it locates the instruction which begins with the word DATA. This time it retrieves the *second* piece of data (remember it made a note that the first piece of data was used). It moves the value 44 to H and again makes a note that data item 2 has been used. One way of looking at this technique is to think of the data items being in a lineup or **queue**. A **pointer** is used to keep track of which data item in the queue has been used.

```
9990 DATA 40, 44, 42, 35
       └─────────POINTER
```

THE DATA STATEMENT

The statement containing DATA may appear anywhere in the program. It may be at the beginning, right after the READ, or near the end. In the example it was placed near the end. The various data items have been separated by a comma. Remember the semicolon was used to separate out the various items to be printed. The comma separates the data items to be READ. If for some reason the programmer wishes to start over again at the first piece of data, the instruction RESTORE resets the data pointer at the beginning of the data.

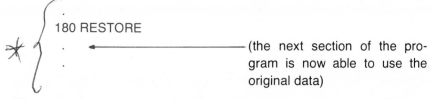

```
     180 RESTORE
```
──────────────────── (the next section of the program is now able to use the
original data)

Obviously it is important for the programmer to know exactly how many data items will be present. This is not always possible. The concepts which follow can be used to solve this problem.

END-OF FILE INDICATOR

In processing a considerable number of data items, it is not always possible to know exactly how many data items will have to be processed. To avoid having to count the number of items in advance, then modifying your program to process that particular number of items, another technique is used. The last valid data item is followed by a dummy data item. This dummy item is a code to indicate to the computer that it has reached the end of the data items. The code is chosen by the programmer who inserts into the program *immediately after the READ* an instruction which causes the computer to check for that code. When the computer runs into that code there is an instruction to cause a branch. Perhaps the branch would be to a wrap-up or summary routine.

```
     140 READ H
     150 IF H = 99999 THEN GO TO 9998 (or to a summarizing rou-
                                              tine)
     160 LET P = H * 6.00

                 .
                 .
                 .

     9990 DATA 40, 44, 42, 35, 9999  (do not confuse the data value
                                         99999 with the instruction
                                         number 9999)
     9998 PRINT "EOJ"
     9999 END
```

More about the IF . . . THEN instruction next chapter.

DATA RECORDS

Sometimes data is recorded in groups, each group representing a **record**. For example, an inventory record might contain i) a part number, ii) the quantity on hand, and, iii) the unit cost. Records with multiple data items may be placed in the DATA statements. The programmer should cause all the data items of one record to be read at one time.

150 READ P, Q, C

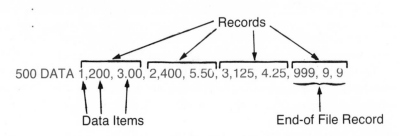

500 DATA 1,200, 3.00, 2,400, 5.50, 3,125, 4.25, 999, 9, 9

In the example each READ will cause the first record, or the first 3 data items, to be moved into P, Q and C respectively. The next READ will find the pointer pointing at the 2 of record #2. The next 3 data items of the next record will then be moved into P, Q and C, that is, the 2 is moved to the P, the 400 is moved to the Q and the 5.50 is moved to the C.

Notice that the dummy record has all three parts of a record. If only the first 999 value were supplied, the computer would attempt to load data into Q and C. Since there would be no more data items, an error message would be produced.

A SHORT REVIEW ON PUNCTUATION

So far you have learned that literals and any number of variables may be printed out in one line as long as each is separated from the other by a semicolon. When reading data, the variables after the READ are separated by commas. In the DATA statements each data item is also separated from the other items by a comma. There is no special punctuation to separate records. The programmer must keep track of the number of items which make up a record. Although this will be covered more thoroughly later you might find it handy to use commas instead of semicolons in a PRINT instruction to space out multiple variables.

Level 2

In this chapter, three ways of inputting data have been discussed. The first was to initialize data right in a program. The second way was to program in an INPUT statement which caused the computer to pause to wait for input. The third way was to have the program READ data from a data file. The data could be supplied in a statement called DATA or it could be found on tape or disc.

OTHER INPUT MEDIA

There are a variety of ways to input data other than through the keyboard of the computer or from the tape. Some of these methods are reaching the point of becoming part of computing history. Others are still widely used.

In the earlier units you were introduced to the computer without being concerned with how data was put in and printed out of the computer. (Some very interesting devices have been developed over the years which have speeded up the rate at which data can be moved in and out of the central processing unit.) As you find out a little about each device, you will likely become quite impressed with the creativity which has been used to develop these devices. Remember these ingenious devices were created by humans!

Before examining these devices, it might be helpful to distinguish between the device itself, that is, the nuts and bolts called **hardware**, and the **medium** of the device. The typewriter for example is considered a *device* and paper that is used in the typewriter is called the *medium* on which the typewriter works.

THE CARD

The standard computer card which is used today has the dimensions of an early American dollar bill. The principle of the card was developed by Jacquard to give uniformity in weaving designs. In 1891 a statistician by the name of Herman Hollerith first utilized the card for mass manipulation of data during the U.S. census of that year. By punching one digit per column, Hollerith was able to put 80 digits of information on one card. The number 5761 would be represented by a "5" punch in column one, a "7" punch in column two, and so on until there is a punch in each of the four columns.

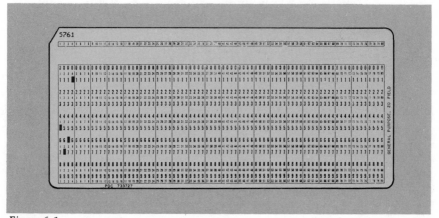

Figure 6.1

Alphabetic information is encoded on cards by using two punches per column. In much the same way that children develop secret codes by assigning numbers to the 26 characters of the alphabet, so the Hollerith code was developed by assigning numbers to the alphabet. However, in order to encode one alphabetic character per column, it was necessary to use one *digit* row punch in combination with a punch in one of the three extra rows on the card. The top three rows of the card called *zone rows* were used for this second punch.

The Hollerith code which was developed is shown below.

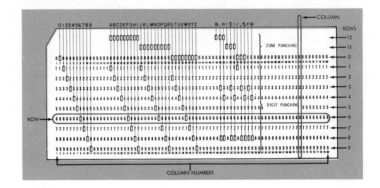

Figure 6.2

CARD FIELDS

A field is a group of columns which represents a piece of data.
The illustration shows 4 fields each requiring 3 columns.

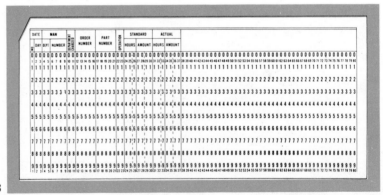

Figure 6.3

THE CARD PUNCH DEVICES

The device which punches the holes in cards is called a key punch. The keyboard is quite similar to that of a typewriter. As the data required in the card is being keyed in, the device activates punching dyes causing them to punch the hole.

Stacker Reading Station Punching Station Card Hopper

Keyboard

Figure 6.4

THE PUNCHED CARD READER

The essential feature of the card is that it can have holes punched in it representing data. These holes are *read* by a device called a **card reader**. This reading is the sensing of the holes by the device and converting the sensed holes into electrical impulses.

Figure 6.5

Most card readers sense these holes in either of two ways. The early card readers had the card pass between a metal cylinder and a series of wire brushes. These wire brushes look like a 19 cm long wire toothbrush with the tufts clearly separated from each other. As the card started to pass between the cylinder and the brushes an electrical current was fed into the metal cylinder. There was a single wire leading from the tuft which was dropped through the hole. The electrical current picked up by the wire brush was fed along this wire into the computer.

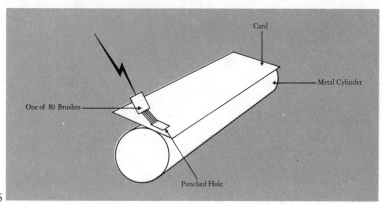

One of 80 Brushes

Card

Metal Cylinder

Punched Hole

Figure 6.6

There were 80 of these wires, one for each column of the card. There was a timing device which enabled the computer to tell from which row the electrical impulse was coming.

Another technique still used to sense holes is one utilizing the principle of the **photoelectric cell**. As the card is being fed through the card reader, a light is played on it. Where there is a hole punched on the card, the light shines through into a light-sensing photoelectric cell. This cell converts the light into electrical impulses and conveys this impulse to the computer. Again, timing is extremely important in determining where on the card the punch is located.

KEY TAPE OR KEY DISC

A device which is proving to be more efficient than the card punch is the key tape or disc. It is similar to the key punch but the medium, instead of being a card, is magnetic tape or disc. Data is recorded onto tape or disc in much the same way sound is put on the tape of a tape recorder. After the data is encoded, the tape or disc permits more rapid transfer of the data into the computer. Tape or disc media are more convenient to store and can be reused.

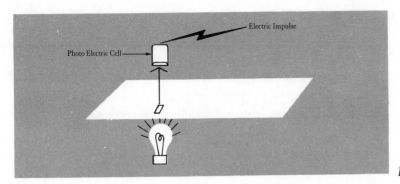

Figure 6.7

MARK READING: THE OPTICAL MARK CARD

There is a trend away from the punched card to a card on which data can be recorded with pencil marks. Industry found serious bottlenecks in the preparation of cards by key punch. The mark cards have been developed for convenience and to reduce the amount of punching of cards by specially trained key punch operators. Certain cards are specially designed to have data recorded on them in pencil.

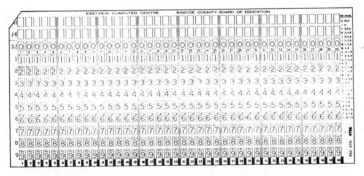

Figure 6.8

Note that the pencil-marked data does not have to be converted to punched holes. Devices to read pencil marks are called **optical mark readers** or OMR. They use the principle of reflecting light into a photo-electric cell. When a mark is sensed, the photoelectric cell generates an electrical current. This electrical current is then carried to the computer.

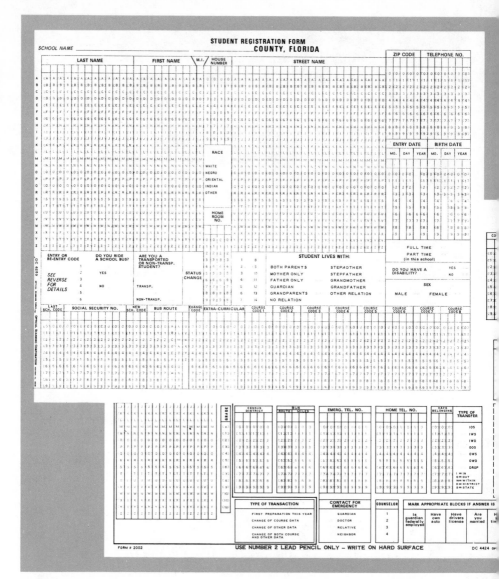

Figure 6.9

THE OPTICAL MARK SHEET

Other devices will accept a full page on which data has been encoded in pencil. These pages contain small box-type areas which can be shaded in with pencil. The device will scan over the page to sense the marks. The device and the computer are then able to interpret what data the marks represent.

There are quite a number of applications for this type of function. Aptitude and intelligence tests, examinations, certain types of questionnaires, and even the census forms are designed to permit encoding by pencil.

Figure 6.10

MAGNETIC INK CHARACTER RECOGNITION

At the bottom of all cheques there are marks which, with a little imagination, could be interpreted as numbers. These are, in fact, numbers representing the bank and the branch of the bank on which the cheque is drawn.

THE TORONTO-DOMINION BANK

64 DUNLOP ST. E. & OWEN ST.
BARRIE, ONT.

PAY TO THE
ORDER OF

SAVINGS
ACCOUNT No.

$1,000,000

DOLLARS

Figure 6.11

The numbers are written in a special ink containing a trace of iron. These characters are called magnetic ink characters and the process of reading these characters is called **magnetic ink character recognition** or MICR. When cheques drawn on a bank in one city are deposited in a bank in another city, those cheques are sent to a clearing house. There is special equipment in that building to handle cheques with these strange looking characters. The cheques are passed through a machine which magnetizes the iron traces in the ink. The cheques then pass through a sorting machine which senses the magnetized spots and interprets them. It is then able to sort the cheques into various pockets called **stackers**. The

Figure 6.12

cheques are then removed and sent out to the appropriate city and the particular branch within the city on which the cheques are drawn. Most of this sorting is done with equipment which significantly reduces the number of clerks involved in clearing cheques.

OPTICAL READER

Certain shapes can be sensed by some sophisticated optical reading devices. Instead of sensing a dot or bar, these devices can sense the shape of the character and send it to the computer for analysis. The computer has stored in its memory the particular patterns of the alphabet characters and the digits. The computer attempts to interpret the character being sensed.

If a character matches one stored in the computer, the character is read into memory. This process is called **optical character recognition**.

Continuing research is being done which will permit a device to understand handwriting. You can well imagine the difficulty a computer will have to decipher some of the writing it may encounter. Without looking too far, you might be able to obtain examples of handwriting which human beings have difficulty in understanding, much less a computer!

When characters are made by hand with a certain amount of care an **OCR** device is able to interpret the shapes.

SOME OF THE OCR FONTS.

OCR - A
The OCR - A font is the standard approved by the American National Standards Institute. This style is available in three sizes.

OCR - A Size 1:
for high speed printers and typewriters

ABCDEFGHIJKLMNOPQRSTUVWXYZ 1234567890
⑂⑁⑀$%|&*{}_-+= —:;"'⑄.?/‡

OCR - A Size 3
for cash registers and adding machine tapes

ABCDEFGHIJKLMNOPQRSTUVWXYZ0123456789
ÜÑÄØÖÆÅ£¥'-{}%?⑁⑂⑀.⑄:;=+/$*"&|

OCR - A Size 4
for embossed plastic credit cards

0123456789
ABCDEFGHIJKLMNOPQRSTUVWXYZ&|
ÜÑÄØÖÆÅ£¥'-{}%?⑁⑂⑀.⑄:;=+/$*"

IBM 1287 & 1288 HANDPRINTED CHARACTERS
Each character should be formed as illustrated and nearly fill its box.

1234567890

Figure 6.13

SCANNING TECHNIQUES

MECHANICAL DISC — The following is the technique used by a mechanical disc scanner.

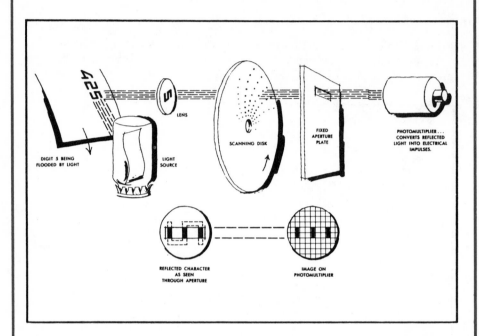

ARRAY OF PHOTOCELLS — Several rows of interconnected photocells, sense an entire character at once.

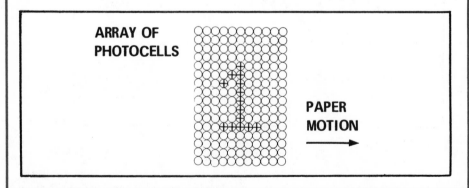

Figure 6.14

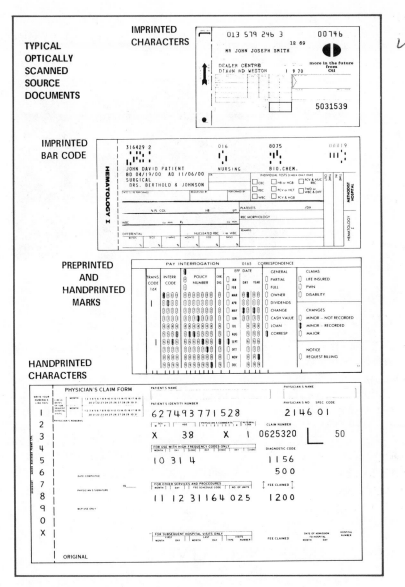

Figure 6.15

OTHER FORMS OF INPUT

Data can be inputted into the computer using interesting devices. Considerable progress has been made with **voice recognition** devices. These devices attempt to match voice patterns with pre-stored patterns. If there is a match the computer will 'understand' what has been said.

The **light pen** and **joystick** are two devices which aid in inputting data. Usually the data is displayed by the computer. The light pen or joy stick are used to *point out* the data which is now to be referenced.

Figure 6.16

CHECKING YOUR READING—LEVEL 1

1. In addition to the LET statement what other statement enables variable data to be loaded into a program?
2. Explain how the INPUT statement functions.
3. What other statements are used to get data into a computer?
4. In what way are data items in the data statement considered to be in a queue?
5. What punctuation separates the various data items in a DATA instruction?
6. What effect has the instruction RESTORE?
7. How is the dummy data item used to identify the end of file of a file of data items?
8. What is a data record?

CHECKING YOUR READING—LEVEL 2

1. Explain how a number such as the number 6379 is recorded on a computer card.
2. Rough out a chart to show how alphabetic data is encoded in a card using the Hollerith code.
3. What is a card field?
4. Illustrate or explain how the wire brush principle was used in the early card readers.
5. In what way is key to tape or key to disc more efficient than key punching?
6. What is the main principle of the optical mark reader?
7. What two types of optical mark readers exist?

8. Explain the principle of magnetic ink character recognition.
9. How is optical character recognition different from optical mark reading?
10. In simple terms how are each of the following used as input devices,
    (a) voice recognition
    (b) light pen
    (c) joy stick

VOCABULARY ASSIGNMENT

Continue developing your vocabulary list by writing a brief definition for the words or phrases in bold type in this section.

PROJECT

Checking For Errors

Identify and correct the errors or poor style which are in the following program segments.

```
1. INPUT "HOURS WORKED", H
2. 20 READ A, B, C
   99 DATA 25; 30; 50
3. 20 READ A, B, C
   99 DATA 10; 15
4. 20 FOR X = 1 TO 5
   30 READ A

       .
       .

   60 NEXT X
   99 DATA, 10; 20; 30; 50
```

Checking For Errors Review

```
5. 30 FOR X = 1 TO 15
   40     FOR Y = 1 TO 10
   50     LET N = N + Y
   60     NEXT X
   70 PRINT N
   80 NEXT Y
6. 30 INPUT "THE RATE OF PAY IS:X"
   40 PRINT "THE RATE OF PAY IS"
```

PROGRAMMING ASSIGNMENTS

On Purchasing an Automobile

1. Write a program to input the price of a new automobile, subtract the value of the trade-in and down payment, and output the balance owing. Use suitable prompting and output literals in your program.
2. Modify the above program to include the sales tax on the balance owing before the pre-delivery service charge is added on.
3. Modify the above program such that the number of months (i.e. 12, 24, 36) over which the balance will be paid is inputted. You could also include the per cent of the carrying charge. For example the carrying charge might be 1.5% per month. Have the computer output the monthly payment which would have to be paid in order to clear off the total debt in the number of months which have been established.
4. Modify the above program so that the time payments may be established for parts of a year, for example 28 months.

Salaries

5. Write a program which will produce under a suitable heading the salaries of the executives of the firm. Use the READ . . . DATA instructions. Provide your own data but keep it in the range of $10 000 and $99 999. The data must be in pure form, however. Do not include the dollar sign, a blank or a comma within the number. Use either a FOR . . . NEXT combination with the READ inside, or the IF . . . THEN and GO TO combination which was illustrated. (Remember this latter combination will be more fully explained in the next chapter.) You should add up the salaries and produce a mini report on total and average salaries.

Inventory Records

6. Write a program which will produce under a suitable heading an inventory report. Create inventory records in a DATA statement. Each record could contain, i) a product number, ii) the quantity on hand, and, iii) the unit cost. Output each record. Use commas to separate the variables following the PRINT. Compute and accumulate the value of the inventory of each product and output the total value of the inventory.
7. Modify the above program to output the product number, quantity, unit cost and *value of each product inventory.* Then output the total value under the last column.

Using RESTORE

8. Write a program which will READ a series of data items, print them

out and accumulate their values. Compute the average. RESTORE the data and read each item again, this time producing the difference between each number and the average of all the numbers.

9. Write a program to INPUT a number. Then read through the data file outputting each item and the item multiplied by the inputted number. After all the data items are read, RESTORE and go back to receive another number from the input instruction. Provide a suitable prompt and suitable headings or comments in the output.

The Time Clock

10. Write a program to input the employee number and the start time and stop time of an employee each day. Input the policy for overtime. (For example if the employee works two hours or more over the basic eight hours in a day, the employee is to receive 'time and a half.' Up to, but not including 10 hours in a day is paid at the regular rate.) Have the computer output the regular hours worked for each day in the week and any overtime if appropriate.
    (a) You might find it easier to use the '24-hour' clock.
    (b) As more of a challenge use the regular time notation—in the a.m. . . . 10, 11, 12, and in p.m. 1, 2, 3 . . .

As A Matter of Interest

11. Write a program which calculates interest, compounded daily.
12. Write a program which inputs the principal, rate and time of a loan in years. Have it calculate the interest compounded quarterly. Also have it calculate the interest if the loan is paid off at other than a quarter segment of the year, for example, one year and 45 days.

ADDITIONAL ASSIGNMENTS

Scientific Applications

1. The frequency of a pendulum is considered to be the number of vibrations per second. Write a program which would input the count of the vibrations and the number of seconds during which the count was taken. Output with a suitable literal the vibrations per second.
2. The **period** of a pendulum is the length of time it takes to swing back and forth once. It is determined by dividing the number of vibrations by the number of seconds over which the count was taken. Program a routine to prompt the inputting of the vibration count and the duration of the count. Output the period.

CHAPTER 7

CONDITIONS

Level 1

IF . . . THEN[1]

Perhaps the one instruction which has really separated the computer from other, so called, programmable machines is the instruction which directs the computer to jump around to various instructions depending on certain conditions. The computer can be programmed to look for a certain condition. If it is not present, it would carry on with one series of instructions. If the condition is present, the computer would branch to a different series of instructions. The BASIC instruction which causes the computer to *make decisions* is the IF . . . THEN instruction.

Example

```
             .
             .
             .
        130 LET X = 26
        140 IF X = 15 THEN (branch to) 9998
        150 LET Y = X * X
        160 LET X = X − 1
        170 PRINT Y
        180 GO TO 140
        9998 PRINT "EOJ"
        9999 END
```

[1]Those instructors and programmers who feel strongly about structured programming will likely be concerned about this chapter being included in the text. Student programmers will have to deal with these instructions as they work on updating and augmenting packaged programs. In addition, in the author's experience, these instructions aid in the understanding of programming concepts in the early stages of programming. Fear not, for these instructions will be put in perspective later.

Instruction 140 asks the computer a question. The answer is either yes or no. Does X equal 15? If this condition is true, 'yes it does equal 15,' the computer will branch to instruction 9998. If the condition is not true, as it will not be true 9 times, the computer will continue with the next instruction in sequence. Statement 180 directs the computer to go back to instruction 140, to check once more if the condition stated is true.

The word *branch* has been used to describe the action which the computer takes. The IF . . . THEN instruction contains a *maybe* branch: IF X = 15 THEN branch to 9998. On the other hand statement number 180 clearly indicates a *must* branch. The difference between the two is significant. In the IF . . . THEN statement the computer would only branch on the existence of a *condition*. This is called a **conditional branch**. The GO TO statement *requires* that the computer branch; there is no choice in the matter. This is called an **unconditional branch**.

Note how similar the IF . . . THEN statement is to the FOR . . . NEXT instruction. It does duplicate much of what the FOR . . . NEXT is able to do. It does, however, add to our bag of tricks.

In a later chapter the concept of structured programming will be covered. Some programmers attempt to write all programs without the use of the GO TO instruction, even if the program must be written in an awkward way. Most programmers, however, find that limited use of this instruction enables efficient, easy to follow programs to be written.

THE COMPUTER HAS A 'CONDITION'

In the above illustration the condition used was the *equal to* condition. There are quite a variety of conditions which could be used.

```
= equals
> greater than
< less than
> = greater than or equal to
< = less than or equal to
< > not equal to
```

Assume that a program is required to calculate the commission on sales of employees. The higher the sale the higher the rate of commission.

```
10 REM *** THIS PROGRAM CALCULATES VARIABLE
    SALES COMMISSIONS
20 REM S = A SALE: C = COMMISSION; T1 = TOTAL
    COMMISSION: T2 = TOTAL SALES; K = COUNTER
100 LET T1 = 0
110 LET T2 = 0
120 LET K = 0
130 READ S
```

```
140 IF S = 999 THEN 400
150 LET K = K + 1
160 IF S< = 200 THEN 190
170 IF S> 400 THEN 240
180 IF S< = 400 THEN 290
190 LET C = S * .10
200 PRINT "SALESPERSON #";S;"      COMMISSION $";C
210 LET T2 = T2 + S

220 LET T1 = T1 + C
230 GO TO 130
240 LET C = S * .125
250 PRINT "SALESPERSON #";S;"      COMMISSION $";C
260 LET T2 = T2 + S
270 LET T1 = T1 + C
280 GO TO 130
290 LET C = S * .15
300 PRINT "SALESPERSON #";S;"      COMMISSION $";C
310 LET T2 = T2 + S
320 LET T1 = T1 + C
330 GO TO 130
```

SUBROUTINES

Did you notice in the program above that, depending on the condition, the computer branched to a section in the program where a special task was done? These sections had a group of instruction numbers. This is a very common practice in programming. Modules of instructions are written to do specific tasks. When the task is to be done, the computer branches to that module. Structuring a program to have special tasks done at certain times has proven to be good programming. The GOSUB . . . RETURN instruction provides another efficient method of doing this.

Assume that within a program the area of a circle is to be calculated a number of times. A **subroutine** to do this task, assigned high numbered instruction numbers, could look something like this:

```
1000 LET R = D / 2
1010 LET A = 3.14 * R * R
1020 PRINT "THE AREA OF THE CIRCLE IS";A
1030 RETURN
```

This routine is now available to the program to be called in and executed on command. For example:

```
120 INPUT "THE DIAMETER OF THE CIRCLE IS";D
130 GOSUB 1000
140 PRINT "IS THERE ANOTHER AREA YOU WISH TO
    CALCULATE? . . . etc.
```

In this example, instruction number 120 is executed. Instruction 130 causes the computer to *call in* the instructions beginning with number 1000. The subroutine is executed. The last instruction in the subroutine directs the computer to return 'from whence it came,' namely, the next instruction after the GO SUB instruction. So there is an instruction which sends the computer to the subroutine, and an instruction, the last one in the subroutine, which sends the computer back to the *next instruction to be executed.*

It is possible that a subroutine might call in another subroutine. The computer would branch to that second subroutine, execute it and return to the *next instruction* in the first subroutine to finish it up. When it was completed the computer would then return to the main part of the program.

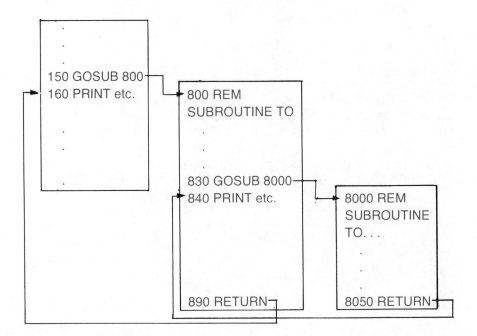

It is extremely important that the logic of what is taking place is clear in your mind as you program. Remember that the word RETURN always causes the computer to return to the *next instruction following the instruction sending the computer to that subroutine.*

It is possible to use GO TOs within a subroutine *but these should be avoided at all costs*. There is a strong possibility that logic errors might be created if GO TOs are used carelessly within a subroutine. It is techniquely possible to use a GO TO to branch out of a subroutine but you should not attempt to branch into a middle of a subroutine. Using GO TOs in subroutines lead to possible logic errors.

The *structure* of programs should be such that there is a main line or basic logic segment which is serviced by modules or subroutines.

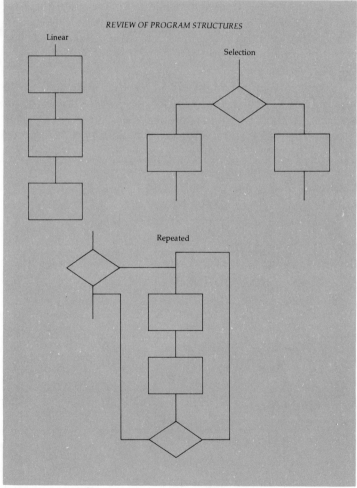

Figure 7.1

Level 2

HOW THE CPU EXECUTES A BRANCH

You will recall that the control section has a number of registers. In addition to the Instruction Register there is an Operation Register, an A-Address Register and a B-Address Register. Also in the control section there is an instruction *address* register. This register tells the computer the address of the next instruction which it will be executing. If the instruction in storage address 0004 is now being executed, the instruction address register would indicate a 0005. After instruction 0004 is executed, the computer would check the instruction register. It would sense the 0005 and go to storage address 0005 to obtain a copy of the instruction. A copy of that instruction would then be moved into the instruction register of the control section. Do not confuse the memory address of an instruction with the instruction number. Instructions are stored in memory in consecutive locations even though there are likely gaps in the BASIC instruction numbers.

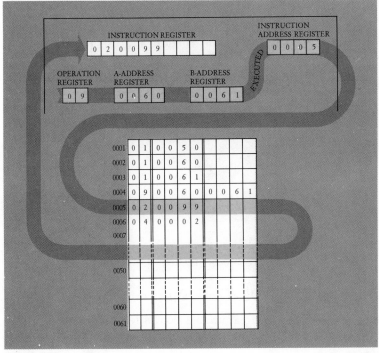

Figure 7.2

At that point, the instruction register would be increased by 1 to 0006.

Frequently programs contain branch instructions. Assume that the instruction 0006 is now in the instruction register. The instruction address register would contain 0007 which is the location of the next instruction to be executed. In a way the computer will be anticipating moving the instruction in address 0007 into the instruction register.

If the instruction *now being executed* was, in effect, GO TO 0002, the operation register would cause the digits 0002 to be moved into the instruction address register.

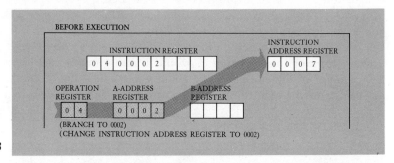

Figure 7.3

After this move is complete, the control section is signalled to obtain the next instruction. It checks the instruction address register which now contains 0002.

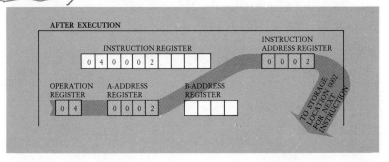

Figure 7.4

It then proceeds to storage address 0002 to obtain the next instruction. The branch instruction has therefore been carried out.

CHECKING YOUR READING—LEVEL 1

1. What one feature of a programmable computer makes it different from the earlier so-called programmable machines such as accounting machines?
2. Differentiate between a conditional branch and an unconditional branch?
3. Make a table of the various conditions which could be tested for in a statement.
4. What is a subroutine?

5. To what point in the program does the subroutine return?

VOCABULARY ASSIGNMENT

Continue developing your vocabulary list by writing a brief definition of the words or phrases in bold type in this section.

CHECKING YOUR READING—LEVEL 2

1. As a program is being executed, what normally takes place in the register which we have called the next instruction register?
2. If a branch is called for, what takes place in that register?
3. Outline how this register is used as a type of 'pointer' during the execution of sequential instructions, and during a branch.

PROJECTS

Checking for Errors

Identify the errors or poor style in the following program segments:

```
1. 130 INPUT "KEY IN VALUE OF THE AUTOMOBILE";V
   140 IF V< = 4000 THEN 400
   150 IF V<    5000 THEN GO TO 500
        .
        .
        .

2. 130 INPUT X
   140 IF X = 5 GO TO 500
3. 130 INPUT Y
   140 IF X = 25 THEN 200 ELSE GO TO 300
   150 FOR Z = 1 TO 20
   160 LET Y = Y + X + Z
   200
        .
        .
        .
   300
        .
        .

4. 150 GOSUB 500
   160 PRINT X
   170 INPUT Y
        .
        .
```

```
500 FOR = 1 TO 10
510 LET X = X + Y
520 GO TO 170
        .

        .
5. 160 INPUT Z
   170 IF Z = 50 THEN GO TO SUB 600
        .

        .

        .
   600 LET Z = Z * 3.14 * 2
   610 RETURN
```

Checking For Errors Review

```
6.   30 READ D, E, F
     99 DATA 10; 20; 40; 50
7. 10 PRINT "THE COUNTING NUMBERS FROM 1 TO 10"
   20 FOR X = 1 TO 10
   30 LET X = X + 1
   40 PRINT X
   50 NEXT X
```

PROGRAMMING ASSIGNMENTS

Sales Commissions

1. Without using subroutines, write a program which will input data structured as follows: salesperson's number and sales. If the salesperson's number is 99, your program has reached the end of file—a dummy record. The commission rate varies with the sales. The rate for sales up to but not including $50 000 is 2 per cent. Between $50 000 and $74 999 the rate is 3 per cent, and from $75 000 to $99 999, the rate is 4 per cent. For sales $100 000 or over the rate is 5 per cent. Output a list of salesperson's numbers, their sales and their commissions. You supply the test data.
2. Revise the above program using subroutines, and accumulate and output the total sales and total commissions.
3. Your employer comes up with a new proposal on how the salespersons should be paid. Each would receive a basic monthly salary of $800 plus a bonus of 1 per cent commission on sales over $10 000. For example, a salesperson selling $55 000 worth of goods would receive $800 basic salary and 1 per cent on $45 000 sales. Program the computer to produce a comparison of the two systems of payment outlined in question #1 and this question.

Example

Sales	Less Base	Bonus
<50 000		(no bonus)
50 000 − 74 999	10 000	40 000 − 64 999 @ 2%
75 000 − 99 999	10 000	65 000 − 89 999 @ 3%
> = 100 000	10 000	> = 90 000 @ 4%

4. In determining commissions, certain combinations of information can produce useful information. The total sales, the commission rate and the commission are the basic components. In order to find the commission the formula is $C = S * R$, where C = the commission, S = total sales, and R = commission rate. Sometimes it is required to find the rate if the sales and commission are known. In this case $R = C/S$. Or, the sales might be required if the commission and rate are known, using $S = C/R$. Write a program to input C, S, and R. One of the three will be a zero. Using subroutines, produce the required output using a suitable literal.

Inventory Inquiry

5. This program is similar to one in the previous chapter. An inventory file is established. Each record has 3 data items. (Only two are used in this program.) Instead of producing an inventory report create an INPUT routine so that an inquiry is able to be made of the computer. Using appropriate prompts, input the product number and the quantity of the product currently being ordered. READ through the DATA until the corresponding product number is located. Check to see if there is sufficient on hand to fill the order. Produce the appropriate message. For example "There is sufficient quantity on hand" or "Insufficient quantity. Only part of the shipment can be made." Of course should your program run into the end of file indicator, it means that there is no such product number on file. A suitable message should be produced in this case as well.

   The logic for this program is a little tricky. After any one of the three situations have been encountered, RESTORE the data and loop back to the inquiry instructions. Perhaps an inquiry for a product number 0 would indicate that the program is no longer needed and should come to a logical end.

Police Inquiry

6. This popular program is patterned on the above but the data file is made up of licence numbers of cars which have been stolen. A police officer makes an inquiry to see if a licence on a suspicious car is on file. If it is on file output a suitable message such as "Apprehend with caution" or some other more creative phrase. If it is not on file output a suitable message, perhaps including a reminder to

"wish the driver a happy day." In either case be sure to RESTORE the data before going back for another inquiry input.

On Renting An Automobile

7. Write a program to input a code representing the type of automobile which has been rented (for example, a subcompact's code might be a 1, compact is 2, standard size is 3 and limousine is 4). Also input the beginning and ending odometer readings, which could be used to calculate the distance driven. Have the computer print out the cost of renting the car if the rental rate is based on the following schedule:

Vehicle Type	Basic Charge	Rate Per Kilometre
1	$15	10¢
2	$18	13¢
3	$22	18¢
4	$35	30¢

Provide in your program the possibility of a sales tax added to the rental costs.

ADDITIONAL ASSIGNMENTS

8. Write program to compute distances. The input is kilometres: feet, yards, and miles are outputted.

   Hint
   Multiply by 3281 for feet
   Multiply by 1093.6 for yards
   Multiply by 0.6214 for miles

9. An electric company charges 5 cents per kilowatt hour up to the first 100 kilowatt hours and 4 cents per kW·h after that. Use data statements containing customer name and total # of kW·h. Output name, hours, and cost. Use a dummy record to tell the computer when to stop processing.

Optimum Ticket Price

10. A theatre company discovers that at a price of $5.00 for each ticket they would be able to sell 300 tickets per performance. Each 10 cents off the price would increase sales of tickets by 15. It would also increase its expenses by 6 cents. His expenses currently are 150 cents per person. Write a basic program to print a table for prices of tickets from $5.00 down to $2.50. At the end print the best price at which to sell the tickets.

Part II: A LOGICAL APPROACH

CHAPTER 8

PROBLEM-SOLVING AND PROGRAM STRUCTURE

Level 1

STEPS IN PROBLEM-SOLVING

When scientists tackle a problem they do so in a very organized fashion. The scientist has a goal, and some organized system is used in an attempt to reach that goal. This approach has been refined over the years and is now called the **scientific approach**.

Problem solving is not the exclusive task of scientists. Any complex problem in the everyday world requires some organized approach before a solution is found. Problems which can be solved on the computer are often quite complex. This type of problem usually requires some organized approach if a satisfactory solution is to be found.

Generally there are 6 steps in solving a problem. Below is a comparison of the logical approach used by a scientist to that used by a programmer.

SCIENTIFIC APPROACH	THE SCIENTIFIC APPROACH IS APPLIED TO COMPUTER PROGRAMMING
1. Establish an Objective—what is it you want to prove?	Define the Problem—what is it you want the computer to do?
2. Develop a method—what equipment, chemicals, etc. are needed and what are you going to do with them?	Analyse the problem and develop a solution.
3. Carry out the experiment.	Test the solution.
4. Evaluate the results—modify and repeat experiment if necessary.	Check the results to make sure the program works as intended—correct and re-test if necessary.
5. Draw a conclusion.	Implement the program.
6. Formally write up the experiment.	Document the program—write up how the problem was solved using the computer.

PROBLEM DEFINITION

Before attempting to write any program the programmer must first of all obtain a thorough understanding of what must be done by the computer. If the program is a payroll program, for example, the programmer must ask questions and obtain payroll information to establish exactly what the program must do.

> OBTAINING A THOROUGH UNDERSTANDING OF A PROBLEM IS ESSENTIAL BEFORE ANY SOLUTION IS ATTEMPTED.

In obtaining that thorough understanding some basic questions could be answered:
1) what is/are the input(s)? are prompts required?
2) what output is required? headings? data lists? summary lines?
3) what processing must be done? computing? counting? accumulating?

The required functions and features of the problem are usually written out in simple English. This statement is called the **problem definition** or sometimes the problem statement.

ANALYSIS AND SOLUTION

Some programming texts have separate steps listed for analysis and solving of the problem. This is a valid way to outline the sequence to problem solving. There is, however, a fine line between analysing a problem and developing a solution. As a programmer identifies what must be done, a solution seems to evolve at the same time.

Generally the programmer must establish the:
1. input which the program will use
2. various processes to be done in the computer
3. output which is required

Usually in a text such as this, the problem definition is given. Your task is to determine how to go about solving the problem, then solve it. Be sure to deal with all parts of the problem definition. If necessary use a pencil to circle key words representing processes. Perhaps input and output processes could be circled twice.

As an aid in getting yourself organized, you could develop a checklist of programming functions which should be considered. Below is an outline of such a checklist which could be used as an aid in the solving of fairly common computer problems.

PROGRAMMING CHECKLIST

INPUT   Source   Structure

PROCESS	Accumulate?	What fields?
	Count?	What?
	Calculate?	What?
OUTPUT	Device	Headings
		Prompts and/or Menus
		Detail Lines
		Summary Lines
		EOJ Indicator

You probably do not know the meaning of all these names and phrases but in time you will.

Another aid in the analysis and solution of a problem is the sketching of an **algorithm** of some type. An algorithm is a representation of the step by step logic used in solving a problem. Although covered more fully later, they should at least be mentioned at this point. Algorithms can be represented by flowcharts, structured diagrams, decision tables and tree diagrams.

TESTING THE SOLUTION AND CHECKING ITS OUTPUT

On running a new program, if there is output the first of *two* classes of test has been done. The program works! But does it work correctly? Is the output correct? Would the output be correct if the input data were a very large or very small number? More later about testing. It is sufficient at this point to plant *the seed* that good programmers take time and pride in making sure their programs do what they are supposed to do.

IMPLEMENTATION OF THE PROGRAM

Most programs written for industry are run repeatedly. Once a new program is written and carefully tested it becomes part of the package of programs run on the computer.

There are a number of safety checks which take place before the program is officially accepted for use on the computer. Once these checks have been made the program is put to work. This stage is said to be the **implementation stage**.

DOCUMENTATION

Documenting a program is the task of putting together all the relevant information about the program. The **documentation** would include:

- The problem definition or description
- The logic representation
- The listing of the program
- Test results (including the data used)

- Layout sheets (more about that later)
- Any special running instructions or special program messages

The programs you have done so far have been fairly simple. There may have been a loop, or even a nested loop, but the programs have been relatively short and simple. Some of the programming assignments which follow in the text are much more complex. The programs require a variety of functions and safety checks. If all functions in a program were simply related to each other, the writing of a long program could be fairly straightforward. Unfortunately, most programming is not like that. Often there are complex **linkages** among programming **segments**. The linkages or GO TOs join various parts of the program. These could result in a nightmare of conditional and unconditional branches.

DEVELOPMENTS IN THE ART OF PROGRAMMING

In the early days of programming there was not too much concern about the organization of a program. Often the programmer simply patched together various sub-programs with conditional and unconditional branches.

Once the program was finished and *appeared* to test out, the programmer went onto other tasks. In addition some programmers used to develop a very complex logic in order to save the computer the execution of a number of operations. In fact some student programs were evaluated to some degree on how short a time it took the computer to execute the program. Many of these programs, however, could only be readily understood by the programmer who wrote them. After a few months, even that programmer often had trouble figuring out just how he/she originally wrote them. The problem arose, and it was a very serious problem, that when the program had to be modified, it was almost impossible to follow the structure of the original program. Even if the original programmer were available, and that was often not the case, the logic and linkages of the program were frequently a mystery to the author.

In order to deal with this problem computer centre managers began to insist on well documented programs. The logic used had to be outlined in some fashion. A list of all instructions used in the program had to be made and this **listing** was kept on file. This made updates somewhat easier to do but the task was often difficult, especially if the program was complex. An even better method was needed.

COMPUTER'S VS. PROGRAMMER'S TIME

It has become an accepted practice in programming to take more care in organizing or structuring a complex program even though careful structuring might require two or three more seconds for the computer to run the program. Computers now process instructions very rapidly. It is thought better to design a program which is easier to update than one which saves the computer a second or two.

In simple terms, a program should be written in such a way that the main functions of the program clearly stand out as one looks down the listing. In order for this to be done, special tasks are removed from the main logic section of the program and relegated to sub programs or subroutines or **modules**. The main or key functions are considered to be the mainline of the program. If one looked over only the mainline of the program the various major components of the program should be easily identified.

```
90  REM   **************************
91  REM   **************************
92  REM   **                      **
93  REM   ** MAINLINE LOGIC       **
94  REM   **                      **
95  REM   **************************
96  REM   **************************
97  REM
98  REM
99  REM
100 OPEN ...              :REM **OPEN FILES**
110 GOSUB 1010            :REM **INITIALIZE VARIABLES**
120 READ...               :REM **INITIAL READ**
130 GOSUB 2010            :REM **PROCESS RECORDS**
140 GOSUB 3010            :REM **SUMMARY ROUTINE**
150 CLOSE...              :REM **CLOSE FILES**
160 END
1000REM   **********************
1001REM   **********************
1002REM   **                  **
1003REM   ** INITIALIZE ROUTINE **
1004REM   **                  **
1005REM   **********************
1006REM   **********************
1007REM
1008REM
1009REM
1010LET X = 0
        .
        .
        .
2000REM   **********************
2001REM   **********************
2002REM   **                  **
2003REM   ** PROCESS RECORDS RTN **
2004REM   **                  **
2005REM   **********************
2006REM   **********************
2007REM
2008REM
2009REM
2010 IF condition THEN RETURN
        .
        .
        .
```

Figure 8.1

MAINLINE LOGIC

In 'top down' programming the program is divided into logical segments. Each segment has an independent function. Within each segment might be an internal control instruction, such as input or output. The segment might also contain a high level process instruction, which might, for example, identify which major modules will process the data. The functional segments of the mainline logic will usually maintain the highest level of internal control—the control most critical to the total program. As a type of servant to the main segments or modules are the lesser utility modules or subroutines.

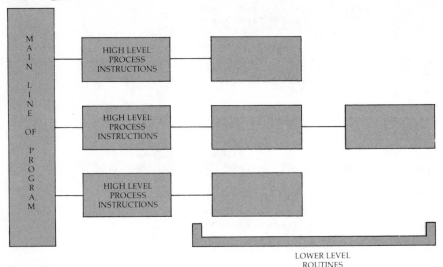

Figure 8.2

ADVANTAGES OF STRUCTURED PROGRAMMING

Modular or structured programming has many advantages. A few of which include:
- additional subroutines may be added if needed, with a minimum of change to the mainline logic of the program
- for security and other reasons a large program might be written by a number of different programmers; the distribution of the programming task is easier if the program is written modularly
- logic errors, particularly those involving GO TOs are reduced if the program is written in modules
- the program can be tested early in its formation and subsequent modules are then integrated and tested in a 'clean' skeleton
- a change in one module usually does not create multiple changes in other modules

STRUCTURE PROGRAMMING VS. GO TOs

Some programmers feel so strongly about writing programs in modules they *will not use* GO TOs. Other programmers avoid if possible these instructions, but periodically find them convenient. These programmers, of course, make sure their program is modular.

You will be urged to structure your programs using a mainline logic and subroutines or sub programs or modules. If you are able to conveniently avoid the GO TOs (other than GOSUB) then do so. If you have to

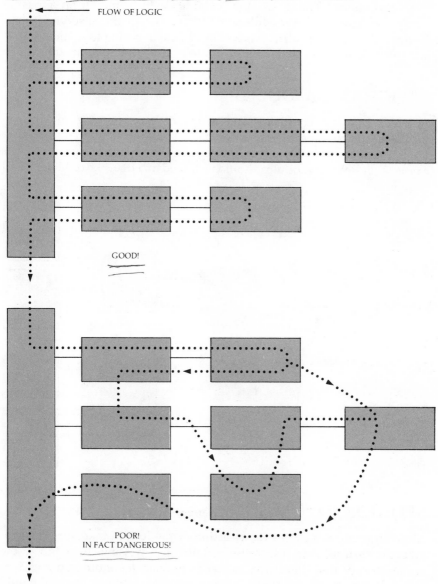

FLOW OF LOGIC

GOOD!

POOR!
IN FACT DANGEROUS!

Figure 8.3

use GO TOs be sure they transfer control either within a module or at least up and down the **hierachical line**. It is very risky to GO TO a module in another branch of the program.

One of the tests of a good program, is how clearly the mainline logic stands out. Refer to the illustrations. In the left column is an outline of the **mainline logic**. The various steps which represent the main objectives of the program are shown. There are no arrows or loops in the diagram. The eye begins at the top of the mainline logic and flows down to the bottom. This approach is sometimes called **top to bottom logic**. To the right, are the subroutines. These are the modules which might be repeated numerous times. Some modules could have sub-modules serving them. Notice that the edit routine has a sub-module available to it such that, if an error is found, the error routine module is called in to look after it.

PROGRAM MODULES

In order to avoid confusing and awkward programming, the use of modules is encouraged. A module does a special task and usually has a limited number of instructions. Usually, *each module has only one entrance and one exit*. Related modules should be linked in a tree-like or hierarchical fashion.

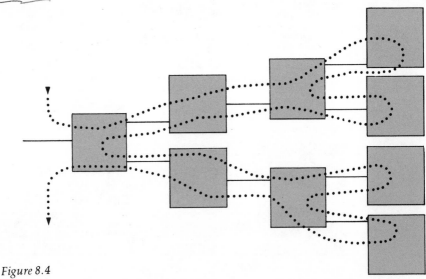

Figure 8.4

SEQUENCE OF MODULES

Avoid jumping around in the selection of modules. Make sure the program flows from *a* to *b* to *c*. Sometimes it is possible to organize the sequence such that there are clear paths of logic depending on the identification of a certain condition. Where possible, repeated routines should be performed *while* a condition is true.

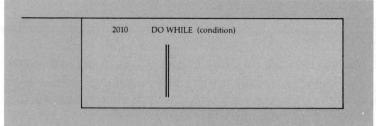

Figure 8.5

PRINCIPLE OF THE INITIAL READ

In the illustration below there are two inputs represented. Sometimes it is more efficient to obtain the first record to be processed in an initial read, then have subsequent reads as part of a module. Notice that the READ which inputs all but the first data record is at the *end* of a module. The READ is performed and end of file is tested. If it is the end of file the condition for performing that routine will no longer be present. Control will pass on down the line. If the READ instruction were at the beginning of a module, when the end of file record is identified, a GO TO would have to be used to avoid attempting to do further processing of the dummy record.

```
10  REM    INVENTORY PROGRAM
       .
       .
90  REM    P = PRODUCT NUMBER
91  REM    Q = QUANTITY
92  REM    C = COST
       .
       .
130  READ P, Q, C
140  IF P <> 999 THEN GOSUB 300: REM CHECK FOR NULL
FILE
       .
       .
300  LET V = Q * C          :REM REPEAT SUBROUTINE
310  PRINT P, Q, C, V
320  READ P, Q, C
330  IF P <> 999 THEN GO TO 300
340  RETURN
```

Although there is no fixed rule, as you gain experience in structured programming you will find that the main line logic will be represented by line numbers 100 to 200 or 250 in steps of 10. Only 10 or 15 instructions are required to:
- open and close files (more about that later)
- initialize some variables (LET instructions)

- the initial READ
- and an instruction to call in a subroutine for a summary line or other 'wrap-up' instructions

Note: BASIC has been enhanced by a group based at the University of Waterloo. With the "Waterloo chip" structured programming in BASIC is much more convenient. For example the subroutine shown above would be coded with the very convenient DO . . . WHILE instruction. GO TOs and IF . . . THEN GO TOs would be eliminated.

Just for fun one could simulate this by replacing the above subroutine with this somewhat awkward routine:

```
300 LET N = 9999
310 FOR X = 1 TO N
320 LET V = Q * C
330 PRINT P, Q, C, V
340 READ P, Q, C
350 IF P = 999 THEN N = 9999
360 NEXT X
370 RETURN
```

HIERARCHY

At the bottom of the illustration is an arrow which indicates the hierarchy of the program sections. The highest in the hierarchy is the mainline

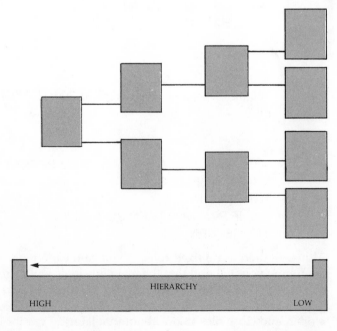

Figure 8.6

logic. Major modules which handle important, significant functions are next in the hierarchy, and the small utility modules are considered to be the lowest in the hierarchy.

Level 2

MATRICES AND SUBSCRIPTING

The FOR . . . NEXT function of BASIC certainly gave us considerable computing power. Another function which is extremely convenient for handling related groups of data is the **subscripted array**. With a name like that one would think that it must be complex and difficult to understand. There are one or two tricky things to remember, but once you understand the logic, you will find it a very convenient tool in your programming bag of tricks.

Before studying this new concept, it is helpful to think through the addressing used in an *apartment building,* of all things! Let us assume that there is an apartment building on Maple Crescent, the only building on the street. There are 25 apartments in the building. Let us further assume that the post office uses the code letter M to represent Maple Crescent. In order to send mail to a family, in say, apartment 17, the address might read: "Maple Crescent, Apt. 17". But since the post office has a code, perhaps the coded address might be M(17). Keep in mind an obvious fact: Apartment 17 has a family living in it—it contains people. Now look at an 'apartment building' which can be created in the computer's memory.

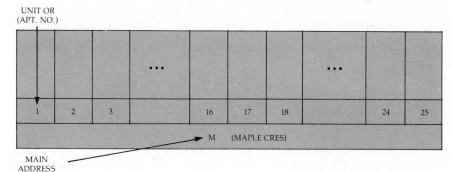

Figure 8.7

To create the apartment building, more properly called an array, an instruction is given to the computer to set aside and organize a part of its memory. The instruction is:

```
10 DIM M(25)
```

The DIM is a short form for the word **dimension**. The M is the label or variable name given to the main address of the apartment building or array. The "(25)" informs the computer of the number of apartments or data cells that are to be in the building or array. Just to see if you have been following this, analyse the following:

> 110 DIM Z(100)

Of course the 110 is the instruction number. The DIM is for dimension which advises the computer that a large group of related items will have to be stored in memory. The Z is the 'street address' or the main address of the array. There would be 100 groups of memory cells which can hold 100 pieces of related data. Now that the memory has been properly reserved and organized with an array let us see what can be done with it.

ACCESSING ARRAYS

First of all, remember that the post office code for apartment number 17 was M(17). Also remember that that apartment had a family in it. Similarly, in storage, any one of the 25 addresses of the array set up by DIM M(25) may be accessed. Data may be loaded into that location or data obtained from it. You are accustomed to using a variable name or label such as C or J. For example, you are quite comfortable using instructions such as:

110 LET C = 0

Using specific elements of an array will soon become just as automatic. To illustrate, assume the contents of apartment 17 must be initialized at 0. The statement would be:

130 LET M(17) = 0

Or one of the elements in the array could be initialized at some other amount:

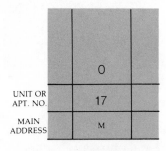

Figure 8.8

140 LET M(20) = 200
150 LET M(21) = 300

In fact, arithmetic can be performed on the contents of these addresses just as it could be done on the contents of simple variables:

160 LET X = M(20) * M(21)

What would be the product of statement 160? Would it be 20 × 21 = 420? If you react with horror to this suggestion, good for you. The numbers 20 and 21 are the *partial addresses* of two pieces of data. The *contents* of these addresses are 200 and 300. The correct value for X, therefore, would be 60 000.

SUBSCRIPTING

Up to now, the only way the addresses of an array have been represented was to have an actual number within the brackets. It is also possible to put a label in those brackets.

```
170 LET C = 13
180 LET M(C) = 400
```

Hmmm, the plot thickens! Here we have a compound address, the second part of which is obtained from the content of another address—the content of the address C! Don't panic yet! Just think through the two or three steps involved. We know that the content of C is 13. We know that the value 400 is to be put into an apartment in a building with the main address of M. What apartment number? The apartment number of the content of C which is 13—yes, the 400 goes into M(13). Got it?

Although the following is rarely used, just to give you the whole picture the apartment number could even be computed right inside the brackets. What apartment or element number is referred to in this statement:

```
50 LET X = M(3 * 2)
```

The answer of course is that address X would be assigned the value of the content of element number 6 in the array M. That is a tough one. Go back over that sentence until it makes sense to you.

It is time to play with this function to get used to using it. Study the following:

Example 1:	*Example 2:*
120 DIM M(25)	120 DIM M(25)
130 LET X = 0	130 FOR C = 1 TO 25
140 FOR C = 1 TO 25	140 LET M(C) = C
150 LET X = X + 2	150 PRINT M(C)
160 LET M(C) = X	160 NEXT C
170 PRINT M(C)	
180 NEXT C	

In example 1 the variable X will contain the 'count by twos.' The values 2, 4, 6, etc. will be loaded into the first, second and third apartments respectively. In the second example, because C varies from 1 to 25 in steps of 1, the value C is moved into the element number C.

This section of program therefore loads the counting numbers into the 25 elements of the array. Just after it loads the one number into the element it causes the content of the element to be printed out so that one can see what is going on. Perhaps this is a little more interesting:

```
110 DIM M(25)
120 LET D = 25
130 FOR C = 1 TO 25
140 LET M(C) = D
150 LET D = D − 1
160 NEXT C
170 FOR C = 1 TO 25
180 PRINT M(C)
190 NEXT C
```

This time 25, the content of D, is loaded into the first element. Then 1 is subtracted from D, so that during the next pass the value 24 is loaded into the second element of M, and so on. A second FOR . . . NEXT statement is used to print out the elements to see what was in them.

CHECKING YOUR READING—LEVEL 1

1. List the six steps in problem solving in computer programming.
2. Why is it sometimes thought that analysis and finding a solution is almost a simultaneous process?
3. What is implementation and what care must be taken during the implementation stage?
4. What major shift has taken place over the years with respect to program design?
5. Why is it no longer necessary to be overly concerned about the apparent efficiency of a program?
6. What is meant by mainline logic?
7. In what way are subroutines or modules servants to one of the major segments in mainline logic?
8. Briefly outline four advantages to structural or modular programming.
9. GO TOs instruction are to be avoided. Under what circumstances may they be used?

10. In what way could a series of program modules be considered to be in a hierarchical structure?
11. If the READ instruction goes at the beginning of a module which was repeated many times, what problem would exist when the end-of-file was reached?

VOCABULARY ASSIGNMENT

Add the key words and phrases found in this section to your vocabulary list along with their definitions.

CHECKING YOUR READING—LEVEL 2

1. In what way is an array similar to an apartment building?
2. Write an example of a dimension statement which sets up an array, and identify each part of the statement.
3. In what way is subscripting like indirect addressing?

VOCABULARY ASSIGNMENT

Add the key words and phrases found in this section to your vocabulary list along with their definitions.

PROJECTS

Checking For Errors

Check and correct errors in the following Basic Program Segments. Logic errors are possible! Study the logic and correct if necessary.

```
1. 120 DIM M25
   120 REM LOADING ARRAY WITH COUNT-BY-TWOs TO
   120 LET M = 0
2. 130 DIM N(100)
   140 FOR X = 1 TO 100 STEP 2
   150 LET M = M + 1
   160 LET N(100) = M
   170 NEXT X
3. 110 REM LOADING COUNTING NUMBERS INTO AN
       ARRAY
   120 DIM N(25)
   130 FOR Y = 1 TO 25
   140 LET M = 0
   150 LET N(M + 1) = Y
   160 NEXT N
```

4. 110 REM LOADING SQUARES OF NUMBERS INTO AN
   ARRAY
   120 FOR A = 1 TO 10
   130 LET B = A * A
   140 LET M(A) = B
   150 NEXT A
5. 110 REM LOADING THE CUBES OF COUNTING NUMBERS
   INTO AN ARRAY
   120 DIM M(30)
   130 FOR B = 1 TO 50
   140 LET M(1) = B * B * B
   150 NEXT M

Review

6. 110 REM PRINTING OUT THE COUNTING NUMBERS
   120 LET X = 0
   130 IF X = 25 GO TO 160
   140 LET X = X + 1
   150 PRINT X
   160 GO TO 130
   170 END
7. 110 REM
   120 INPUT X
   130 IF X = 100 GO TO 190
   140 IF X = 200 GO TO 200
   150 PRINT "THE VALUE INPUTTED IS EITHER 100 or 200"
   190 REM ROUTING DEALING WITH THE VALUE 100 etc.

PROGRAMMING ASSIGNMENTS

Note: Wherever possible, use modules or structure programming with actual or implied subroutines.

Hotel Management

1. Write a program which would create a matrix which would correspond to the number of rooms in a hotel or motel. Load the matrix with zeros. The matrix represents the reservation log for one day. As each room is reserved, place a 1 in the matrix element representing the room. A person reserving the room may request a certain room, or the rooms may be assigned in some sequence such as ascending. Provide a routine which would output the available rooms, as the motel becomes full.
2. Expand the above program to handle reservations for a one-week period.
3. Assuming that not all the rooms are in fact used on any one night,

have the computer prepare a report for the house-keeping staff, out-putting the rooms which require cleaning the following day.
4. Prepare a routine which produces a report for management which outlines the percentage occupation of the motel from the previous night.
5. Instead of recording a simple "1" in the matrix element if a room is reserved, record a code which indicates the cost or charge for the room. For example a '1' might mean the room is worth $25 per night, a '2' $30, and a '3' would mean the room is worth $35 per night. Produce a report showing the income which should have been generated from the previous night's bookings.

ADDITIONAL PROGRAMS

Tax Tables

6. Load an 8 element array with the values .40, .38, .36, .34, .32, .30, .28, .26, which will represent rates of tax.
Input employee number, hours worked, rate of pay and tax code (1, 2, 3, 4 . . . 8). Calculate the gross pay and, using the table, determine and output the amount of the tax and the net pay. For example, if an employee has a tax code of 2, the rate of tax would be 38 per cent. Use structured programming. Include an initial read.

Discounts

7. Load a 7 element array with discount data (75%, 50%, 33%, 25%, 15%, 10% and 5%). Input from DATA statements the product number, quantity ordered, unit price and discount code. Use structured programming. Include an initial read. Output:
PRODUCT NO. QUANTITY PRICE EXTENSION DISCOUNT NET COST

Calculating Currency

8.(a) Write a BASIC program which will input an amount of money. Output the value of the amount along with the denominations of currency such as 1s, 2s, 5s, 10s, 20s etc., which could make up the amount. For example:
The amount is $143. The currency required is:
1—100s
2— 20s
3— 1s

(b) Write a module to calculate the necessary coins.
The amount is 68¢. The coins required are:
2—25s
1—10s
1— 5s
3— 1s

CHAPTER 9

LOGIC REPRESENTATION

Level 1

It has been found that, no matter how clever a programmer might be, fewer programming errors are made if the solution to a programming problem is carefully thought out and outlined in some fashion on paper. As the solution is outlined by the programmer, problems might become evident. The logic of alternative solutions could be explored on paper, even before the writing of instructions is actually begun. This is somewhat similar to an architect or draftsperson making the plans for a house even before the sod is turned to dig the basement. Without a plan a flight of stairs might end in a clothes cupboard, or a wall on the upper floor might not have sufficient support under it on the lower floor. Careful planning in the early stages often prevents frustration later. So it is with programming. A plan of attack, sketched out in some fashion, aids the programmer in exploring various approaches which could be taken in solving the problem.

Over the short history of programming, various methods of representing logic have become popular and have then been replaced by something thought to be better. This chapter attempts to give you a brief overview of the major systems which have been, and are being used. The two reasons for this overview are:
1) you have in your bag of tricks a variety of tools you could use depending on the type of program you must solve, and
2) you might run across one of these methods in books or in documentation as you modify or update an older program.

ALGORITHMS

The step-by-step solution to a problem is called an algorithm. An algorithm can take a variety of forms. Perhaps the most common form is the list of instructions which come with a toy or device which must be assembled after it has been purchased. If you follow these instructions, the toy or device should go together smoothly.

A second form of algorithm is a block diagram. Key steps are set out in blocks to make easier the understanding of the relationship among the various steps.

A block diagram which uses standardized symbols or shapes is called a **flowchart**. A flowchart could be used to represent a variety of things. The flow of material on an assembly line could be represented by a **process flowchart**. The flow of data in business could also be represented by a **data flow flowchart**. The logical flow of instructions which represent a computer program set out in a flowchart is called a **logic flowchart**. Programmers usually leave out the word logic when discussing logic flowcharts. When they use the word flowchart it is assumed to be a *logic* flowchart.

THE LOGIC FLOWCHART

The using of special shapes and giving them special meaning is not new. Look at the symbols in Fig. 9.1.

Figure 9.1

These symbols are commonly used. Frequently the shape alone is sufficient to communicate the meaning.

Someone familiar with the flowcharting symbols shown in the two examples in Fig. 9.2 would be able to quickly scan the diagrams and understand what is going on without having any words in the symbols. You will be able to do this very soon.

Example A is used extensively in solving mathematical problems. Business programmers, on the other hand, use symbols shown in example B.

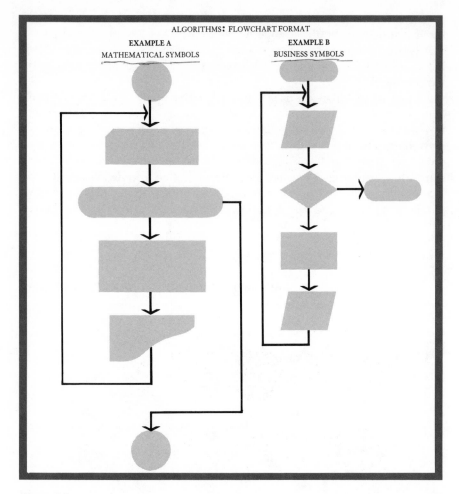

Figure 9.2

STANDARDIZING SYMBOLS

After considerable experience, business programmers and mathematicians found it extremely helpful to agree on certain symbols having certain meanings, much in the same way there is now international agreement on traffic signs. This agreement results in one programmer, with a glance, being able to obtain general understanding of another programmer's flowchart.

It is unfortunate, however, that there is not agreement on symbols between mathematicians and business programmers. With very little practice, however, the main symbols for both can be learned.

There are five computer operations which are most commonly used in solving problems. These operations are:

1. start or stop
2. inputting
3. outputting
4. doing a move or an arithmetic calculation
5. testing for a condition

} *Most commonly used computer operations.*

The symbols for these commonly used procedures are shown in Fig. 9.3.

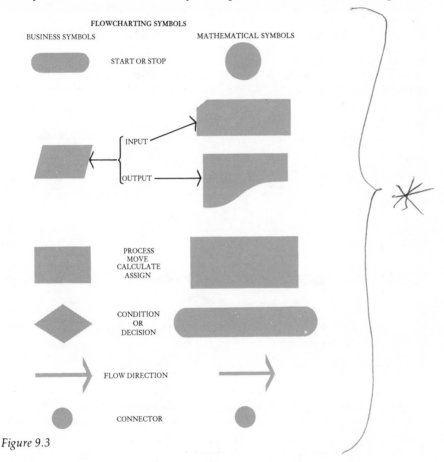

FLOWCHARTING SYMBOLS

BUSINESS SYMBOLS   MATHEMATICAL SYMBOLS

START OR STOP

INPUT

OUTPUT

PROCESS
MOVE
CALCULATE
ASSIGN

CONDITION
OR
DECISION

FLOW DIRECTION

CONNECTOR

Figure 9.3

To demonstrate how convenient these symbols are, see if you can determine just from the symbols what logic is being used in the flowchart in Fig. 9.2.

There could be a number of interpretations of this flowchart because it does not contain any words which would help to make the meaning of each symbol absolutely clear. One interpretation of this flowchart would be:

START
INPUT DATA

END OF DATA? STOP
CALCULATE SQUARE OF NUMBER INPUTTED
OUTPUT THE SQUARE
GO TO INPUT DATA

Already, without a great deal of training, you are probably having some idea of the usefulness of these symbols.

AIDS TO HELP MAKE FLOWCHARTING EASIER

A special form has been designed as an aid in keeping flowcharts well spaced and easier to understand. The flowcharting form of Fig. 9.4 enables the programmer to keep uniform spacing.

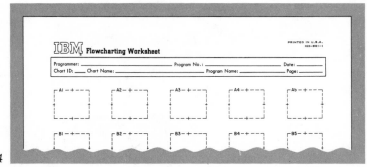

Figure 9.4

If you have flowcharting paper available, here are some tips on using it.

✓1. Begin in the second column from the left.
2. Wherever possible have your logic flow *down*. If a horizontal flow is necessary, try to arrange to have it flow to the right.
3. Arrowheads may be omitted as long as the flow is down and to the right, but they help in making the flowchart clear. Arrowheads are a must if, as sometimes will be the case, the flow will have to go to the left or up.
4. If you reach the bottom of a column and your flowchart is not quite complete, use a connector symbol. (See Fig. 9.5) A template is used to help make symbols more accurate and make them easier to draw.

Flowcharts representing straightforward logic tend to have a number of flow lines looping back to specific points in the flowchart. When the logic is complex flow lines begin to cross each other. The author has seen some flowcharts which look like a plate of spaghetti and meat balls! To improve on this instead of flow lines, circle connectors are sometimes used. Connectors eliminate or reduce the number of flow lines.

Again there is a convention or agreement among programmers on how to use these connectors. Obviously, connectors join two parts of the flowchart. The *exiting* connector *drops out the bottom* of a flow, or *goes out to the*

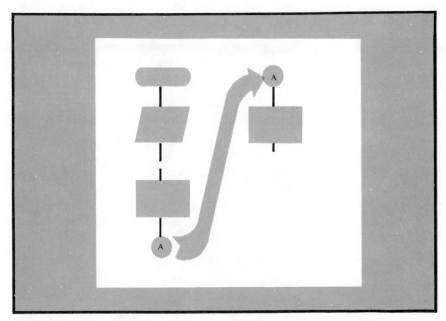

Figure 9.5

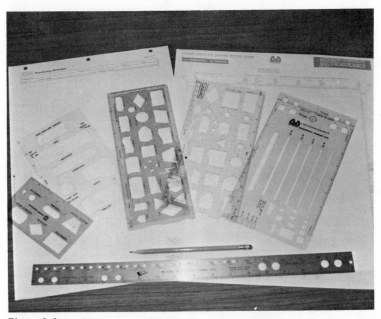

Figure 9.6

right. The *entering* connector *comes in from the top or comes in from the left*. It is possible that there might be more than one exiting connector to match up with only one entering connector.

Figure 9.7

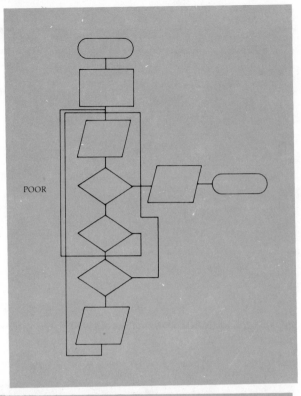

POOR

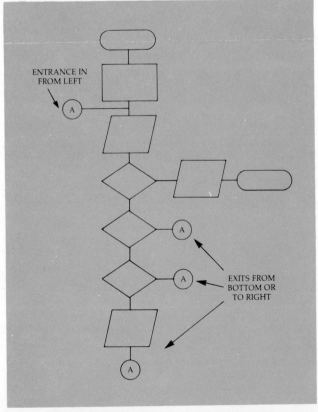

ENTRANCE IN
FROM LEFT

EXITS FROM
BOTTOM OR
TO RIGHT

Due to the shift away from the *looping* flowchart, few illustrations of this exist in this book. Be advised that this type of flowchart has been a very popular method of representing logic and if you come across it, or are required to use it, treat it with respect.

STRUCTURE DIAGRAMS

There are a variety of ways to represent structured programs in the form of a diagram. Some diagrams could be as short as a series of circles and lines. The circles contain a letter and represent a subroutine. A legend is supplied to indicate how many times or under what conditions that subroutine is to be performed.

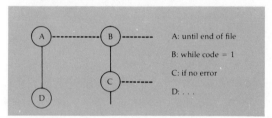

Figure 9.8

It has been found that some students find this skeleton-type of diagram too brief to allow ready identification of what is going on. By marrying the skeleton diagram with the traditional flowchart, a compromise system has been worked out and found to be very successful. The result could be called a structured flowchart but a better name is **structured diagram**. The mainline logic is represented using business symbols of the traditional flowchart. The circle and letter are put in the mainline flow to represent a module. The legend is provided to indicate under what conditions the module is to be performed. Sometimes a structure diagram can become a little complex. Again, a convention must be established as to how to interpret various conditions. In our classes we have agreed that, where there are two paths from a circle or node, the path to the right will be taken under either of three circumstances. Go to the right if the condition is

UNTIL
WHILE
TRUE or "YES"

If the condition is satisfied, or the answer to the question is 'no,' take the downward path. The 'T' at the end of a branch indicates the 'end of that routine, return to process another record.'

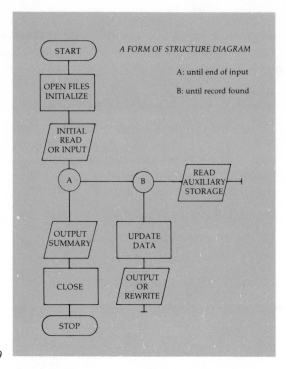

START

OPEN FILES
INITIALIZE

INITIAL
READ
OR INPUT

A — B

READ
AUXILIARY
STORAGE

OUTPUT
SUMMARY

UPDATE
DATA

CLOSE

OUTPUT
OR
REWRITE

STOP

A FORM OF STRUCTURE DIAGRAM

A: until end of input

B: until record found

Figure 9.9

DECISION TABLES

There is another technique that is sometimes used in conjunction with or instead of the flowchart. This technique is the designing and use of a **decision table**. To make a decision table, divide a page into three areas. The first area contains situations called **conditions** which might arise in the problem such as 'is the number greater than zero' or 'is the employee a hard worker.' *The wording of the conditions is such that the answer is either yes or no.* There could be a number of conditions in the condition entry section.

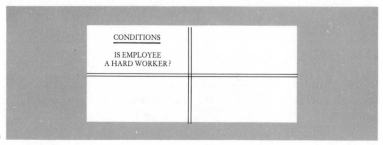

CONDITIONS

IS EMPLOYEE
A HARD WORKER?

Figure 9.10

The second area contains all the *actions* which could be taken within the program such as 'square the number' or 'give employee a raise.' The series of actions are independent of each other. Some actions might be taken while others may not, depending on the conditions.

CONDITIONS	
IS EMPLOYEE A HARD WORKER?	
ACTIONS	
GIVE RAISE FIRE HIM	

Figure 9.11

The third area contains **rules** showing the relationship between certain conditions and certain actions. A rule is built up by placing a Y or N representing yes or no in a column opposite the conditions and by placing check marks opposite the appropriate action.

		RULES				
CONDITIONS		1	2			
IS EMPLOYEE A HARD WORKER?		Y	N			
ACTIONS						
GIVE RAISE FIRE HIM		✓	✓			

Figure 9.12

A rule is required for each unique combination of conditions.

			RULES			
			1	2	3	4
CONDITIONS	IS IT A GIRL?		Y	N		
	IS IT TWINS?		N	N	Y	
	IS IT TRIPLETS?		N	N	N	Y
ACTIONS	BUY PINK CRIB		✓			
	BUY BLUE CRIB			✓		
	BUY TWO CRIBS				✓	
	PUT AD IN PAPER					✓

Figure 9.13

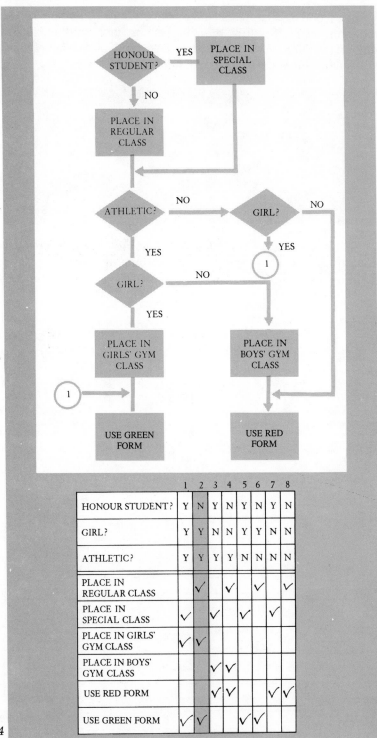

Figure 9.14

A decision table enables the programmer to place all the logic on one relatively compact outline. In Fig. 9.14 both parts show the logic for the same problem. The problem deals with the placement of students in a class. Note the conditions and actions.

When there are a series of conditions, one following another, the subsequent rules of the decision table tend to be more compact and easier to follow than a flowchart.

USING THE DECISION TABLE IN PROGRAMMING

Each rule is converted to a section or module of a computer program. For example, rule 2 in the illustration would be programmed as a module. An experienced programmer should have no difficulty working directly from the decision table to write the necessary modules. After all the rules are programmed, all that remains to be added would be the programming of main logic, including input and output routines.

TREE DIAGRAMS

There is another technique which is sometimes used as an aid in showing the logic of a program. This technique is the construction of a **tree diagram**. The tree diagram is a series of lines, each representing a series of sequential situations. It is most often used to represent the logic in programs in which succeeding actions depend on previous computed results. For example, tree diagrams are useful in planning programs

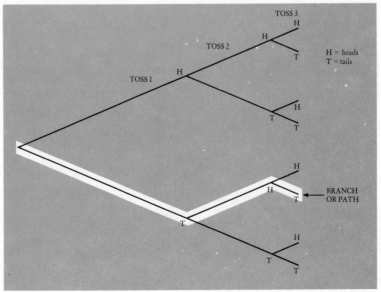

Figure 9.15

involving games. Although tree diagrams could become very complex in nature, for illustration purposes, we will do a rather simple one.

Assume that we want to study the probability of obtaining three heads in a row when flipping a coin. The first toss of the coin would produce either a head or a tail. If it were a head, the second toss of the coin could produce either a head or a tail. If that toss happened to be a head, the third toss of the coin could be either a head or a tail. By examining paths along the tree diagram, one could count the number of times out of eight possible situations that there would be three consecutive heads or three consecutive tails or two heads and one tail, etc. In the diagram, the possibility of obtaining three consecutive heads would tend to be one out of every eight experiments.

In computer programming there could be a series of chain reactions similar to the heads and tails illustration above. A tree diagram such as this could be used as an aid to programming, for example, by constructing a module for each branch of the tree.

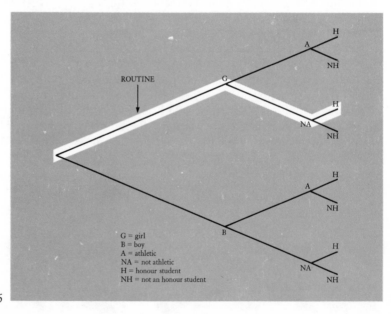

Figure 9.16

PLEX AND P.E.R.T. STRUCTURES

An extension of the tree diagram technique is the plex structure. Whereas the tree diagram shows two options leading from an event, the **plex diagram** shows how events might be dependent on a combination of other events.

In the illustration, the **nodes**, represented by circles, are linked to other nodes, showing their relationship to each other. For example, node B is independent upon nodes A and C for its existence.

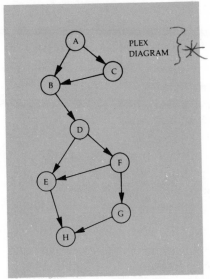

PLEX
DIAGRAM

Figure 9.17

Similar diagrams are used to represent **time flowcharting**. The timing and relationship of events in construction and in factory assembly procedures are often represented by such a diagram. These diagrams are called P.E.R.T. structures—*P*rogram *E*valuation and *R*eview *T*echnique. Sometimes they are called **Critical Path Networks** because events crucial to the timing of the total project can be determined. For further information on, and instruction in this technique, refer to chapter 26 of *Information Processing—The Computer in Perspective* by the same author.

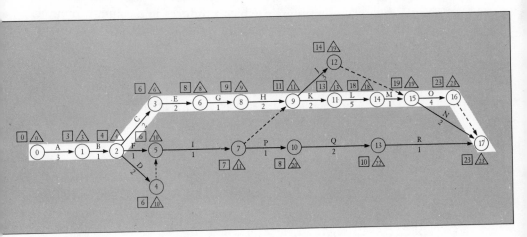

Figure 9.18

PSEUDO CODE

Using short simple English words or phrases to represent the logic of a solution is called **pseudo coding**. The most common terms used in pseudo code are:

GET	inputting data
WRITE	outputting data
IF-THEN-ELSE	conditional branching
DO-WHILE	repeating a module
ASSIGN	load a constant, the content of a variable, or the result of an algebraic expression, *into* the variable which is named.
STOP	every program must come to a logical stop

Just so you will realize that you are not learning a whole new language notice the close relationship there is between pseudo code and BASIC. In fact one could substitute BASIC reserved words for the pseudo code.

PSEUDO CODE	BASIC
GET	INPUT, READ
WRITE	PRINT
IF-THEN-ELSE	IF . . . THEN . . . ELSE*
WHILE DO	FOR . . . NEXT
ASSIGN	LET
STOP	END

Use your knowledge of BASIC to analyse the pseudo code below. It represents the logic of a program which produces in a column counting numbers from 1 to 10, under a heading, with the sum of the counting numbers printed at the end.

```
ASSIGN COUNTER THE VALUE 0
ASSIGN ACCUMULATOR THE VALUE 0
WRITE "COUNTING NUMBERS AND THEIR TOTALS"
WHILE COUNTER IS LESS THAN 10
    ASSIGN COUNTER OLD VALUE PLUS 1
    WRITE COUNTER
    ASSIGN ACCUMULATOR OLD VALUE PLUS COUNTER
WRITE "SUM OF COUNTING NUMBERS", ACCUMULATOR
STOP
```

As you can see, pseudo code is similar to BASIC.

---

* The "else" feature is not available on all BASIC interpreters.

HIPO DIAGRAMS

The term **HIPO** comes from the phrase *h*ierarchy *p*lus *i*nput, *p*roces ;ing and *o*utput. You will recall from the previous chapter that processing and input-output instructions could be identified as having some degree of importance to the main logic of a program. This approach could be represented by a HIPO diagram.

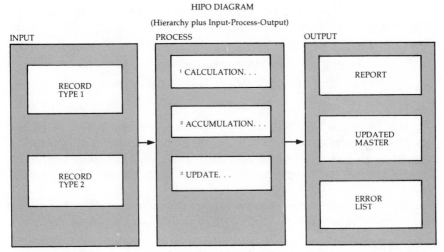

HIPO DIAGRAM

(Hierarchy plus Input-Process-Output)

INPUT   PROCESS   OUTPUT

RECORD TYPE 1

¹ CALCULATION. . .

REPORT

² ACCUMULATION. . .

UPDATED MASTER

RECORD TYPE 2

³ UPDATE. . .

ERROR LIST

Figure 9.19

WHY REPRESENT LOGIC?

There might be a temptation to by-pass the writing of a logic representation because the program itself indicates the logic. When first learning programming, however, a quick outline of the logic is extremely helpful in organizing one's approach. Complex solutions, particularly, should not be attempted without some type of logic representation done in advance. The time taken to rough out the logic of a complex program is usually saved many times over in debugging. Once the program has been written, a neat representation of logic is required for documentation.

More about that in Chapter 11, dealing with documentation. Logic representation, therefore, has two important purposes:

1. A rough outline aids in developing a correct solution to a problem
2. neat representation becomes part of documentation

Level 2

ALPHA STRINGS

Up to now, numeric data has been manipulated, read, and printed.

Alphabetic data has been outputted using the print instruction: 150 PRINT "TODAY IS SUNNY." In business data processing in particular, there are many applications requiring **alphabetic** data to be inputted, moved in memory and outputted. In order to do this in BASIC, the programmer advises the computer that a variable will be required to hold alphabetic information. The variable name to hold **numeric** data could be any single letter of the alphabet, or, an alphabetic letter and a digit. *Variable* names which will hold alphabetic data are constructed in the same way except the dollar sign($) forms a suffix. Variable names which the computer would identify as holding alphabetic data could be A$ and A1$. Study the following program:

```
130 INPUT "INPUT YOUR NAME";N$
140 PRINT "HAVE A GOOD DAY, ";N$
9999 END
```

The variable name N$ advised the computer to set up memory in such a way as to hold alphabetic data. During execution, the computer prints the phrase "INPUT YOUR NAME" and pauses. When the person does key in his or her name, the computer loads the characters into the address called N$.

This takes a little different approach for the computer than if it had to load numeric data into a variable. The PRINT statement causes the computer to retrieve the person's name from the address N$ and output it. The READ . . . DATA statements can also be used for alphabetic data.

[Note:] The computer you are using might require that the alphabetic data be enclosed in quotation marks. Check the user manual if you have trouble with this.

A string variable may also be used in an IF instruction. One has to be careful, however, to use quotation marks around a string which is not held in a string variable address.

```
 90 REM ***MAINLINE LOGIC***
100 INPUT "WHAT NAME DO YOU WISH TO VERIFY?";N$
              (keyboard input usually does not have to be in quota-
              tion marks)
110 IF N$<> "AAAAA" THEN 220
198 PRINT "EOJ"
199 END
200 REM
205 REM ***READ FILE ROUTINE***
210 REM
220 READ D$
230 IF D$ = "ZZZZZ" THEN 250
240 IF D$ = N$ THEN 300
250 PRINT "NAME NOT ON FILE"
```

```
260 RESTORE
270 GO TO 100
300 PRINT "THE NAME   ";N$;"  IS ON FILE"
310 RESTORE
320 GO TO 100
990 DATA JAN SMITH,JOE KELLY,IAN BROWN,ZZZZZ
```

Note that the 5 As and 5 Zs were put in quotation marks in the IF instruction of line number 110 and 230. Also note, however, that the two string variables D$ and N$ were compared in line 240 without quotation marks. The data items did not require quotation marks either.

An extra space was included within the quotation marks in line 300, after the word NAME and before the word IS. When string variables are printed separated by a semi-colon no space is automatically inserted by the computer as appears to happen when printing numeric variables. (Technically the computer is not leaving a space for you when it does print numeric variables. It just does not print the plus sign.)

COMBINATION OF INSTRUCTIONS

Now might be as good a time as any to provide you with another trick for your bag of programming tricks. You know that the IF instruction requires a condition. With most BASIC interpreters you may use a combination of conditions. For example:

```
140 IF X = 100 OR Y > 0 THEN GO TO . . .
250 IF A = 1000 AND N$ = "ZZZZZ" THEN GO TO . . .
```

In line 140 above, should either X = 100 or should Y > 0 the branch will take place, otherwise the computer will drop to the next instruction. In line 250 both conditions must be present before the branch will take place. Otherwise the computer will drop to the next instruction.

Although one has to be careful in making an IF instruction complicated, it is possible to have more that two conditions.

```
350 IF D = 100 OR C > 0 AND E = 1 OR N$ = "ZZZZZ" THEN
```

In this case the computer requires at least one condition either side of the AND to be true before it will branch.

The word NOT may also be used but its need would be rare.

```
200 IF NOT X = 100 THEN . . .
```

There are better ways around this, right?

In some computers, the AND and OR features require that the conditions must be in brackets. The OR is represented by a + sign and the AND is represented by a * sign.

300 IF (X = 100) + (B > 0) * (N$ = "ZZZZ") THEN . . .

WHEN SHOULD MULTIPLE CONDITIONS BE USED?

In this chapter decision tables were outlined. Some programs do have multiple conditions for which the computer must test. In cases such as these, the multiple condition IF instruction is very handy. Before you start to use it in a major program, however, experiment with it on a small scale. Perhaps you could set up some LET instructions and use some of the examples above for a test.

CHECKING YOUR READING—LEVEL 1

1. What is an algorithm?
2. What three forms do algorithms traditionally take?
3. Name three different types of flowcharts.
4. Why are special symbols used in logic flowcharts?
5. Summarize the four main rules of flowcharting.
6. In what way must care be taken in structuring the wording of a condition in a decision table?
7. What is a condition table rule?
8. How are rules used in programming?
9. Under what circumstances, or what type of program, are tree diagrams used for outlining logic?
10. In what way is a plex diagram similar to, and different from, a tree diagram?
11. In what way are pseudo code terms a condensed version of almost all program functions?
12. What does the term HIPO represent?
13. What is the major stress in a HIPO diagram?
14. For what two functions or purposes may a programmer use logic representation.

VOCABULARY ASSIGNMENT

Continue developing your vocabulary list by writing brief definitions of the words in bold print in this section.

CHECKING YOUR READING—LEVEL 2

1. What is the difference in the content between a numeric variable and an alpha string?
2. In determining the name for an alpha string what is the only difference between a numeric name and an alpha string name?
3. What are the rules with respect to quotation marks when using string

variables, i) in condition instructions using only the address names, ii) in condition instructions using an actual string, and iii) in a data statement.

4. What care must be taken to have suitable output if string variables are printed, along with literals, separated by semicolons?
5. What are the combinational *operation* words used in a multiple condition IF instruction?
6. Complete the following truth table:

X = 5, Y = 1

	True	False
IF X = 5 OR Y = 0		
IF X = 5 AND Y = 0		
IF X = 0 OR Y = 1		
IF X = 5 AND Y = 1		

7. Complete the following truth table:

X = 100, Y > 0, N$ contains the value ZZZZ

	True	False
IF X = 100 AND Y = 0		
IF X = 100 AND Y = 0 OR N$ = "ZZZZZ"		
IF X = 100 AND Y > 0 AND N$ = "ZZZZZ"		

PROJECTS

Testing For Errors

1. 120 READ N, N$, S
   999 DATA J. JONES, 25, 3000, A. ADAMS, 30, 35000, . . .
2. 130 INPUT "KEY IN YOUR NAME"; N
3. 130 INPUT "KEY IN YOUR NAME AND ADDRESS";NM$

Testing For Errors Review

4. 110 REM LOADING SQUARES OF NUMBERS
   120 DIM M(N)
   130 FOR X = 1 TO 10
   140 LET M(X) = X * X
   150 NEXT X
5. 110 REM NESTED LOOPS
   120 FOR X = 1 TO 10
   130 FOR Y = 1 TO 5
   140 NEXT Y
   150 PRINT N
   160 NEXT X

PROGRAMMING ASSIGNMENTS

Information Processing—Using Structured Programming

1. Produce under a suitable heading the names of five of the largest companies operating in Canada. (General Motors, Ford, Imperial Oil, Canadian Pacific, George Weston). Make a simple representation of the logic in your program.
2. Under a suitable heading, rank the top 4 provinces of Canada having the greatest revenue from farm products. (They are, in order: Ontario, Saskatchewan, Alberta and Quebec. Include a ranking number beside each province). Make a simple representation of the logic in your program.
3. Produce under a suitable heading an alphabetic list of the major religions of the world. (Christian, Jewish, Moslem, Zoroastrian, Shinto, Taoist, Confucian, Buddhist, Hindu)
4. Program the computer to produce a sales report of salesperson's number, name and sales. Include a total for the sales. You supply at least four data items. Make a simple representation of the logic in your program.
5. Program the computer to produce a payroll similar to question #6, Chapter 8, but include names of employees and output a summary line. Make a simple representation of the logic in your program.

ADDITIONAL ASSIGNMENTS

Scientific Applications

6. Under a suitable heading produce a report showing the densities of a sample of elements.

Densities in Grams Per Cubic Centimetre at 20°C

air	0.00129
alcohol	0.80
aluminium	2.7
brass	8.5
gold	19.3
lead	11.3
platinum	21.4

7. Although the formula should be adjusted for extremes in temperature, the density of an element is calculated by dividing the mass (weight) by the volume. Write a computer program to input the mass and volume, and output the density.
8. Relating to the above question, the measured volume of an irregular object can be determined by lowering it in water and determining the increase in the volume. Modify the above program so that the initial volume of water is inputted, then the total volume after the

object has been immersed. Have the computer determine the volume of the object, then its density.

ADDITIONAL PROBLEMS FOR PRACTICE IN REPRESENTING LOGIC

Using the type of logic representation suggested by your instructor, outline the logic which could be used to solve the problems which follow. Logic representation *should* be language independent. That is, special programming words or symbols should not be used in the representation. Although many BASIC words would be suitable to be included in logic representation, perhaps you should go out of your way to select other than BASIC words.

Assume a file of information about students. You are required to output the following information:

9. The names of all girls.
10. The names of all boys, the count of all students and the count of the boys which have been listed.
11. The names of those students who are 18 years old and who have the highest mark in computer programming.
12. The names of those students who are 17 years old, have a part-time job, and have an average over 75 per cent.
13. The names of those students who are 19 years old, who have a career goal of either computing or social work.
14. The names of those students who have an average of 75 or better, and are athletically or are artistically outstanding.

The following two problems are ideal for tree diagrams:

15. Sketch a logic representation for a program which would simulate probabilities or combinations of an automobile driving through a small town with only three traffic lights. Each traffic light is either red or green—no caution light.
16. Similar to the above question, but include the caution light, such that the driver might have one of a green, red or yellow light at each intersection.

And finally, represent the logic involved in sorting an ordinary deck of playing cards. Decide in advance if rejected cards are set aside or added to the bottom of the deck. The joker could be used as end of file.

17. Sort out all aces.
18. Sort the deck into a euchre deck that is all cards of a value 9 or greater.
19. Sort the deck to obtain 13 cards in ascending order from 2 to Ace.
20. Sort the deck until a card is obtained with the same value as one already separated out.

CHAPTER 10

TESTING AND DEBUGGING

Level 1

TESTING

After programming a number of relatively simple programs the beginning programmer obtains the impression that after eliminating the odd little problem, "the program works!" If the program *appears* to do what is expected of it, it is "correct." This is not necessarily the case. The actual output must be **verified**. If the program is to be used for a variety of data, some **acid test** runs should be made to test all parts of the program with data at the extreme.

The computed output is easy to verify when the program multiplies numbers such as 5 × 12. When one gets into the heavy calculating in a computer program, the results are too often not verified to make sure that the program is doing all that it is supposed to do.

Of course, there is a limit as to how much verifying one must do. There has to be some point in time when the results of the computer program are accepted as being correct! Certainly, but a good programmer should not assume the program is correct until a variety of sample data is used to test the program. The computer output should then be checked against hand calculated results.

In addition to checking the handling of a variety of data all parts of the program should be tested. Good programs should have tests for bad data, improper operating procedures and in general a test for any wrong situation which could occur. In fact anything that could seriously affect the correct operation of the program should be planned for.

After these safety routines have been programmed, each should be tested to see if they do what they are supposed to do. One of the major difficulties of error routines is, if the error routine does identify a problem, does it enable the program to recover satisfactorily or does it 'hang it up.' Good testing will establish, if after an error is discovered, the action of the program is what the programmer wants.

In business and industry, programs are usually thoroughly tested before being accepted into the whole system of programs. Even then, the output is watched and spot-checked to make sure the program is working as it should. Testing becomes increasingly important in relation to the importance of the program. The more important the program, the more testing is required.

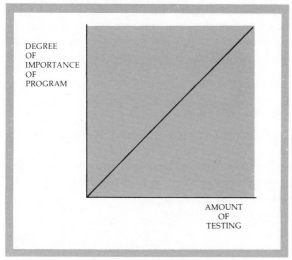

DEGREE
OF
IMPORTANCE
OF
PROGRAM

AMOUNT
OF
TESTING

Figure 10.1

TYPES OF ERRORS

There are a number of types of errors found by testing:
- logic errors which repeat themselves each and every time the same test data is presented
- errors in establishing the limits within which the program will operate correctly; for example sending out in error an invoice for $0.00 (more about that in the next chapter)
- recovery errors should bad data be inputted, or should there be a hardware problem such as a power failure during execution

THOROUGH TESTING IS REQUIRED TO PROVE THAT YOUR PROGRAM DOES WORK UNDER *ALL* ANTICIPATED CONDITIONS AND WITHIN THE LIMITS YOU HAVE ESTABLISHED.

HOW IMPORTANT IS TESTING?

Surely, the odd little test applied to your program would be sufficient. As long as a life does not literally depend on the accuracy and completeness of your program, half-hearted testing is fine. But if your program is to be used to navigate a big jet or produce the correct combination of drugs for a person on chemotherapy then every aspect of your program should be checked and re-checked. Similarly in industry, if your program is to be *managing* millions of dollars of funds it had better not have any *leakage* in it.

HOW MUCH TESTING IS NORMAL?

Of the total time given by management to produce a program the per cent of that time dedicated to testing will vary depending on the degree of complexity and the importance of the program. NASA in its space program, might establish that 80 per cent of the total project time must be given to thorough testing. Programs involving thousands or even millions of dollars of accounts receivable for a company might require the same percentage of testing time.

APPROACHES TO TESTING

As stated earlier, having the computer produce output is not necessarily proving that your program works. After you have just finished a program you tend to input data which suits what you have just written. One of the ways to more thoroughly test your program is to feed in data which is out of the ordinary. For example you could feed in:

- data of large numbers or very small numbers
- large volumes of data
- bad data, with special characters or alpha characters where they are not supposed to be
- no data, a null file

If your program is able to handle each of these situations and logically recover from the bad data or null file, then you have increased confidence that your program will work under unusual circumstances.

 In the case of data of large (or very small) values, make sure that the variable accumulators are not overflowing and dropping off or truncating the totals.

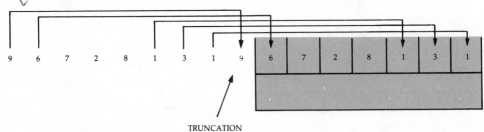

TRUNCATION

Figure 10.2

In BASIC one does not have to be too concerned about this problem but it is a serious problem in some of the other languages. Often this overflow or truncation problem arises during the *move* of the data to a print statement which has only a limited number of print positions available for the results.

SYSTEMATIC TESTING

There are two approaches to a systematic testing of a fairly complex program. The one is to do **bottom up testing**. Each module is tested thoroughly. Extreme data or bad data is tested in the module. Error recovery routines are tested. The program is tested to make sure that the main program goes to the module when it is supposed to and the module returns to the correct location in the mainline of the program.

Another approach to testing a complex program is to do **top down testing.** In this case, the mainline of the program is tested skipping many of the modules. Dummy data could be provided by the modules if required to keep the mainline of the program processing. If the mainline of the program appears to work, then modules can be added perhaps one at a time. Each module is then thoroughly tested *within* the context of the mainline of the program.

Either approach might not be the best approach in any one case. A combination of the two approaches might likely be the best. It is important, however, that some systematic approach be used.

TESTING TRICKS

To monitor what is going on in your program, extra instructions called *testing* or *debugging instructions* could be inserted. For example a test instruction within a module might be:

311 PRINT "INTEREST MODULE"

or more generally

151 PRINT "POINT 1"

The programmer is able to trace the path taken by the program by studying these extra print statements. The programmer might also have certain key variables also printed each time a module is executed to make sure it is obtaining the data which is expected. If instruction 311 was in a module which was repeated, its output could trace the value of the variable I1.

311 PRINT "INTEREST MODULE";I1

Another example is a **conditional trace** or **breakpoint** such as:

209 IF A = 0 THEN GO TO 9997
9997 PRINT "A = 0"
9999 END

If A should not equal zero instruction number 209 would check for such a condition.

There are some debugging routines available on most computers which 'trace' the contents of all or specified variables. The output is often difficult for beginning programmers to follow and too often gives much more information than is required.

ACCEPTANCE TESTING

Once a program is thoroughly tested in the 'laboratory,' it is then moved to the **user environment** for more testing. Again using sample data, the program is tested along with the programs which form part of the whole system. It is possible that a new program might *mess up* the data which is common to a number of programs. This type of testing is designed to make sure that this does not happen. Ultimately, a parallel run is made, using the new program to process the real data along with the old program or other method used up to this point. If repeated parallel runs show identical output to the old system, then the program is 'accepted' into the system.

DEBUGGING

From the early dawn of the computer age, programmers, no matter how clever, found they made errors. It is difficult for some programmers, to accept the fact that their more complex programs *will* have errors. Some of these errors or **bugs**, as they are called, are very difficult to find. Perhaps hours of frustrating searching will be required before a simple little bug is identified and corrected. You too must accept this fact! Part of the art of programming includes:

1. accepting the fact bugs will occur
2. developing the *patience* to track down those troublesome bugs

THINK TESTING AND DEBUGGING WHEN DESIGNING YOUR PROGRAM

If you keep in mind the need for testing and debugging as you initially plan or layout your program, you might modify slightly the design of your program to make testing and debugging easier. Certainly if you construct your program modularly, you are already making easier these two tasks.

MURPHY'S LAW

There are a variety of things which can go wrong in a program. Keeping in mind **Murphy's Law** that anything which could go wrong will go wrong, one should take extra care with each module. If a bug should show up during testing there are a number of things you might have to do. The method of correcting the bug might be obvious. Or the behaviour of the bug might be a mystery. If this latter situation occurs, you have to develop a system of tracing down why the bug does what it does.

DESK CHECKING

The first approach to finding a mysterious bug is to do some **desk checking**. Coding sheets or listings of your program should be carefully gone over to see if the reason for the bug suddenly becomes obvious. Usually, after a short time of studying the code, you will say, 'there it is, how dumb can I/that machine be,' or words to that effect!

A second approach which could be used if the initial desk checking does not provide the solutions is to ask someone else to look over the coding with you. The trick here is to have you explain what your program is doing and 'why there should not be a bug where it appears to be.' The author has found that about 8 out of 10 times the original programmer discovers the error during his/her explanation—the listener contributed nothing but an ear!

VERIFY SECTIONS

If all this fails then you might have to begin modifying the program, to zero in on the bug. One approach is to run only part of your program. If that part is clean, keep adding sections or modules to it until the bug shows. Or you could have the first half of your program run, then have it pause using the instruction:

        199 STOP (assuming a 400 instruction program)

If a 'dump' statement were also included the programmer would be able to see what is going on in the variables to that point:

        198 PRINT A,B,C,D
        199 STOP

If the first half does not check out, have the computer run the first quarter:

        148 PRINT A,B,C,D
        149 STOP

The computer programmer could continue limiting the number of instructions run, executed until the bug is narrowed down to the actual instruction with the error. If the bug appeared to be in the second half of the program a stop could be put in ¾ down the program and the same approach used.

TRACES

Of course you could also use debug instructions much in the same way that special test instructions are used during testing. Sprinkle throughout your program, in logical places, extra instructions such as:

```
124 PRINT "POINT 1"
149 PRINT "POINT 2"
```

Then study the output to see which parts of the program are being repeated when they should not be repeated, or being missed completely. Dumping certain variables along with these literals could help in determining what is happening.

DETECTIVE HERCULE

In looking for bugs, play detective. You could, if you had the imagination, put yourself inside the program. You could then ask yourself, 'what section or module of this program would likely be causing the bug?' Then study that section to see if you are able to 'detect' it. There might be two or three prime suspect modules. Use a logical approach to ruling out the suspects. If a number of modules are equally suspect check out the module which is the *shortest* or least complicated. Then check out the next shortest or least complicated module, leaving until the last the longest most complicated section.

Do sit back and think. If you are flustered and angry and under pressure of a deadline, all the more reason to take time off, think about other things and then have a fresh start. The mind appears to continue working on a problem subconsciously while a person is doing something else. The author once had an unusual experience along this line. After giving up on a particularly stubborn problem and going skiing, the solution popped into his head on the way up on the ski lift, at a time when the scenery was uppermost in his mind. Immediately after skiing the solution was tested and it did work.

CORE DUMPS

As a last resort a procedure to dump memory could be used. The output is extensive, often in code and is sufficiently difficult that programmers avoid using it.

COMMON TYPES OF ERRORS

Below is a checklist of common errors which you could examine if, at some future time, you run out of things to do in trying to find a bug:
1. variable name modified or changed partway through the program (A1 became A)
2. the zero was used instead of the alphabetic o (oh) or vice versa
3. wrong data or data used was beyond the limits you have set for your program
4. instructions you thought were present are, in fact, missing
5. variables which should have been initialized were not, resulting in 'garbage' left from another program being included in this program

6. the program was not instructed to branch when it should have, or not instructed to return to the correct place.
7. subscripting went out of bounds

```
DIM M(25)
FOR I = 1 TO 26
LET X = X + 2
LET M(I) = X
NEXT I
```

8. end of data not handled correctly
9. wrong information being passed from one module to another
10. an accumulator is overflowed and results truncated
11. improper print formats
12. nesting problems
13. flag combination problems (more about flags in chapter 12)
14. counters are too small
15. errors in complicated (Boolean) expressions

```
IF A = B AND NOT A = C AND B = C
```

16. directing the computer to divide instead of multiply
17. instructing the computer to do something it cannot do
18. operations done in an order not intended by the programmer

Level 2

CONTROLLING OUTPUT

Up to this point in your course you have learned two different ways of spacing output. In order to output data items consecutively on a line the semicolon is used. To use the built-in zone or tabulation feature of BASIC the comma is used. The comma enables four columns of data to be spaced out. On one computer the data begins on the first, 12th, 22th and the 31st output positions. (Some computers have different spacing.)

There is even more flexibility available to you. Often the outputted data does not suit four columns of information. Sometimes more columns are needed or fewer columns needed but the data should be laid out more evenly. In order to accomplish this additional flexibility the TAB feature is available in BASIC.

THE TAB FEATURE

TAB is a shortened form of the word **tabulation**. This word has a variety of meanings but in the context of printing or typing it means the skipping over to a certain column of the output device.

```
130 LET A = 77
140 LET B = 88
150 LET C = −98
160 LET D = 99
170 PRINT A;B;C;D
180 PRINT A,B,C,D
190 PRINT TAB(19);A;TAB(28);B
```

On most output devices instruction 170 would print the values of A,B,C and D leaving one space between them (plus a space for the sign). Instruction 180 would use the automatic tabulating feature of BASIC, outputting the amounts in 4 evenly spaced positions across the output area.

Instruction 190 demonstrates the flexibility of the TAB instruction. The computer would space over 19 spaces and begin outputting the value for A in the 20th output position. It would then tab over to position 28 and begin outputting the value of B in the 29th position. Because B is a positive number, the first digit is outputted in position 30 (the plus sign is suppressed). If B were negative, the minus sign would be placed in position 29.

Within the brackets of the TAB statement, a variable could be used. For example:

```
120 LET X = 0
130 FOR Y = 1 TO 8
140 LET X = X + Y
150 PRINT TAB(X);"*"
160 NEXT Y
```

The computer will space along the value of X before printing the *. Remember that TAB means that the computer will *leave* that many spaces from the beginning of the output before it begins outputting in the *next* output position.

Just for fun the above program segment could be added to with something like this:

```
170 FOR Y = 8 TO 1 STEP −1
180 LET X = X − Y
190 PRINT TAB(X);"*"
200 NEXT Y
```

Try it—you'll like it!

HEADERS AND DETAIL LINES

An output report usually has three parts to it: the headings, the body, and the summary or total line. These parts are traditionally identified as

header, detail line and **total line.** There could be a number of header lines, including a column heading line.

	ABC Company			header -1
	Balance Sheet			header -2
	As of January 31, 19XX			header -3
Acc't No.	*Account Name*	*Debit*	*Credit*	header -4
1	Cash	2 000		detail line type 1
4	Inventory	5 000		
	.			
	.			
	.			
30	Accounts payable		1 000	detail line type 2
35	Bank Loan		4 000	
	.			
	.			
	.			
	Total	25 000	25 000	total line

Most output lines have the same detail line format. There are cases, however, where two or three detail line formats are required. In the illustration, there are two types of detail line. One is used to output a debit account and the other is used to output a credit account. (If you have not taken a course in accounting, do not be concerned about the terms. A programmer must learn to work in unfamiliar areas. After acquiring an understanding of what has to be done the programmer does it without becoming unnecessarily involved in special terminology.)

Note: More information on planning computer output is found in the chapter on Forms Design.

CHECKING YOUR READING—LEVEL 1

1. What invalid assumption is sometimes made when a program is tested using simple data?
2. What rule-of-thumb could be used when determining how much time and effort should be put into a particular program?
3. What three classes of errors are found during testing?
4. In testing your program to establish how well it handles data, what four types of data, or approaches, should you use?
5. What two approaches could be taken to systematic testing?
6. What is meant by a testing, or debugging instruction?
7. What is the key difference between *routine testing* and *acceptance testing*?
8. If you 'think testing' when you begin writing a program, in what way might your program design be altered?

9. What is meant by 'desk checking' in attempting to locate a bug?
10. What approach could be used to 'zero in on' a bug?
11. If you suspect that a bug exists in one of three modules, what approach would you take in identifying which module contains the bug?
12. What is a core dump?

VOCABULARY ASSIGNMENT

Continue developing your vocabulary by writing brief definitions for the words and phrases in bold print in this section.

CHECKING YOUR READING—LEVEL 2

1. In a print statement how does the action of the semicolon differ from the comma?
2. What flexibility does the tab instruction provide?
3. If an instruction caused the computer to tab over eight spaces, in what output position would the first digit of a positive number be printed following the tabulation? Why would that be the first output position of the number.
4. Name the 3 different types of output lines commonly found in a report.

VOCABULARY ASSIGNMENT

Continue developing your vocabulary by writing brief definitions for the words and phrases in bold print in this section.

PROJECTS

Checking For Errors

Detect and correct the errors in the following BASIC programming segments.

```
1. 110 REM READING AND WRITING
   120 READ N, NM$, S
   130 IF N = 99 GO TO 150
   140 PRINT N: NM$:S:
   150 GO TO 120
   199 DATA 25 J. JACKS 10000; 30 A. ADAMS 5000; 99 E
       OF 0
2. 110 REM OUTPUTTING SENTENCES
   120 INPUT "KEY IN YOUR NAME", N$
   130 PRINT "HELLO", N$
```

3. 110 REM TABULATING: NAME (NM$) HAS 18 CHARAC-
   TERS MAX. NUMBER N HAS TWO DIGITS
   120 READ N: NM$; S
   130 IF N = 99 GO TO 198
   140 PRINT TAB(5) N,TAB (4) NM$, TAB (6) 5
   150 LET T = T + S
   160 GO TO 130
   170 PRINT TAB (30) T
   198 DATA etc.
   199 END

PROGRAMMING ASSIGNMENTS

Spacing—Business Programs

1. Under a suitable heading, produce a sales report which lists a number
   of salespersons and the value of the sales, making sure that the
   amounts begin at the 24 output position. At this stage, have your
   amounts in the thousands of dollars, for example:

J. Jones	3450.00
F. Fram	5231.25

2. Under a suitable heading, produce a report which lists a variety of
   inventory products, their regular price, the discount rate and the discounted price. Have 5 spaces between each column of information.
   Again, use similar values for price, discount and discounted price.

kettles	$25	10%	$22.50
dryers	30	15	25.50

3. Assume there is required an inventory report similar to the data above,
   with the names of the items listed down the left column. There is a
   special requirement, however. The value of the inventory is to go in
   two columns, depending on the 'class.' For example, 'class 1' should
   go in the first column after the item name, whereas 'class 2' amounts
   should go in the second column. Accumulate separate totals for each
   column.

tennis racquets		$500.00
tennis balls	$125.00	
baseballs	300.00	
squash racquets		200.00
lacrosse sticks		215.00
	$425.00	$915.00

4. Under a suitable heading, produce a report listing the used cars available for sale in a car lot. Make a plan to use all the output positions

available to you, spacing out the data fields in a reasonably balanced fashion. The data might include:
i) year and make of car, ii) cost, iii) asking price, and iv) mileage on odometer.
5. Develop a program which produces a multi-column report of data or statistics concerning a sport of your choice (such as hockey, basketball, or volleyball). Provide your own data, either actual data or hypothetical data.

ADDITIONAL ASSIGNMENTS

Graphing

6. Use the TAB function to produce a curve on the output device of the function $y = x^2$.
7. Use the TAB function to produce a diamond shape, the top point of which begins at about the centre of the output line.
(See chapter on Forms Design for an aid in planning this output.)

CHAPTER 11

DOCUMENTATION AND PROGRAM MAINTENANCE

Level 1

Having the combination of a padlock or the serial number of your bike written down and stored in a safe place is of little value in itself. In fact, one sometimes feels foolish or over-organized when writing down and saving information such as this. The information is of no value until the combination is forgotten and the padlock cannot be opened. Similarly the serial number of a bicycle is of no value until the bicycle has been stolen and the police request the serial number to aid in their search.

DOCUMENTATION

Saving these slips of paper containing what might prove to be valuable information is a form of documentation. Documentation is the writing down and saving of information which might be used later to understand how something works or how something was done.

When programming the computer, beginning programmers are more interested in obtaining the correct solution to the problem than in writing down how the solution was obtained. As long as the method of solution will not have to be re-examined, documentation is of no value. If the program has to be reviewed, corrected or updated, good documentation is a must!

Some programs such as payroll programs are used repeatedly. It is extremely important that proper information about the program be organized, bound together, and stored under the proper label. Should, or perhaps a better word is *when*, a problem arises or a change in the program is required, it would be fairly easy to look up the structure of the program and modify it. Remember, almost all good programs which are regularly used are updated or modified from time to time.

The documentation of a program is a *package* of the different aspects of the program. There are different parts to it. Each part is outlined below.

PROGRAM DESCRIPTION

The **program description** would be included in this documentation. The statement would be a summary of the problem or what the program can do. It might also include any controls or tests which were written into the program. For example, a payroll program might be written to test the amount of the cheque just before it is printed to verify that it is not over a certain amount, say $500. This information should go in the problem statement.

PROGRAM DEFINITION
. . . ALSO INCLUDED IN THE PROGRAM IS AN ERROR TRAP. THIS ROUTINE TESTS THE VALUE OF THE OUTPUT BEFORE THE CHEQUE IS WRITTEN. IF THAT VALUE IS OVER $500.00 A PAUSE OCCURS AFTER OUTPUTTING A MESSAGE TO THE OPERATOR. THE OPERATOR IS PROMPTED TO SELECT ONE OF THREE OPTIONS:
   1) CONTINUE THE PROGRAM
   2) SKIP OVER THE PRINTING OF THAT CHEQUE
   3) TERMINATE THE PROGRAM

Figure 11.1

At one time program documentation had both a problem description and a program definition. The former was just a little more than the name of the program. The latter defined all the parts of the program. Lately these have been combined.

LOGIC AIDS

Any structure diagram flowchart, decision table, or sketch which outlines how the problem was solved would also be included in good documentation. If a complex program must be analysed and updated by a different programmer or even the original programmer, without the logic representation, the programmer might as well start from scratch. It would not take too long to re-structure the logic for a short simple program, but it is extremely difficult to determine the logic from the listing of the instructions of a complex program. The task is more complex if the program is not written with a structure.

PROGRAM LISTING

A list of the program's instructions should also be included. Remarks or comment statements should be included at various critical locations in the listing, especially heading up modules.

Changes can sometimes be made easily by changing one module or adding a new module. The new instructions must be consistent with other instructions in the module, and in some cases consistent with the balance of the program. The listing also provides a basis for the programmer to write additional modules which are consistent with the original ones.

PUTTING THE FINISHING TOUCHES TO THE LISTING

Various programming techniques have been outlined which give your program some style. These techniques do not make your program run any faster or run any better but they do make your program easier to understand. You will recall that the first 100 lines are available to properly identify your program. This identification could include the following:

- program name
- program description
- author's name
- copyright notice
- references
- list of variables
- list of arrays
- important messages to the user, etc.

In documenting a program, take the time to do a good job of this. Make this section attractive. In fact make it a work of art!

Then go through the program and add REMARKS statements in places which seem appropriate. Have key parts of your program stand out clearly. Make sure nested loops are indented. Have the end part of your program clearly identified. Perhaps the data, and end of job notation should be near the end statement unless there is a good reason to have them elsewhere.

Take pride in this aspect of your work. If your program is a good one, then give it the appearance of a professional program!

Figure 11.2

```
 5:
 6:
 7:
 8:
 9:
10 REM                    **** CAR SALE PROGRAM ****
11:
12:
13:
14:
15 REM                    **** BY JOE PROGRAMMER ****
16:
17:
18:
19:
20 REM                    **** 19-- 01 06 VERSION 3 ****
21:
22:
23 REM ************************************************************
24 REM ************************************************************
25 REM **      THIS PROGRAM IS DESIGNED TO AID AN           **
26 REM **      AUTOMOBILE SALESMAN. INPUTS ARE              **
27 REM **      PROMPTED, FOR FINANCIAL DATA                 **
28 REM **      CONCERNING THE SALE OR POTENTIAL             **
           **      SALE OF A CAR.                              **
29 REM **                                                   **
30 REM **      THE PROGRAM CALCULATES THE TOTAL             **
31 REM **.     COST OF PURCHASING A CERTAIN CAR.            **
32 REM **                                                   **
33 REM **      A SECOND OPTION ENABLES THE                  **
34 REM **      CUSTOMER TO HAVE AN ESTIMATE OF THE          **
35 REM **      MONTHLY CHARGES IF THE CAR IS                **
           **      PURCHASED ON THE INSTALMENT PLAN.          **
36 REM ************************************************************
37 REM ************************************************************
38:
39:
40:
60 REM ************************************************************
61 REM ************************************************************
62 REM **                                                   **
63 REM **      VARIABLES                                    **
64 REM **                                                   **
65 REM **      P    = PRICE      I    = INTEREST RATE       **
66 REM **      T    = TRADE-IN   G    = GROSS COST          **
67 REM **      D    = DELIVERY   N    = NET COST            **
                        COST
68 REM **      ST   = SALES TAX  TX   = TAX                 **
                        RATE
69 REM **      M    = MONTHS     F    = FINAL COST          **
70 REM **                                                   **
71 REM ************************************************************
72 REM ************************************************************
80:
81 REM ************************************************************
82 REM ************************************************************
83 REM **                                                   **
84 REM **      ARRAYS (NONE)                                **
85 REM **                                                   **
```

```
 86 REM ••••••••••••••••••••••••••••••••••••••••••••••••••••••••••••••
 87 REM ••••••••••••••••••••••••••••••••••••••••••••••••••••••••••••••
 90 REM ••••••••••••••••••••••••••••••••••••••••••••••••••••••••••••••
 91 REM ••••••••••••••••••••••••••••••••••••••••••••••••••••••••••••••
 92 REM **                                                         **
 93 REM **              MAINLINE OF PROGRAM                        **
 94 REM **                                                         **
 95 REM ••••••••••••••••••••••••••••••••••••••••••••••••••••••••••••••
 96 REM ••••••••••••••••••••••••••••••••••••••••••••••••••••••••••••••
100 INPUT "KEY IN THE PRICE OF THE CAR";P
110 PRINT
120 INPUT "THANK YOU. NOW ENTER THE VALUE OF THE
    TRADE-IN";T
130 PRINT
140 INPUT "O.K. ENTER THE DELIVERY CHARGES";D
150 PRINT
160 INPUT "THANK YOU. NOW ENTER THE SALES TAX";ST
170 GOSUB 1000
180 INPUT "IS A ROUGH ESTIMATE OF THE MONTHLY PAYMENTS
    REQUIRED? (YES/NO)";A$
190 IF A$ = "YES" THEN GOSUB 2000
200 INPUT "IS THERE ANOTHER CUSTOMER? (YES/NO)";B$
210 IF B$ = "YES" THEN 100
220 PRINT "END OF JOB"
230 END
990 REM ••••••••••••••••••••••••••••••••••••••••••••••••••••••••••••••
991 REM ••••••••••••••••••••••••••••••••••••••••••••••••••••••••••••••
992 REM **                                                         **
993 REM **         COST OF CAR CALCULATION SUBROUTINE              **
994 REM **                                                         **
995 REM ••••••••••••••••••••••••••••••••••••••••••••••••••••••••••••••
996 REM ••••••••••••••••••••••••••••••••••••••••••••••••••••••••••••••
997 :
998 :
999 :
1000 LET G = P + D
1010 LET N = G − T
1020 LET TX = N * ST / 100
1030 LET F = N + TX
1040 PRINT "THE COST OF YOUR CAR WILL BE";F
1050 RETURN
1990 REM •••••••••••••••••••••••••••••••••••••••••••••••••••••••••••••
1991 REM •••••••••••••••••••••••••••••••••••••••••••••••••••••••••••• **
1992 REM **                                                         **
1993 REM **       ESTIMATED MONTHLY COST SUBROUTINE                 **
1994 REM **                                                         **
1995 REM •••••••••••••••••••••••••••••••••••••••••••••••••••••••••••••
1996 REM •••••••••••••••••••••••••••••••••••••••••••••••••••••••••••••
2000 INPUT "KEY IN THE NUMBER OF MONTHS OVER WHICH
     PAYMENTS WILL BE MADE";M
2010 PRINT
2020 INPUT "THANK YOU. NOW KEY IN THE CURRENT INTEREST
     RATE";I
2030 REM INSERT INTEREST CALCULATION ROUTINE WHICH
     REPRESENTS THE CURRENT ACCEPTED METHOD OF
2040 REM INSTALMENT PAYMENT CALCULATION
2090 RETURN
```

The listing would be improved if the variables are spelled out in full words. A program done this way is almost self-documenting.

```
...; PRICE              ...; SALESTAX
...; TRADEIN            ...; MONTHS
...; DELIVERY           ...; INTERESTRATE

Other variables would be:
        G becomes GROSSCOST TX becomes TAX
        N becomes NETCOST     F becomes FINALCOST

Among the changes which would therefore be made are:
1000 LET GROSSCOST = PRICE + DELIVERY
1010 LET NETCOST = GROSSCOST - TRADEIN
1020 LET TAX = GROSSCOST * SALESTAX / 100
1030 LET FINALCOST = NETCOST + TAX
1040 PRINT "THE COST OF YOUR CAR WILL BE";FINALCOST
1050 RETURN
```

Figure 11.3

OUTPUT OF TESTS

An outline of the test data used to test the original program should also be included in the documentation package. The output of the test data should be kept with the program listing. Should the program begin to produce unusual output, the tests could be run and compared with the original test output. If the output is different it is probable that one or more instructions in the program have been altered. (Perhaps part of the program was not copied correctly during some operating system updates.)

After a program has been updated it is sometimes reasonable to rerun the original test data to make sure the changes have not (in error) altered the basic program.

LAYOUTS

Included in good documentation should be a sketch outlining the fields in any data records used as input for the problem. When re-examining a program it is sometimes necessary to change the input. If the original *record layout* is available, a change can be made with a minimum of effort.

A copy of the output should also be included. For example, if the output format or design was a report, an **output layout** should be made, outlining the headings, the placement of the data, the placement of page numbers, the spacing of the detail line, and the location of any totals. If appropriate, the layout of the video screen should also be saved. More about layout diagrams in the chapter on Forms Design.

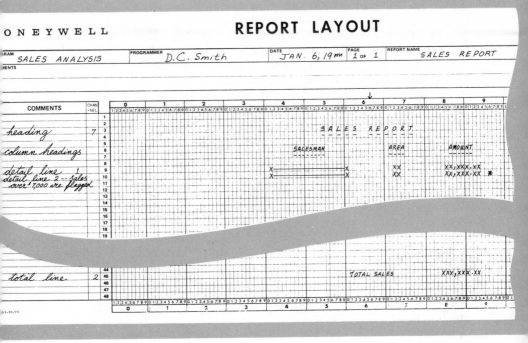

Figure 11.4

The layout of the disc or tape files is called auxiliary storage record layout. These layouts should form part of good documentation.

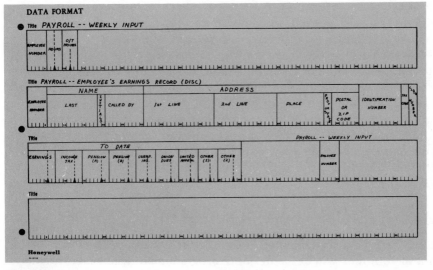

Figure 11.5

THE RUN BOOK

The **run book** is a guide for the computer operator to follow while running that particular program. It serves two main purposes. It guides the operator in setting up the computer to run the program. It also provides information should there be some difficulty during the run. The run book would tell the operator:

1. the type of input cards, if cards are used
2. the label, or file name on the tape or disc which is used
3. any special switch settings on the computer console
4. the meaning of any program error messages that the computer might print out while running the program
5. special paper to be used such as cheque forms

PROGRAM MAINTENANCE

If a program is to be used once and once only, there would be no need to document it. If a program is to be used repeatedly, well into the future, there is a good chance that it will have to have some **maintenance** or **augmentation**. The need for **program maintenance** arises due to any one of the following situations:

- procedures *within* the firm change and the program must be altered to reflect those changes
- changes occur *outside* the control of the firm such as government regulations requiring a different way of processing certain information, such as payroll
- an additional safety check or edit feature is thought to be necessary
- an additional routine or module would produce a new report or new statistics which would expand the decision-making tools of management
- a bug has been found in the programs and requires correcting

Some programmers have a very pessimistic view of a *clean* program. They define such a program *as one in which an error has yet to be found!* How is that for pessimism! Perhaps you should not be quite so pessimistic, but you should realize that any major program you write which will be used regularly might have a bug or two still in it waiting to expose itself. The author once wrote a program which was used daily for 18 months before a certain card count, never before encountered, caused the program to write only page headers on page after page of paper! (It was the fatal combination of end of file and a new page routine occurring simultaneously).

MAINTAINING SOMEONE ELSE'S PROGRAM

If you become a programmer in industry, chances are that over 70 per cent of your time will be spent doing program maintenance. Fortunately, or unfortunately, depending on how you look at it, most of the maintenance will be done on programs written by another programmer. Too many of the packaged programs for micros contain errors which have to be patched. Another reason for maintenance is that you or your employer might want some improvement in a pre-packaged program.

In industry there is considerable mobility of programmers, especially good ones. The author of a custom written program quite likely will have left the firm. If the author left good documentation, your task will be easier. Your task will be difficult if:

1. there is no documentation
2. the quality of documentation is poor
3. the program was poorly structured

There are a series of steps which you should take in approaching a maintenance problem. Assume that a bug has surfaced in a program and your task is to find it and correct it.

APPROACHES TO MAINTENANCE ✳

1) The first step is to become familiar with the program and the documentation which is available. Study the program and documentation until you are familiar with its overall function.
2) If there appears to be a logic error, check over the original logic representation. For example, check the structure diagram flowchart, decision table or pseudo code to make sure it appears logical. If it does appear logical, compare the **coding** or list of instructions with the logic representation to make sure all parts of the logic found their way into the program.
3) If the logic representation is missing, it will likely save time in the long run to sketch or outline your own, using the listing as reference.
4) As you look over the documentation and program, note any deficiencies in the documentation and make the appropriate *pencil* notations. Add remarks or comment statements in the program as an aid.
5) Make a list of the variable names and their apparent use. Also make a list or table of when files are opened and closed, and of any routines using flags. (More about these last two concepts in later chapters.)
6) Be very careful when you make changes. Remember that a change may affect other parts of the program and begin a chain of other compulsory changes. If the program is not structured and not written in modules, each module having one entrance and one exit, be even more careful when making changes. A change in one section might pop something out in another section.
7) Make neat pencil notations on the original listing of any changes you make. Pencil notations are suggested because frequently the changes you want to make at first, subsequently are found to be unwise. Sometimes there is a good reason for coding which initially appears to be illogical. Avoid making changes just to clean up a **glitch** or awkwardly coded section of the program. The more changes you make which are

not absolutely necessary, the more additional problems you might be creating.

8) Be sure to add your own error checking routines in any additional modules you write. Or add error checking routines in sections previously written which, in your opinion, should have had them.

RE-TEST

Once you believe you have found the error and corrected it, or have put in the new routines which were required, you must now see that a thorough test is carried out. The same approach is used in testing programs which have just had maintenance done on them as is used on new programs.

DO NOT OMIT THIS VERY IMPORTANT ASPECT OF PROGRAM MAINTENANCE!

RE-DOCUMENT

Be sure to carefully document *any changes* you make. Resolve that the documentation you return to file will be in better shape than you received it. Remember that this program which you have augmented or maintained will very likely have to have further maintenance at some future time.

Level 2
ON . . . GO TO

One of the most important functions of a computer, which makes it different from any other so called programmable machines, is its ability to 'make decisions.' You know about the IF . . . THEN instruction. A type of decision is made by the computer when executing this instruction. There is an implied decision in the FOR . . . NEXT instruction as well. There is a very handy 'decision maker' which can also be used. It is the ON . . . GO TO instruction. Essentially the computer is able to make a branch to any one of quite a number of instructions using this instruction. Here is how it works.

The computer checks the value of the variable or computes the value of an expression which follows the word ON.

The value of the variable or expression should be one of the counting numbers, 1, 2, 3, 4. . . . If the value is 1, the computer branches to the *first* instruction number after the GO TO. If the value is 2, the computer branches to the instruction number listed *second* after the GO TO, and so on.

```
130 INPUT "INPUT A NUMBER FROM 1 TO 6";X
140 ON X GO TO 200, 300, 400, 500, 600
150 PRINT "ERROR IN INPUT, TRY AGAIN"
```

160 GO TO 130

.

.

.

200 REM ROUTINE FOR A 1 INPUT

.

.

.

300 REM ROUTINE FOR A 2 INPUT

If X has the value of 1, the computer will look at the first number listed after the phrase GO TO to find the instruction number to which it should then branch. In this case the instruction number is 200. The series of instructions beginning with instruction number 200 will be the module which will be processed as a result of a '1' input. Similarly if the value of X happened to be a 4, the computer would obtain the number of the next instruction to be executed from the *fourth* number after the GO TO. In the illustration, it would be instruction number 500.

Instruction number 140 might have in it an expression instead of a variable name, following the word ON.

120 Z = 0
130 Y = 3
140 ON (Y * $^2/_3$) − Z GO TO 600, 700, 800

The computer first calculates the value of the expression, then uses that value to determine where it is to branch to next. It is important that the value of the expression be either a 1, 2 or 3. The programmer must make sure that one of these three numbers will be the result. In this case, if the result of the expression is 1, the computer will branch to instruction 600 for its next instruction. Similarly if the result were 3, it would branch to 800. As an option GOSUB may be used in place of GO TO. The rules of GOSUB, of course, apply.

TRICKS TO USE ON ON . . . GO TO

Assume that during your program, you obtain a variable which you wish to use in the ON . . . GO TO statement, but the variable could be a −1 or a zero, or a +1. This problem can be solved with a little ingenuity. Study this:

120 LET X = −1

130 ON X + 2 GO TO 200, 300, 400

Because the value of the variable or expression following ON must be a counting number, by adding 2 to X if −1 ⩽ X ⩾ +1, we can create the required results.

Keep this in mind while programming. You will discover similar tricks to make full use of this programming feature. In the next chapter the INT and ABS functions are explained. These are useful operations when used with the ON . . . GO TO instruction.

MENUS AND MAPS

Many programs used today provide a variety of options for the user. A whole program would not have to be run if the user wishes to access and run only a part of it. To provide this option the user is informed at the beginning of the program just what the program will do and how to select the part required.

A **menu**, sometimes called a **map**, of what is available is displayed as soon as the program is called for execution. Instructions are provided as to how to use the menu, that is, how to select the routine desired. The operator makes the selection and follows the instructions to direct the computer to that section.

For example, a program might be available to do a wide variety of tasks relating to an accounts receivable file. When the program is called in, the first thing it does is to display a series of **prompting instructions**, and, if requested, a menu.

Message 1   Do you wish to see a menu, (Y or N)?

Message 2   (Assuming N) What routine number do you wish to run?
(Assuming Y) Which Of The Following Do You Wish To Access:
Menu A
1. Current/Total Receivables
2. Subtotals by Age of Receivables
3. Amount of Receivables over a specified age
4. Information concerning a specific customer's account

.
.
.

Message   Input a Number

After the particular routine is requested the program branches to the suitable module.

If from Menu A the number 3 or 4 is selected, the corresponding module might continue prompting the user. It might even produce another menu outlining the various ages of accounts which could be produced and requesting a selection of one of these ages. Or, in the case of a 4 being selected, a list of all customers might be produced so that the user may select the customer involved. If there were many customers, the program might prompt the user by asking for the customer number, if available, or the first four characters of the customer's name. A menu of all customers with those same first four characters could be produced by the program for the user to examine.

CHECKING YOUR READING—LEVEL 1

1. What is a simple definition of documentation?
2. What is the purpose of documenting a program?
3. What is the problem description of a computer program?
4. What is the prime function of logic aids, such as a structure diagram or a flowchart?
5. What is the listing of a program?
6. Why are the various tests of a program and a copy of the test data kept on file?
7. List four types of layouts which might accompany program documentation.
8. Briefly explain how a computer operator uses a run book.
9. Briefly list five reasons why a program might have to be maintained or updated.
10. What trend is there to indicate that most of a programmer's time will involve program maintenance?
11. Write two or three simple sentences to outline the general approach to program maintenance, especially identifying and correcting an error in a current program.
12. Why would it be important to carefully re-test a program after it has been maintained?
13. Why is it extremely important to re-document after changes have been made to a program?

VOCABULARY ASSIGNMENT

Continue developing your vocabulary by writing brief definitions of the words or phrases in this section in bold type.

CHECKING YOUR READING—LEVEL 2

1. Outline the function of the ON . . . GO TO statement.
2. Why is it important that the value of the expression, or the variable, following the word ON be a digit?
3. In computer programming, what is a menu, or a map?
4. What is a prompting instruction?

VOCABULARY ASSIGNMENT

Continue developing your vocabulary by writing brief definitions of the words or phrases in this section in bold type.

PROJECTS

Debugging Practice

Review

Identify the errors in the following program segments:

1. 110 LET AA = "SALES REPORT"
2. 130 PRINT X, TAB(150)
3. 130 PRINT "THE TOTALS ARE", TAB(3) ;X; TAB(4) ;Y
4. 120 READ A,B
   199 DATA, J. JONES; $25; F. FRANKS; $70; KIM KIMBERLY; $100
5. 110 LET X = 1.5
   120 GO TO 100 IF X
6. 110 LET X = 2
   120 FOR I = 1 TO 5
   130 LET Y = X + I
   140 ON Y GO TO 1, 2, 3, 4, 5
   150 NEXT I
7. 110 LET A = −2
   120 LET B = 2
   130 ON A + B GO TO 200, 300, 400
   140 IF A + B = 4 GO TO 999
   200 PRINT "A + B = 1"
   210 LET B = B + 1
   220 GO TO 130
   300 PRINT "A + B = 2"
   310 LET B = B + 1
   320 GO TO 130
   400 PRINT "A + B = 3"
   410 LET B = B + 1
   420 GO TO 130
   999 END

Note: You will be pleased to learn that you have just finished the last of the debugging assignments in this text. By now you should have developed a critical eye as you look over instructions. All subsequent practice will be provided by YOU. The more errors you make, the more practice you will get. Hopefully you will have very little opportunity for practice!

PROGRAMMING ASSIGNMENTS FROM BUSINESS AND INDUSTRY

Up to now you have been practising your programming by writing relatively short programs. Little or no documentation has been required. Most of the programming assignments which follow in the text are based on problems from business and industry. Some have been watered down. Others are quite challenging. A variety are supplied so that you could choose assignments which interest you. In some cases the assignments are linked together, each successive one building on the programming which was done previously. Not all parts of these programs have to be done.

This chapter provided an extensive outline as to what documentation is and how it is used. Clearly, now is the time for you to develop your documentation skills. You are urged to fully document *some* of these programs. At the absolute minimum you should fully document a program at least three times during the term.

And a word of caution is in order. Usually the first few efforts at documentation are not too satisfactory. Your instructor will be very hard on you until you reach certain reasonable standards. At that point helpful hints still will be given, but generally your instructor will give full credit for the good work you do.

In the early stages of developing documenting skills most students are deficient in the following areas:

1) Problem definitions vaguely written, or written in poor English. They must be clearly written, providing the reader with a good understanding of what the program is all about.
2) The logic representation is:
   - not correct
   - not neatly done
   - contains special words or phrases not commonly understood by programmers
3) Layout sheets are not neatly done or not done in the traditional style.
4) The listing is missing, or the listing does not include remarks statements where it would be reasonable to expect them. The listing lacked style. Parts or all of the identification section are missing.
5) All parts of the program were not tested, or the various tests did not become part of the documentation.
6) The run manual (more likely a run *sheet*) was missing or important parts of the information about the program were missing from it.

DOCUMENTATION IS ALMOST AN ART. DO NOT EXPECT A PERFECT GRADE OR MARK FROM YOUR INSTRUCTOR TOO SOON. BE PATIENT. LEARN FROM YOUR MISTAKES AND FROM THE SUGGESTIONS OF YOUR INSTRUCTOR. IN TIME, BOTH YOU AND YOUR INSTRUCTOR WILL BE PROUD OF THE QUALITY OF THE DOCUMENTATION YOU DO.

By the way, keep in a safe place some of your better efforts. If you go looking for a position as a programmer, or other computer related jobs, showing the interviewer a sample of your work will certainly make an impression.

If you begin writing programs to be sold, either directly or through a software house, part of your reputation will be established on the quality of your documentation.

Annuities

In simple terms an annuity is a contract in which the customer or policy holder puts in or deposits money so that at some future time the money will be paid back. Generally, the money is deposited during the annuitant's earning years and paid back during retirement. Usually, periodic deposits are made and, at some point in time, regular payments, say monthly payments, are paid back from the company. Sometimes, a lump sum is paid instead of regular deposits, and sometimes a lump sum is taken to close out the annuity, instead of regular payments.

The following individual assignments should be done keeping in mind that they could be put together into one large program. (Read assignment number 6 before you begin with assignment number 1).

1. Write a program to calculate the amount which would accumulate in an annuity if a principal amount or lump sum is compounded at a certain interest rate for a specific number of periods. The formula to be used is $A = P(1 + I)^N$ where A = the end amount, P = principal or deposit, I = rate of interest *for the period* and N = the number of periods. Remember that in BASIC the exponential symbol is an arrow. Also remember that if the interest is compounded semi-annually for 6 years and the rate is 10 per cent per annum, the rate for the **period** would be 5% and the number of periods would be 12.

2. Add to the above program the capability of inputting N and any two of A, P, or I, and solving for the third item. (When the program solves for P, it is said to be solving for the 'present value' of A, such that if the accumulated amount in the future would be say, $5 000, what would have to be deposited now?)

3. In the case where regular deposits are made into an annuity over a period of time, a modification of the formula would have to be made. It is $S = (D(1 + I)^N - 1) \div I$ where S is the accumulated value of the annuity, in other words, the sum of the payments and the interest; I = the rate of interest for the period; N = the number of periods; and D = the regular deposit. Write a program to calculate the sum after inputting the other variables.

4. Modify assignment #3 so that the sum of the payments and interest is given and the amount which must be regularly deposited is required.

5. In paying out an annuity, the annuitant could decide that instead of receiving a certain payment per month for a certain length of time, (leaving the balance to earn interest), the total value of the policy is requested. The present value of all individual payments may be determined by the formula $PV = P(1 - (1 \div (1 + I)^N)) \div I$. PV = present value and P = potential individual payments. Write a program to find the present value of an annuity given the variables.

6. Combine the above five programs and write a menu to guide the user. You might wish to improve each module of the program by inserting a sub-menu or prompting routine to lead the user along.

7. FULLY DOCUMENT YOUR PROGRAM.

ADDITIONAL PROGRAMMING ASSIGNMENTS

Volume of a Sphere
8. (a) A manufacturing firm produces hollow spheres of varying sizes. Generally the spheres are used as storage tanks for certain types of hazardous liquids. The spheres are custom made. Write a program to accept into memory the radius of a sphere and have the computer output its volume. ($V = 4/3 \pi r^3$)
(b) Add a routine to the above program such that the circumference of a sphere could be measured and inputted and the computer would calculate its volume. (Hint: $C = 2 \pi r$; therefore $r = \ldots$)
(c) Add still another routine such that the volume could be inputted and the computer would calculate the radius required for a sphere of the necessary volume. (If you are not sure how to handle the cube root problem, use the bulldozer method of incrementing r by 1 until the volume equals the inputted value).

Space Science

9. Write a program to input a person's mass and a digit representing the planet the person 'plans on visiting.' Display the planets in a type of menu along with their reference number. Have the computer calculate the equivalent weight of the person. Use the following table:

PLANET	GRAVITY RATIO
Mercury	0.25
Venus	0.85
Earth	1.00
Earth's Moon	0.16
Mars	0.38
Jupiter	2.64
Saturn	1.17
Uranus	0.92
Neptune	1.12

10. (a) *Dates* Write a program which will accept into memory a digit representing the day of the week (Sunday = 1, Monday = 2, etc.). Also input the number of the month (January = 1, etc.) and the day of the month. Have the computer output the date as in the following example: Monday, April 19.
(b) Some firms use the number of the day in the year for the code used in the Lot designation (the chemical 'mix' that particular day). Write a program to input the day and the month and output the day number in that particular year. For example the lot number of February 20, 1983 would be "Lot 05183). If you have time, add a routine to your program to handle leap year.

CHAPTER 12

PROGRAMMING TRICKS

Level 1

Over the last few chapters you have discovered that programming is not just putting together a series of instructions, obtaining an output from the computer and saying, 'that's a job well done.' A complex program which will be used repeatedly should be thoroughly tested, debugged and documented. There have been a few concepts which were mentioned in the earlier chapters which now require additional explanation.

EDITING

The editor of this text has the job of checking over each sentence and paragraph to make sure each makes sense. If the editor finds something vague or discovers some bad or awkward grammar the red pen is activated. In addition to correcting vague sentences or bad grammar the editor also looks for spelling errors and poor punctuation.

A programmer should program the computer to be an editor. Certainly the compiler has an automatic editing feature which looks for reserved words spelled incorrectly or wrong punctuation (syntax errors). The programmer should plan for the mishandling of the program. The type of **editing** you could write into your programs could take two forms:

1. For reasonableness
2. For output

EDITING FOR REASONABLENESS

Editing for reasonableness is using a long word to describe a programming feature which checks the input data to make sure it falls within certain parameters. (Hmmm, editors are also supposed to make sure that big words are not used when short common words will do! I should have used the word 'limits' instead of the word parameter). For example, if, in a payroll program, it is known that no one ever works more than 50 hours in a week, the variable holding the number of hours worked would be checked to make sure that the number is equal to or less than 50.

> 130 INPUT "HOURS WORKED THIS WEEK" ;H
> 140 IF H > 50 THEN 600   (statement 600 would be the begin-
> ning of an error message and 'error
> recovery' module)

Similarly the rate of pay could be edited to make sure it is less than, say $12.00, assuming that is the maximum hourly rate paid by the company.

As a safety feature, the output should also be edited. Periodically one reads about the 'error the computer made,' printing out a $2 000 000 cheque when in fact it should have been a $200 cheque. Jumping to the defense of the computer, the error was likely made as a result of two people errors. The first person at fault was likely the operator, or data entry clerk, who inputted incorrect data, resulting in this serious mistake. The other person at fault would be the programmer who did not include a satisfactory edit routine in the program. Output could be edited using instructions such as:

> 150 LET P = H * R
> 160 IF P > 600 THEN 800   (instruction 800 would be the begin-
> ning of another error routine
> module)
> 170 PRINT "THE PAY IS" ;P

OUTPUTTING

As was mentioned earlier, publishers' editors correct any punctuation errors or omissions so that the written material reads smoothly. Within the computer numbers are computed in 'pure form' uncluttered by commas, spaces or dollar signs. Some amounts when outputted, particularly large amounts, are awkward to read. The programmer should insert a routine to make these numbers easier to read. Where possible, commas or blanks should be inserted and the dollar sign added. In working with accounting, sometimes it is appropriate to add the letters CR or DR after an amount representing an unusual status of an account. More about that later. The PRINT USING statement will be explained in the second section of chapter 16 but the following will give you some idea as to what it is all about:

> 120 LET A$ = "###,###.##"
> 130 LET P = 222333.458 + .005
> 140 PRINT USING A$;P

The output should be 222,333.46. The amount has been 'edited' and the correct punctuation has been inserted. (Note: At the time of writing, no routine was available in BASIC to produce metric editing. In metric the commas, usually put in large numbers are deleted leaving a space between each group of 3 digits.)

ERROR ROUTINES

If, during the edit routines an error is discovered, some suitable action should be taken. There are three common procedures.
1) Produce a suitable error message and go to the end of the program.
2) Produce a suitable error message and cause the program to pause.
3) Produce an error message and have the program carry on with the next data item.

FATAL ERRORS

Again, assume that no employee works more than 50 hours in one week. If the program is to stop should the hours inputted be over 50 hours the error is said to be a **fatal error**. Here is an example of how this type of error routine could be accomplished:

```
130 READ H
140 IF H > 50 THEN PRINT "ERROR IN HOURS WORKED":GO
TO 200
150 . .
```

Instruction 140 is really two instructions in one. Using the ":" following the IF statement causes the execution of the instruction and the GO TO 200, *only if* the condition is true. If it is not true the computer skips over the PRINT and the GO TO 200 and proceeds to the next instruction— instruction 150. If the program is caused to branch to 200 END due to the error, the computer stops executing the program.

THE CHOICE IS YOURS

Instead of stopping the program, a programmed pause could be inserted. If the operator wishes to continue with the program the appropriate control instruction would then be given. If the error appears to be sufficiently serious that the program should be stopped, the operator is then able to make that decision.

```
130 READ H
140 IF H > 50 THEN GO TO 800
        .
        .
        .
800 INPUT "ERROR IN HOURS WORKED, IF YOU WISH TO
        CONTINUE WITH NEXT DATA ITEM INPUT A '1'. IF YOU
        WISH TO TERMINATE INPUT A '2' ":J
810 IF J = 1 THEN GO TO 130
820 IF J = 2 THEN GO TO 200 (END)
830 GO TO 800
```

Even in the error routine an input error is anticipated. What a pessimist! Should the operator enter other than a 1 or a 2 another chance is given.

NOTE IT AND CARRY ON

[If the program is to continue in spite of a detected error, an error message may be outputted or some indication that there was an error could be stored, and the program would carry on. This could be considered a **non-fatal error.**]

```
130 READ H
135 LET C = C + 1
140 IF H > 50 THEN GO TO 800
    .
    .
    .
800 LET K = K + 1    (K is the subscript of the matrix E.
                     C is the count of the records. This
810 LET E(K) = C     routine builds a matrix of the count of the
                     records which have errors).
820 GO TO 130
    .
    .
9950 REM            PRINT ERROR-IN-DATA MESSAGES
9960 PRINT "ERROR IN THE FOLLOWING RECORD COUNT"
9970 FOR L = 1 TO K
9980 PRINT E(L),
9990 NEXT L
9998 PRINT "EOJ"
9999 GO TO 200 (END)
```

or, using the preferred modular structure:

```
130 READ H,R            (Initial READ)
140 LET C = C + 1
150 IF H > 50 GOSUB 800
160 LET P = H * R
    .
    .
    .
800  PRINT "ERROR IN RECORD NUMBER";C (where C is the
        record count)
810 READ H,R            (Regular READ)
820 LET C = C + 1
```

```
830 IF H > 50 GO TO 800
840 RETURN
```

In this case, the error message is outputted in the subroutine. The next data set is read and checked to see if the hours worked are within the limit. If so, the return takes the program to instruction 160 for processing the data.

ERRORS IN INTERACTIVE DATA ENTRY

In each of the examples used above, data was READ. If data is inputted interactively the program would immediately go into an edit module. If there was an error, a suitable error message would be outputted. The message would likely prompt the data entry clerk to try again, correcting the error. The programming for this would be similar to the approach used above.

RESTARTS

If a programmer is to assume the worst, (yet hope for the best) the program should have features which enable it to be logically and orderly terminated should a problem develop. A routine should be included to enable a **restart** to take place without requiring duplicate processing or producing distorted data.

Assume that a program is processing a massive data file. If the operator makes a mistake or if there is a power failure, the program quite likely would have to be restarted. The author had a very unfortunate experience early in his programming career. He was running a timetabling program on a file of about 1600 records. The program was slow and literally took hours to run. Just near the end of a run there was a power failure. The program did not have a restart feature. The data had to be tediously loaded again and the program rerun. Many hours of valuable time were lost. It was very frustrating. As soon as there was time, a restart routine was written and inserted. Other special instructions were also included so that during subsequent runs the operator had much more control over the running of the program.

One technique used to do this is to have the program ask right at the beginning if this is a restart.

```
130 LET R = 0
140 LET C = 0
        .
        .
        .
170 INPUT "IS THIS A RESTART? IF YES INPUT 1, IF NO
    INPUT 2";Z
```

```
180 IF Z = 1 GOSUB 7000
190 READ #1, R1, A$, V
```

> (where #1 is the device number,
> R1 is the assigned record
> number, A$ is the name of the
> record and V is the price of
> the item).

```
7000 REM          RESTART ROUTINE
7010 INPUT "INPUT THE VALUES FOR THE ACTUAL
     RECORD NUMBER ";R
7020 INPUT "INPUT THE VALUE FOR THE RECORD
     COUNT";C
7030 INPUT "INPUT THE VALUE FOR . . . etc.
```

> (routine to read through the file until
> appropriate record is found)

```
7070 RETURN
```

Restart routines are extremely useful in programs which process quantities of data on a tape or disc file. Use them wherever they might apply.

OTHER SAFETY CHECKS

As implied in the above segments, it is traditional to output a **record count** at the end of a program. At the end of the run, the number would be outputted and compared with the record count of other runs. This is especially appropriate in file processing as opposed to data base processing. If the number of records processed differs unaccountably, an error has occurred. If there were some bad data, that information might also be recorded during the program and outputted at the end of the run.

Another safety check is to do a **sequence check** of the number assigned to the records in a sequential file. Usually the record numbers are in ascending order.

```
120 REM          SET UP A VARIABLE TO STORE RECORD
                 NUMBER
130 LET R2 = 0        (R2 stores previous record number)
140 READ #1, R1, A$, V   (#1 indicates source of data—tape)
150 LET C = C + 1
160 IF R1 < = R2 THEN GOSUB 800
170 LET R2 = R1
```

```
200 END


800 REM          ERROR IN RECORD SEQUENCE ROUTINE
810 PRINT "ERROR IN RECORD SEQUENCE—RECORD
COUNT";C; "RECORD NUMBER";R1
820 INPUT "INPUT 1 TO TERMINATE RUN OR 2 TO
ATTEMPT TO CONTINUE";Q
830 ON Q GO TO 200, 850
840 GO TO 820
850 READ #1, R1, A$, V
860 LET C = C + 1
870 IF R1 < = R2 THEN 810
880 RETURN
```

HASH TOTALS

In file processing, in addition to counting the number of records processed and checking the sequence of the records, a **hash total** could be computed. A hash total is a meaningless value which is computed by adding up an item, or field of the record not usually processed. For example, in doing payroll, the employees' social insurance number might form part of the record. Adding up all the social insurance numbers would produce a hash total. This total in itself is of no value, but it is saved to compare with the same hash total of future runs. If the totals are the same, then likely all records have been processed—none have been accidentally missed. If, for some reason, they are different, then one of the records may have been missed.

FLAGS

Outside of computing, flags have a variety of purposes. Certainly the most common flag is the national flag—the symbol of a nation. Flags of a different sort are used for signaling. In computer programming, **flags** are used to indicate a condition or a change in a condition. A flag is simply a variable. It is initialized at some value, likely zero. During the program an instruction would keep checking to see if it is still zero. Under some circumstances an instruction might give the variable the value '1.' The next time the flag is checked 'it would be waving' the 1, and some alternative programming action would then be taken.

For example sometimes a flag is used to signal the end of data.

```
120 LET F1 = 0
```

```
150 READ #1, R1, A$, V
160 IF R1 = 998 THEN
        GOSUB 1000              (assume the last
            .                   valid record
            .                   number is 998)

            .
240 REM           TEST FOR FLAG
250 IF F1 = 1 THEN 8000
            .

            .
1000 REM          SET FLAG
1010 LET F1 = 1
1060 RETURN

            .

            .
8000 REM          WRAP UP ROUTINE
```

In this case after each record is processed, the flag is checked (instruction 250) to see if it is equal to 1. If it is not, the program continues. If it is equal to 1, the program branches to the wrap-up routine.

You probably are able to see a more efficient way of doing this, avoiding the flag. If so, you are reading this book critically and with good insight. The flag could be avoided in this case but the example illustrates the use of flags, keeping the program as simple as possible. Flags are a handy tool to have in your programming bag of tricks, especially when processing the merging of multiple files. More about that later!

Level 2

INT AND ABS

Another feature which might be useful at this time is the ABS(X) and INT(X) instructions. If in computing X its value is a negative number but a positive number is required, ABS(X) would cause the absolute value of X to be determined; that is, the negative value of X has its sign changed to positive.

Value of X	ABS(X)
−2	+2
−8.5	+8.5
+4.3	+4.3

The feature is sometimes useful to use just before an ON . . . GO TO. Remember the expression or variable after ON must be a (positive) counting number. ABS(X) would convert a negative amount to positive.

The decimal amount is also a problem with the ON . . . GO TO instruction. The instruction INT(X) cuts off or **truncates** everything after the decimal, reducing the decimal number to the next *lowest* whole number.

Value of X	INT(X)
25.4	25
7.9	7
−9.9	−10

Notice that the next *lowest* whole number to −9.9 is −10. Think about it for a minute until you are sure why this is so. Also, notice that no rounding takes place. If you required the value of X to be rounded, simply add .5 to X before you take its integer value:

Value of X			INT(X)
25.4 + .5 =	25.9		25
7.9 + .5 =	8.4		8
−9.9 + .5 = −	9.4		−10 (next lowest whole number)
−8.4 + .5 = −	7.9		−7

If necessary, the above can be combined:

```
130 LET X = −3.3
140 ON ABS(INT(X + .5) ) GO TO 200, 300, 400
```

Are you able to figure out to which instruction the computer will branch? If you determined to 300 you are correct. Here is why:

$$
\begin{aligned}
&\text{ABS(INT(X + .5))} \\
&= \text{ABS(INT(−3.3 + .5))} \\
&= \text{ABS(INT(−2.8))} \\
&= \text{ABS(−2)} \\
&= +2
\end{aligned}
$$

Now try this one.

```
130 LET X = −4.3
140 ON INT(ABS(X + .5) ) GO TO 200, 300, 400
```

This time the computer will branch to 400.
Here is why: (working from the inside out)

$$
\begin{aligned}
&\text{INT(ABS(X + .5))} \\
&= \text{INT(ABS(−4.3 + .5))} \\
&= \text{INT(ABS(−3.8))} \\
&= \text{INT(+3.8)} \quad \text{remember that ABS changes the sign to +} \\
&= +3 \quad \text{the INT truncates that which follows the decimal, lowering the number to the next lowest whole number.}
\end{aligned}
$$

The ABS and INT are commonly used in gaming applications. You will likely have to review this section if and when you get into that exciting computer application. These functions are infrequently used in general vocational programming but are introduced here just in case *you* come up with a problem which could be solved by one or both of these operations.

TWO DIMENSION ARRAYS

You will recall that you could set up what we called an apartment building with one major address and sub-addresses for each apartment. Perhaps the analogy used should have been that of a one-storey model. When learning about a two dimensional array the apartment building analogy still works well, but the number of the floor on which an apartment is located becomes important.

Assume that apartments have a unique numbering system. The floor on which the apartment is located is included in the apartment's number. For example on floor 1, the apartments would be numbered 1,1; 1,2; 1,3 . . . etc. On floor 2 the apartments would be numbered 2,1; 2,2; 2,3 . . . etc. Apartment number 12 on the 15th floor would have what number? If your answer is 12,15 you are wrong. If your answer is 15,12 you are correct. The number of the floor is always given first.

In order to set up memory for a two dimension array the DIM instruction is changed slightly from what you now know it. Remember to set up a 25 apartment array the instruction is:

```
10 DIM M(25)
```

The instruction to set up an array with 10 'floors' with each floor having 15 apartments would be:

```
10 DIM T(10,15)
```

Notice that the number of 'floors' are designated first, then the number of apartments per floor.

If you wanted to output the content of the 6th apartment on the 10th floor, which of the following would be the correct instruction:

```
130 PRINT T(6,10)     or     130 PRINT T(10,6)
```

The instruction on the right is the correct one. The instruction on the left would output the content of the 10th apartment on the 6th floor. Got the idea?

FOR . . . NEXT AND THE TWO DIMENSION ARRAY

Often the FOR . . . NEXT instruction can be used to efficiently manage arrays. The floors of the apartment building become rows and the apartment numbers become columns. If you wanted to output the contents of a 10 row array, with each row having 15 elements, the following should do the job:

```
130 FOR R = 1 TO 10      :REM     R IS FOR ROW
140 FOR C = 1 TO 15      :REM     C IS FOR COLUMN
150 PRINT T(R,C)
160 NEXT C
170 NEXT R
```

To gain a little practice, try loading the above array with the counting numbers. Use instructions similar to the following if you want:

```
110 DIM T(10,15)
120 LET K = 0
130 FOR R = 1 TO 10
140 FOR C = 1 TO 15
150 LET K = K + 1
160 LET T(R,C) = K
170 NEXT C
180 NEXT R
```

Experiment with different outputs. In experimenting, you might like to output all of column 1, then, all of column 2, etc. Or you could output the array in reverse.

CHECKING YOUR READING—LEVEL 1

1. What two general classifications of editing are there in a computer program?
2. Give an example of how inputted data could be checked to make sure it was below a certain maximum limit.
3. If there is an error in output, what two people were likely at fault?
4. In addition to editing output to be within certain prescribed limits, what other type of output editing is frequently done?
5. What three types of error routines are available to a programmer?
6. What is a re-start, and how is it accomplished?
7. In file processing, what three safety checks could be included in a program?
8. In computer programming, what is a flag?

VOCABULARY ASSIGNMENT

Continue developing your vocabulary list by writing a brief definition of the words and phrases in bold type in this section.

CHECKING YOUR READING—LEVEL 2

1. What is meant by the absolute value of a number?
2. What does the integer function in BASIC do?
3. How could the absolute value and the integer functions in BASIC be used with the ON . . . GO TO function?
4. What is the conceptual difference between these two arrays DIM A(20) and DIM B(4,5)?
5. Describe a two dimensional array in simple terms.

VOCABULARY ASSIGNMENT

Continue developing your vocabulary list by writing a brief definition of the words and phrases in bold type in this section.

PROJECTS

Programming Assignments from Business and Industry

Theatre Tickets

The printing and issuing of tickets for performances has changed significantly due to the capabilities of the computer. Computers can produce: simple, un-numbered tickets on plain paper
   simple tickets but sequentially numbered for maintaining control
   tickets with variable data produced on pre-printed ticket forms
   tickets with seat and row designations
   on the spot tickets for the best available seat to a particular performance.
Summaries of the total values of all tickets printed, average value and value of all the tickets of a particular price range aid the theatre manager. Certain promotional decisions and auditing the revenue after the performance are made easier because of the report.

1. Design a simple ticket for a particular function related to some student activity. Provide for the inputting of the number of tickets wanted, the price, the place, time, name of production or performing group. (The chapter on forms design could provide some suggestions on layout.) Output sample tickets. Include the sequence number on each ticket. Produce a report on the total number of tickets printed, and the total value of the tickets printed.
2. Modify the above program so that two price ranges are available. The input to the program would include the number of tickets at each price. Again produce a report on the total tickets printed, the value of the tickets in each price range, the total value and the average price of all the tickets.
3. Program a routine which would put seat numbers on the tickets. Assume the 'house' has rows label A to T. Each row has 48 seats in it.

4. The seats are arranged in 3 blocks of 16 seats each. An aisle goes down the outsides and two aisles split the seat groupings into thirds. Add a module to the above program to have the computer put the aisle designation on the ticket. (For example all seats numbered 1 to 8 would have an aisle 1 designation. Seats numbered 9 to 24 would have an aisle 2 designation, etc.).

5. (a) Simulate the issuing of tickets on the best available basis. Set up the seats in a two dimension array. Assume that all seats in row 1 are better than all seats in row 2, etc. Seat number 1 is better than 2, etc. (This certainly is not a valid assumption but it will do to make things reasonably straightforward). Put the program in a loop such that it waits for an input. When the input comes, have the computer 'issue' the best seat available and return for the next input. (You could set up a dummy alpha string on a micro, say A$, and have it available for the input prompt. INPUT "IF YOU WANT A TICKET HIT ENTER";A$)

(b) Modify the program to issue tickets beginning at the centre and working to the outside.

ADDITIONAL PROGRAMMING ASSIGNMENTS

6. With reference to problem 5 above, block off the extreme corners of the seating arrangement and designate these 'wing' seats as being poorer than the last row in the house.

7. Write a program to issue tickets, combining as many features as suggested in problems 1 to 6 above.

8. Write a program for issuing tickets for a theatre, or auditorium in your place of learning or community.

Biorhythm

9. Some people believe that a person has cyclical highs and lows. The cycles are thought to exist for 3 human characteristics—physical condition, emotional well-being and intellectual alertness. Each component has its own cycle:

physical	23 days
emotional	28 days
intellectual	33 days

Write a program to input the birthdate of a person and the current date. Have the program calculate the current status of each cycle for the person. Assume that the cycles begin at birth on an upward direction, peaking at about ¼ into the cycle. The cycle turns downward and reaches the neutral point by half way through the cycle, continuing downward for the next ¼. At the ¾ point in the cycle it turns upward. Be sure to deal with leap year. Output for the person whether each component is in the 'up' part or 'down' part of the cycle and whether the current trend is upward or downward.

Part III: INFORMATION PROCESSING

CHAPTER 13

BUSINESS DATA PROCESSING

Level 1

Anyone operating a business, whether the business is large or small, must maintain certain types of information. The information is helpful in running a business and making business decisions. In addition, the law *requires* that certain information be obtained and kept on file. Important documents such as corporate or personal tax statements are made up from information carefully kept by a business.

This information is kept in an employee file or in a **book of accounts**. The phrase, book of accounts, is a general term used to represent the keeping of business information. The information might actually be kept in one book. More likely it is kept in a number of books, each book con-

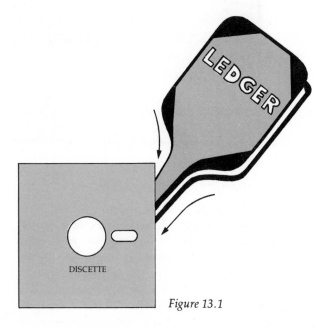

Figure 13.1

taining different types of business information. In fact the information might not be kept in a physical book at all! It could be kept in file folders, or on cards in a drawer full of cards. Since the widespread use of equipment in business, especially the use of computers, the information is often now kept on magnetic tape or magnetic discs. So it is possible, in fact likely, that the 'book of accounts' is really business information on a small magnetic disc. Are you totally confused? Read on.

TYPES OF INFORMATION

Whether kept in a physical book or on magnetic tape or disc the important thing is that the right type of information be kept. The right information must be available so that reports can be made from it. These reports, as mentioned earlier, could form the basis of a business decision. If a report showed that a business operation was losing money, certain decisions could be made to prevent further losses. In fact, actions could be taken to turn losses into a profit. Information which would be useful for this type of decision would include the amount of income of the business operation and the amount of expenses.

INCOME	$20 000
EXPENSES AND OTHER COSTS	16 000
PROFIT	4 000
INCOME	$21 000
EXPENSES AND OTHER COSTS	23 000
LOSS	− 2 000

Figure 13.2

BUSINESS DECISIONS

The various types of expenses which have been recorded could be analysed. It might be found, for example, that too much money is being spent on advertising. The manager of the business might reduce the advertising budget and find that the income from sales remains constant, whereas the expenses are reduced, resulting in a profit. There might be other possible decisions but you have the general idea of how income and expense information could be used.

Other types of information which are also kept by businesses include:

- how much money there is in the bank
- the value of the land and buildings
- how much money is owed to the business
- how much money the business owes to others

RECORDS AND FILES

A piece of information about some aspect of business is called a **record**. A group of related records is called a **file**. For example, the writing down of the fact that the business owns a delivery truck creates a record. A collection of the records of all other things that the business owns is called a *file*—in this case a file of **assets**. Businesses have a variety of files. Look over the following table:

RECORD: the written down . . .	*FILE: the collection of records is called . . .*
value of delivery truck	asset file
amount of money owed to XYZ Co.	accounts payable file
amount of money owed to us by J. Jones	accounts receivable file
data on what an employee has been paid, and tax forwarded to the government, etc.	employees' file
quantity on hand of a product which is in stock, but available for sale	inventory file
the monthly sales of salesman X	sales file

It should be clear by now that a collection of similar types of records make up a file. The medium on which a file is kept does not matter as long as the information is kept and can be retrieved.

REPORTS

Information kept but never retrieved is not of much value. Only when certain information is obtained from the files, then organized into some meaningful form, is it useful in running the business or making key business decisions. Retrieved information put together into a meaningful form is called a **report**. There are many types of reports. Perhaps the most obvious which comes to mind would be the profit (or loss) report. A businessperson is vitally interested in whether the operation has made a profit or a loss.

There are many other types of reports. In simple terms, there could be a report made up of the important changes in each of the files listed above. For example, there could be a report on the total value of the inventory. Another report on inventory might list those items which are too few in number. Reordering should be done before the company completely runs out of stock. Another inventory report might highlight those items in stock which are 'slow moving.'

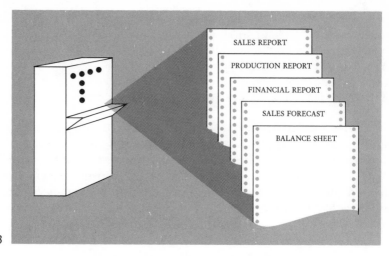

SALES REPORT

PRODUCTION REPORT

FINANCIAL REPORT

SALES FORECAST

BALANCE SHEET

Figure 13.3

Similar types of reports are made from the information in the other files. One of the most important reports made from the employee earnings record file is the annual report to the federal government. The report outlines the total earnings of each employee and the income tax withheld and forwarded to the federal government during the year.

Reports are also made using the accounts receivable file. Obviously the total receivable would be of interest to management. If the total receivable keeps going up, perhaps too much credit is being given to customers and not enough effort is being made collecting overdue accounts. But before panicking, a report showing an analysis of the age of each account would be in order. If sales on account are increasing but almost all accounts are paid off within 30 days, then there might not be as much concern as if most of the accounts were, say, 90 days old. It is important to realize that wrong conclusions could be made by taking a quick look at a report. Further studying of the report or additional reports on the same file might result in a different conclusion.

Some reports are made from a combination of a number of files. For example, a report called a **balance sheet** is made up of information from assets, accounts receivable, accounts payable, and from a few other records. If the files are being managed by a computer, it would be important for the computer to be able to access almost simultaneously a number of files.

THE COMPUTER'S ROLE AS A FILE MANAGER

As has been stated, records may be kept on magnetic tape or disc. The computer has the capability of recording records on the tape, retrieving those records and even making up reports by taking information from each record. In fact the computer is able to do to its electronic files almost anything a human would do to files kept in file folders in a filing cabinet.

It is able to:

- initially record the data
- add records to the file
- remove records (permanently) from the file
- change or update records
- extract certain information from the file

To illustrate these operations assume we are setting up an employee's earnings record file. The basic information about the rate of pay and tax deductions of each employee would be inputted into the computer. The computer would put it out on tape or disc in some organized fashion planned by the programmer. New employees might be hired and their records would have to be removed, (but not before tax information is reported to the federal government). An employee's marital status might change from single to married. Or an employee might have an addition to his or her family. The employee's record would be changed to show another dependent added to the number of dependents. The record would have to be updated to show a different tax code and therefore a new tax rate.

Table of Net Claim Codes Table des codes de réclamation nette	
Net Claim for 1980 Réclamation nette pour 1980 From – De To – A	Net Claim Code Code de réclamation nette
$2,890 — $2,940	1
2,941 — 3,430	2
3,431 — 3,760	3
3,761 — 4,030	4
4,031 — 4,470	5
4,471 — 4,800	6
4,801 — 5,300	7
5,301 — 5,890	8
5,891 — 6,380	9
6,381 — 6,870	10
6,871 — 7,300	11
7,301 — 7,740	12
7,741 — 8,040	13
8,041 and up – et plus	X
Exemption from Tax Deduction as claimed below Exonération de la retenue de l'impôt réclamée ci-dessous	0

Figure 13.4

THE COMPUTER AS A REPORT WRITER

Among other things, the computer is able to do computations—very difficult computations—very well. Also it is able to manage massive amounts of data very efficiently.

Part of the management of data is the ability to produce reports. The computer can be programmed to look through a file of many records to find a certain special record. For example, we could ask the computer to find the record of an employee who has worked for the firm for 23 years, has 3 dependents and is less than 41 years old. This task would be easy for the computer. If a record meeting these requirements existed, the computer could find it very quickly.

The computer might be required to produce a report by extracting information from all records. For example, management might want to verify the total amount of money paid out in wages so far this year. The computer would locate each record, extract the wages paid so far this year from each, accumulate the information, and after the last record had been processed, would produce a statement outputting the total. Obviously the amount of information produced in a report, and how attractive the report looked, are both programmed by a programmer.

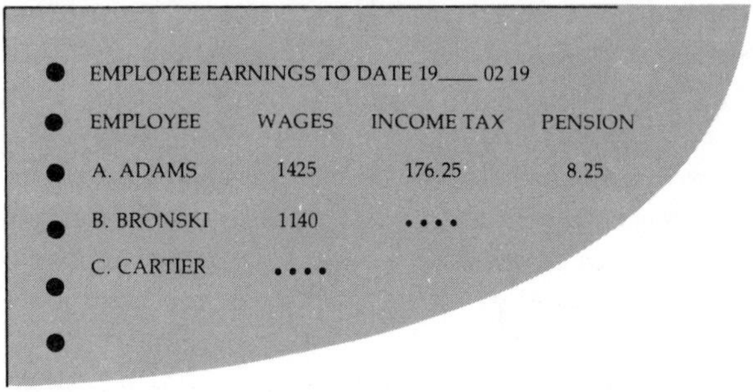

EMPLOYEE EARNINGS TO DATE 19___ 02 19			
EMPLOYEE	WAGES	INCOME TAX	PENSION
A. ADAMS	1425	176.25	8.25
B. BRONSKI	1140	••••	
C. CARTIER	••••		

Figure 13.5

Level 2

HOW THE COMPUTER DOES FILING

The organization of a file is established by the programmer. After considerable discussion with other people in the firm, the programmer selects the most appropriate combination of options for a computerized file. For example, it is possible that an employee file could be organized alphabetically by the employees' last names. This is possible but unlikely. Initially the file could be organized in this way, but soon it would be altered significantly as employees leave and new employees are signed on. The computer could be programmed to maintain the file alphabetically, but this is very inefficient. More likely each employee would be assigned a number and the employees would be recorded on tape or disc in the sequence of their employee number in ascending order. If an employee left the firm, likely his or her assigned number would remain inactive. It is possible after a year or so that a new employee take over an old number, but usually a new employee is assigned the *next* available number.

If a certain record must be located by the computer, the number of the record is inputted and the computer uses the number to locate the record. The computer would then carry out the required task on that record.

SEQUENTIAL FILES

A great many files are organized in sequential order. Naturally, these are called **sequential files**. Just what the sequence is could be determined by the programmer and other management personnel. The sequence of a computer managed employee file would likely be numeric—employee numbers in ascending order. Other types of files might be organized by date and time. In this case a record would have as its identifying element the date and time the record was created. In processing sequential files the computer begins at the beginning and reads each record in sequence, whether or not a change must be made to that record. Obviously, if it were a large file, this would be very inefficient. There are, however, some applications such as inventory control which are processed sequentially.

RANDOM FILES

Other types of files lend themselves to random processing and are called **random files**. In this case the record to be updated is located directly on disc, without having to read each record from the beginning of the file until the required record is located.

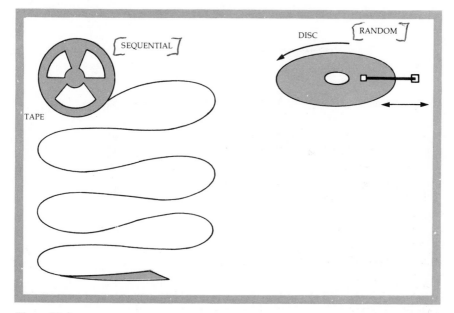

Figure 13.6

INDEXED SEQUENTIAL FILES

There are two methods the computer uses for managing random files. The first method is **indexed sequential**. An indexed sequential file usually contains records in some type of sequential order. After the file is initially recorded, a special computer program causes the computer to examine each record and make a note of its number and its relative location on the disc. The program then records these two pieces of information in a separate place on the disc in the form of an **index**.

If a record is required from an indexed file, the record number is inputted. The computer uses the record number as a **key** to check the index. It scans down the index until it locates the number of the record which matches the key. It then reads the *disc address* of the record and goes right to that disc location to retrieve the record.

For indexed sequential files the computer does not have to read over every record. Even in looking over the index the computer is able to check blocks of record numbers until it finds the block in which the record is located. Once the block is located, the computer then checks each record number within the block until it finds the number of the required record.

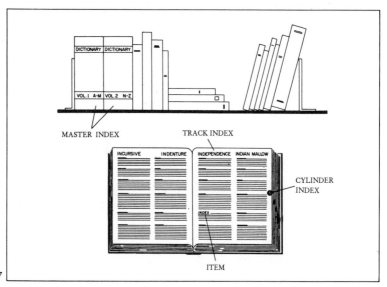

Figure 13.7

PURE RANDOM

Another organization of a random file is to have its records on disc, not in sequential order, but in **pure random** order. As a record is added to the file the computer finds any empty space on the disc and puts that record there, noting its number and the disc address. Again an index is maintained of the record number and its disc address. When a record is required for updating, the computer looks for the record number in the index it has created and retrieves the disc address of the record. (More about disc addressing in chapter 19.)

RECORD DESIGN

A certain amount of planning must be done in designing the record of a computerized file. First of all it must be decided what would be the minimum amount of information which would be required for each record item or field. The following might represent the fields of a relatively simple employee file:

EMPLOYEE NUMBER
EMPLOYEE NAME
   FIRST GIVEN NAME (including a space for a code to indicate which
                         name is commonly used)
   SECOND GIVEN NAME
   FAMILY NAME
ADDRESS
   APPARTMENT
   STREET OR RURAL ROUTE
   PLACE (city, town or village)
   POSTAL CODE OR ZIP CODE
SEX
DEDUCTION CODES
   TAX
   UNION
   PENSION
   HEALTH INSURANCE
RATE OF PAY
   REGULAR
   OVERTIME
TO DATE
   EARNINGS
   DEDUCTIONS
      INCOME TAX
      OTHER TAX
      UNION DUES
      PENSION
      HEALTH

SIZE OF FIELDS

Once the number of fields has been established, the programmer must determine the size of each field. For example if the examination of samples of last names indicates that most names are about eight characters long, but some names are sixteen characters long, what size of field would you select, the eight character or the sixteen character? Because most people are sensitive about the use of their name, you would likely have to assure your manager that *all* employees will have their name correctly and fully spelled out. You would, therefore have to select the sixteen character field. Unfortunately, with this system, each field containing the last name of employees will have an average of eight characters wasted.

There is a technique which enables the person inputting data to inform the computer how many characters there are for a data item. The number is put at the beginning of the field. The computer then uses exactly the number of spaces to store the data. By using the two extra characters to record the size of the data, no additional spaces are left empty.

√ RECORD LAYOUT SHEETS

Once the fields and their sizes have been established, a sketch is made of the record. This sketch is called a **record layout sheet**. If the record is to be kept on disc, usually the word disc appears in the title. Instead of just *record layout sheet,* the title might be *disc layout for employee record.*

RECORD CODES

One cannot help but notice the number of codes in the record. Computers work best with numbers. Each of these codes take a minimum of space on the disc or tape. The codes are used to look up the appropriate table or formula during the processing of the payroll.

BASIC FILES

In file processing each file must be given a name. For example an employee file could be given the name EMPL. Depending on the computer you are using, you may have to tell the computer in advance the name of the file and the particular cassette drive or disc drive on which the file is to be located. In creating a file, data is inputted and outputted on the cassette or disc. Again depending on the computer, you may have to identify the device being used for output, immediately following the word PRINT. A statement is given to signal the computer that 'that is all the records' and that the file should be saved. The computer automatically records an **end of file marker** after the last record on the tape or disc. This marker is used by the computer to prevent a programmer from attempting to read records which are not there.

ACCESSING STORED RECORDS

On accessing a saved file the program includes a statement that a file is to be accessed. The READ statement is used to read each record in sequence. (Random processing will be dealt with in chapter 19.) Usually the disc drive or cassette drive number is included immediately after the READ statement.

        150 READ #1, _____

After each read a check must be made for the end-of-file marker. If the marker has not yet been read, process that record. If the marker has just been read, some other action would have to be taken, such as doing a summary module.

Remember, variable names should give a clue as to the nature of the field or data item. The following are possible variable names which could be used with the record, just previously outlined:

FIELD NAME	BASIC VARIABLE NAME
Employee Number	N
Employee Name	
First Name	N1$
Second Name	N2$
Name Code	C1
Family Name	N3$
Address	
Apt	A1$
Street or R.R.	A2$
Place	A3$
Postal or Zip Code	A4$
Sex	S
Deduction Codes	
Tax	D1
Union Dues	D2
Pension	D3
Health	D4
Rate of Pay	
Regular	R1
Overtime	R2
To date	
Earnings	E1
Deductions	
Income Tax	T1
Union Dues	T2
Pension	T3
Health	T4

If it is possible on your computer use a full word for a variable. This makes easier the reading of your program by other people. A listing of your program would be a much better form of documentation.

Because the BASIC compiler only uses the first two letters in the word, care must be taken that two words used as variables do not have the same first two letters.

CHECKING YOUR READING—LEVEL 1

1. What are the various forms used to record the book of accounts?
2. What two classes of information are required to calculate the profit or the loss?

3. Give two more examples of types of information which might be kept in books of account.
4. Differentiate between a file and a record.
5. With respect to financial data, what would be a good definition of the word *report*?
6. Give at least two examples of types of reports prepared in business.
7. In what way is a computer a file manager?
8. Give an example of how the computer could be used to produce a report by selecting certain information from some or certain records and selecting out information from all records.

VOCABULARY ASSIGNMENT

Continue developing your vocabulary list by writing a brief definition of the words and phrases in bold print found in this section.

CHECKING YOUR READING—LEVEL 2

1. Which is more efficient for the computer, to maintain a file alphabetically or by sequence number?
2. What is the difference between a sequential file and a random file?
3. How is the index used in locating records which have been stored in an indexed sequential file?
4. What is the difference between an indexed sequential file and a pure random file?
5. What is a record field?
6. In determining the size of a field, why is the minimum size equal to the maximum length of the data that goes in the field?
7. Why should a file be given its own unique name?

VOCABULARY ASSIGNMENT

Continue developing your vocabulary list by writing a brief definition of the words and phrases in bold print found in this section.

PROJECTS

Programming Assignments from Business and Industry

Files

1. *Inventory* Using the DATA statement, create a file of three records representing three inventory items. Design your own fields, but it is suggested that each record have at least three fields, such as a field for each of: part number, description, and quantity on hand. Have the program produce a report under a suitable heading, which would indicate the status of the inventory file.
2. Expand the records of programming assignment #1 to include the

price per unit of each item. Modify the report so that it shows not only the quantity on hand but the value of items on hand. Of course, make the computer calculate the value of each item, and the total value of the inventory.

3. Enhance the above program to include the maximum and minimum quantities on hand for each record. Have the computer compare the number of items on hand with the minimum. If the quantity on hand is less than the minimum, have the computer produce a report which you could call a reorder report. This would list the items to be re-ordered and the quantity to be ordered. (Hint: obviously the quantity to be reordered would be the difference between the quantity on hand and the maximum which should be on hand.)

4. *Employee Records* Design a simple record for an employee. The record might only include the employee's number, the employee's name, and the rate of pay that the employee receives. If you have the capability, write a program to save on some auxiliary storage medium, such as cassette, an employee file of at least three records. If there is no auxiliary storage available to you, use the DATA statement. Now write a program or a major module for the file creation program. Then write modules to input the employee's number and the number of hours worked that week. Have the computer produce a report under a suitable heading which would include the employee's name, employee's number, the rate of pay, the hours worked, and the gross pay for that week.

5. Expand the records in the above question to include certain deductions. For example, there could be union dues, United Appeal, medical insurance, pension plan, and unemployment insurance payments. Find an arbitrary constant value for each of these additional fields for each employee. Have the computer produce a report which now includes the various deductions which you have selected.

6. Modify the above records to put a **tax code** in the record in place of the tax rate. The content of the code could be the digits 1, 2 or 3. Now create an array or table of three elements. Element #1 should hold a tax rate such as 10 per cent, number 2 could hold a tax rate such as 15 per cent, and number 3 could hold a tax rate such as 20 per cent. Remember to convert each percentage to a decimal fraction before you store it in the table. Now, have the computer calculate each employee's pay using the tax code to look up in the table of the tax rate so that the income tax could be calculated. In this assignment make sure that the pension plan and unemployment insurance deductions are made *before* the income tax is calculated.

ADDITIONAL ASSIGNMENTS

7. *Student Files* Create a file of student data. The field names might include the student's name, student's sex, student's age, student's

average mark, and the student's grade, level or year. Have the computer produce two or three different types of reports which would require the computer to select out from the data file certain records. You choose the particular combinations of fields the computer would select. For example, you might wish the computer to produce a list of all girls who have an average mark of 75 per cent or over. Or, you might have the computer print a list of all the boys who are in a certain year or grade. You determine the combination.

8. *Roof Construction* In constructing a sloping roof, the degree of slope is called the pitch. The pitch is calculated by dividing the run into the rise divided by 2. (Pitch = (Rise/2)/Run. For example if the run of a roof was scaled at 1m and the rise 2m then the pitch would be 1. (P = (2/2)/1)

   (a) Program the computer to input the run and the rise of a roof. Have it output the pitch.

   (b) Enhance the above program to calculate the length of the slope of the roof (called the top chord) if any two of the run, rise or pitch were given. The chord would be calculated using the Pythagorean Theorem. The square of the top chord would be equal to the sum of the squares of the other two sides. (Review: To square a number either multiply it by itself or use the 1^2. To find the square root of a variable such as the variable X, use the BASIC operation SQR(X)).

   (c) Augment the above program to input the length of the roof in metres. Calculate in m^2 the area of roofing plyboard which would have to be acquired if it comes in 2.88 m^2 pieces.

   (d) Also have the computer output the number of bundles of shingles which would be required if each bundle of shingles covered 2.89 m^2.

   (e) Add a module which would calculate the roof with gable as illustrated in the diagram. Reduce from the area of the main roof a triangle formed by the gable roof.

CHAPTER 14

BUSINESS COMPUTER APPLICATIONS

Imagine, if you will, the chain reaction which you would cause if you purchased a small item, such as an 8-track tape, from a large retail store. The purchase first must be recorded by entering the product number and the amount into a cash register. The amount of the purchase would be included in that cash register's total sales for that day. An inventory rec-

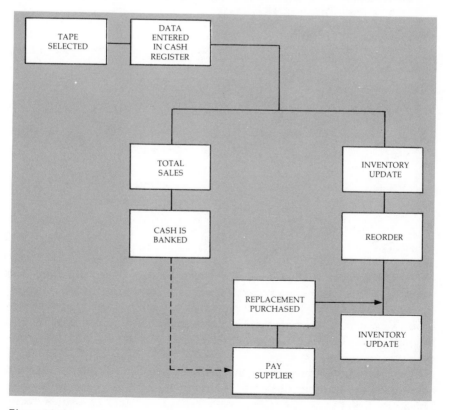

Figure 14.1

ord might be changed to show that there is one fewer of that item in stock. Perhaps the item will be re-ordered and later received into stock. The inventory record would be updated to record the tape being received into stock and some record would be made of the supplier being paid. Notice all the steps which resulted from the sale and replacement of one 8-track tape.

ORIGIN OF DATA

The example above seemed to illustrate a circular chain reaction which began with your purchase of an 8-track tape. Your purchase *created* data which started the chain reaction. In almost all business computing, a **transaction** such as this one takes place to start the chain reaction. A *transaction* in business causes *value to flow both ways* between the 2 parties involved. You received something of value, the tape, and the store received something of value, your money. With respect to the store, this transaction caused 2 things to happen—inventory to go down by one tape, and, money in the till to go up the amount received for the tape.

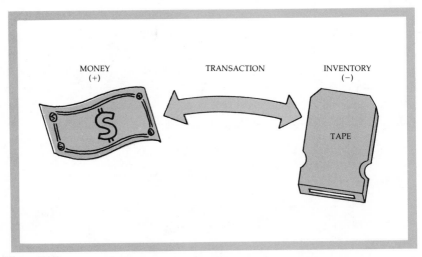

Figure 14.2

The transaction is, therefore, the origin of data or information. The transaction is recorded in a variety of ways. It could be recorded on paper in characters which are machine readable. Later the paper tape becomes input for a computer program. Or the data could be keyed directly into the computer. In this case the cash register becomes a computer terminal.

In recording the transaction, the product number or code is recorded along with the number of items which are sold (in this case, only one). The price ticket is considered to be the origin of data or **source document**.

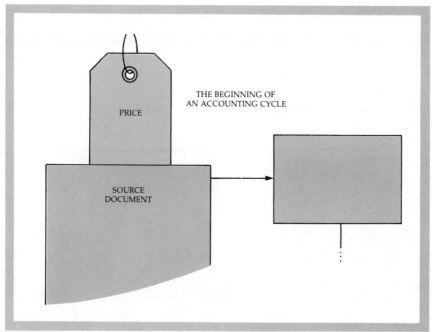

Figure 14.3

It is the source document which provides the necessary information to set the chain reaction going. Once data has been originated, a number of operations could be performed on it as it moves through the chain reaction. These operations on the data include: **recording**, **classifying**, **calculating**, **sorting**, **storing**, **summarizing**, and **communicating**.

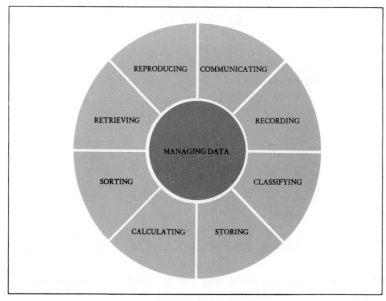

Figure 14.4

MANIPULATION OF DATA IN BUSINESS

At the point of sale, basic information is *recorded* from the source document. The recording would involve keying in the data into the cash register. Once recorded, the data is inputted into the computer.

After data has been recorded and inputted into the computer, a number of operations or manipulations can be performed on it. For example, data can be *classified*.

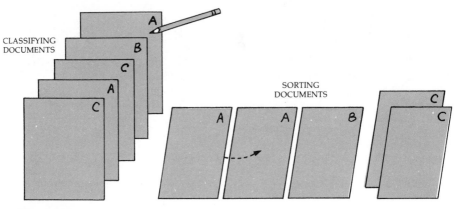

Figure 14.5

In the above example the purchase of the tape would be classified as a sale. A sale affects two things. It would affect the total sale figure for that day. It also would reduce the inventory record by one.

Other types of information such as the paying of wages or other store expenses are also fed into the computer. It is important that each type of data is classified so that it could be properly processed.

Once classified the various similar items can be *sorted* into groups.

For example after each item sold during the day has been classified as to type, all the sales of 8-track tapes for the day could be grouped together.

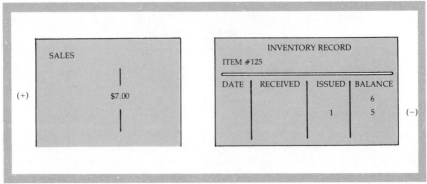

Figure 14.6

Expenses, such as wages, once classified could also be sorted and grouped together.

The data also causes some *calculating* or computing to be done. As stated earlier the amount of the sale is *added* to the total sales for the day and the product is *subtracted* out of the inventory record.

Finally various reports are produced or outputted by the computer. These would likely show only a summary of many transactions, including your purchase as part of total sales.

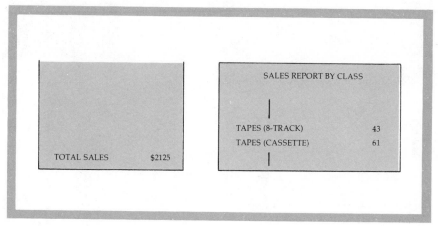

SALES REPORT BY CLASS

TAPES (8-TRACK)   43
TAPES (CASSETTE)   61

TOTAL SALES $2125

Figure 14.7

These reports are then distributed or *communicated* to a person or persons who would make decisions based on the reports. For example, one decision might be to re-order tape of the type you purchased from the store.

The computer, if programmed to do so, would not only produce summary reports but also produce **purchase orders** which could be mailed to the supplier.(See Figure 14.8)

When the supplier fills the order, the receipt of goods would be recorded in the store's computer using the packing slip as the source document. The computer would record in the appropriate record that the supplier is owed some money and that the particular tape is now in inventory, available for sale.

TYPES OF COMPUTER APPLICATIONS IN BUSINESS

1. Inventory Control

As has been suggested earlier, a major task for certain businesses which have to have quantities of products on hand is the task of **inventory control**. The products on hand may be various parts and raw materials which

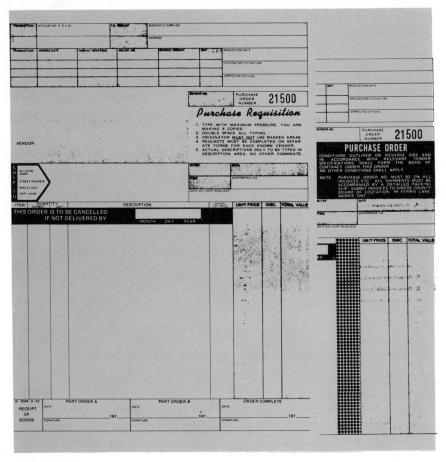

Figure 14.8

go into the manufacture of a product. Or the products may be finished goods, ready for sale. In some firms some finished goods are purchased and **warehoused**, available for sale along with related goods which are being manufactured by the firm. For example, a firm making shoes might have considerable inventory of leather, but also an inventory of shoe laces which have been manufactured by another firm.

Many hours are spent keeping track and updating inventory records. The computer is able to assist in reducing the number of hours spent on this type of recordkeeping. It is also able to produce more quickly status reports and reports of slow moving items. The computer can almost instantly revise the value of any one item in stock. Should the price of an item be lowered, for example, the computer could be informed and that new information would almost instantly become part of the inventory information in its file.

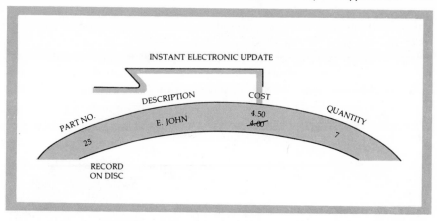

INSTANT ELECTRONIC UPDATE

DESCRIPTION

COST

4.50
4.00

QUANTITY

PART NO.

E. JOHN

25

7

RECORD
ON DISC

Figure 14.9

2. Accounts Receivable

In the days of the good old-fashioned country store, credit was given and recorded in a counter book. Often each charge customer was assigned his/her own book by the storekeeper, and all products purchased were recorded in the book. If the customer wanted to pay off the account, the storekeeper simply added up the totals of each bill to obtain the total owing.

Things have changed somewhat from the simple days of charging at the general store. Large retailers have encouraged customers to open charge accounts. Gasoline companies have encouraged charging of gasoline purchases. Credit card firms such as Master Card, Visa and American Express have thousands of customers using their credit. As a result, the management of any one of these credit files has become a major task. The computer is able to take over the routine management of these files, and do the job very efficiently. Each customer's purchase is recorded on his or her file by the computer. Payments made on account are also recorded. As the amount of the debt increases the computer calculates the new monthly payment which should be made. (For example, if the outstanding amount were $100 the computer would send out a bill, outlining the transactions that month. The total outstanding balance of $100 would be shown. The computer would calculate the amount currently due, say $10 or 10% of the balance. Interest and other charges would be calculated automatically by the computer.)

One of the situations which has caused the computer to acquire a bad reputation has been the program which causes the computer to send out those nasty letters to people who are behind in their payments. Every so often we hear of a person paying off all that is owed, yet the computer keeps sending out letters outlining what might happen if the account is not paid. When interviewed by the press the customer usually says something to the effect: "How do you get that computer to listen to you—I've paid the bill yet it keeps sending out these letters." It appears as if the programmer of this part of the programming system had not put in sufficient options for the computer. You know enough programming methods to know how this type of programming error could be corrected.

By the way, did you hear about the letter generated by the computer which threatened that if the account was not paid up, the case would be turned over to a human? Now there's a switch!

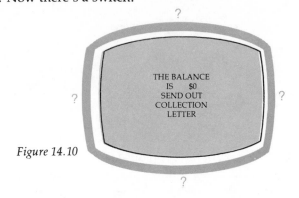

THE BALANCE
IS $0
SEND OUT
COLLECTION
LETTER

Figure 14.10

3. Accounts Payable

Some firms, particularly large firms, purchase thousands of dollars worth of products and materials every month. Very few of these purchases are made by cash. The order is placed, and the goods are shipped and received. The invoice is prepared and submitted to the company purchasing the goods. By tradition, that company has from 10 to 30 days to process the invoice and to issue the cheque. If a firm is dealing with many purchases from many different suppliers, the keeping track of the purchases and the payments becomes another big job for someone to manage. Again, the computer is able to do a very good job managing this type of file.

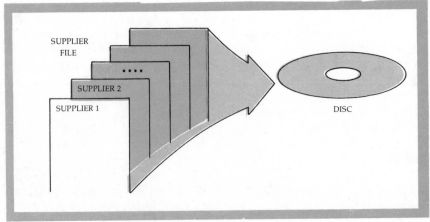

Figure 14.11

4. Budget Control

Sometimes a budget for each department is fed into a computer at the beginning of the year. As orders are made, the computer is informed and it sets aside the estimated cost of the order. When the invoice is received and the computer is authorized to make the payment, it generates the cheque. Should a department use up its budget and attempt to order something else, the computer would reject the order. Someone in authority would have to make a decision whether or not the computer should permit the order to be processed.

Other similar safeguards could also be programmed. For example, a routine might make sure that no order was made from a company which produces inferior quality products. Or the computer might have programmed limits for the amount of any purchases from any one supplier. As long as the order was within any pre-set limits, the computer would process that order. If the estimated cost of the order was over that limit, or over budget, the computer could be programmed to either reject the order completely, or downgrade it so that it did fall within the prescribed limit.

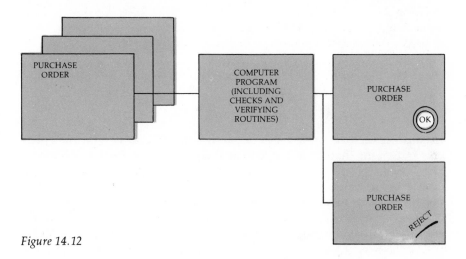

Figure 14.12

5. Payroll

In firms with a large number of employees, during the pre-computer era, the last two or three days before payday were set aside for the preparation of the payroll and the making up of the cheques. Often large numbers of office staff would have to leave their regular jobs and pitch in to get the payroll done on time. With the computer, payroll information could be fed in on a daily basis. When the day comes that the payroll is to be done, the computer operator calls in the payroll program and out come the necessary reports and cheques.

In addition to the weekly or bi-weekly cheques, the computer is programmed to do another task, equally as important. The employee earnings records must be maintained accurately. An annual record of the total pay of each employee must be maintained. In the record, all deductions must also be recorded. At the end of the calendar year, a full report must be made to the federal government. Of course the employee uses the report for the accurate preparation of his/her income tax return.

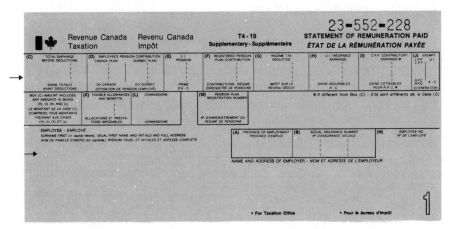

Figure 14.13

6. Management Information Systems

If a business is to be well run, or run sufficiently well to avoid bankruptcy, it is important that there be good managers making the key decisions. This makes the difference between success and failure. Good decisions cannot be made unless those making them have the correct information and all the information necessary to form the basis of the decision.

 The computer can be programmed with a series of programs which provide management with any type of information concerning the operation of the firm. A series of programs to provide this type of information is called **management information system.** For example, the computer could produce comparison reports of various types of annual financial statements over the past few years and a comparable statement on the operation of the company so far this current year. The computer could also be programmed to extend or *extrapolate* the current information into the future so that management would know that if everything were left as is the report would tell them what likely would be the financial situation three or four months from now.

The quality of the reports would only be as good as the program which was written and the type of information to which the computer has access. For example, if the computer had access to last year's file of cus-

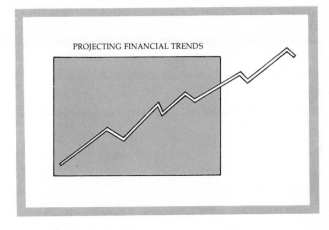

PROJECTING FINANCIAL TRENDS

Figure 14.14

tomer orders, it could compare it with the orders so far this year. The computer program would then produce a comparison report with percentage changes from one year to the next. It could even modify its 'forecast' if last year's records indicate that the company is now going into its annual slow time.

Having considerable information available, and having excellent programs would not necessarily mean that management would make excellent decisions. The number of business failures per year indicate that some people are unable to either

1) get a feel for the marketplace,
2) adequately finance their operation to withstand the slack times, or
3) make the hard decisions which have to be made.

So the computer is able to assist management by providing information, but it (at least at the time of writing) still leaves the ultimate decision to management.

Level 2

ACCOUNTING IN THE COMPUTER

You may or may not have had a course in accounting or double entry bookkeeping. If you have, the information which follows should be fairly easy for you to understand. If you have not, then do not be overly concerned. The information will be presented with as few technical terms as possible.

All complex businesses have a series of accounts in which the financial changes or transactions are recorded. The group of all these accounts is called a **ledger**.

The ledger could be in some computer accessible file, such as on disc. Each account would be a record in the file.

Figure 14.15 shows a sample of accounts which will be used to demonstrate computerized accounting.

The account number is really a three part code. The first digit is used to classify related types of accounts. More about that later. The second part is the account number traditionally assigned to each account. The third part is used to show subgroups of accounts. More about that later as well.

There are 7 classes of accounts in the illustration. Accounts classed as "1" are **asset** accounts.

These accounts represent what is *owned* by the business. For example, account 1 20 0 is land and building. The amount in the account represents the value of the land and building owned by the business.

The class 2 accounts are **liability** accounts which represent what the business *owes* to its creditors.

For example, in the illustration the firm owes the bank $8 000. Class 3 accounts are **equity** accounts which represent the amounts the firm owes to the owners of the business. (Technically, the firm does not really own anything. All that it appears to own is really owed to the owners of the firm.)

There is a simple formula which describes the relation of these three classes of accounts. It is:

$$\text{Assets} = \text{Liabilities} + \text{Equity}$$

This formula can be used indirectly to show the **accounts in balance**. The value of all the assets the firm appears to own is equal to the value it owes to its creditors and its owners. If all class 1 or asset accounts were added together the total would be the value the firm appears to own. All class 2 or liability accounts and class 3 or equity accounts added together would be the value of all the firm owes. The two totals would be equal or "in balance." According to the formula, total assets should be equal to the total of liabilities and equity.

Accounts classified as 1, 2 and 3 represent the *current status* of the accounts. Classes 4 and 5 represent a short history of *what has been happening*. For example the class 4 account is an accumulated total of all the income or sales which have taken place over a period of time, such as one month, or a whole year.

The amount shown would not necessarily be in cash in the bank. To illustrate why this is the case, *you* might not have in your bank account every cent you earned or were given as an allowance last year. Some money would have been spent. The $51 000 shown is just the *accumulated total of all income*. Most of this money will have to be used to pay expenses. Similarly class 5 accounts represent the payouts or expenses which have been paid or incurred over the same period of time, perhaps a year. Many or most of these expenses will have been paid by now. The amounts are just a record of the total expenses which were incurred in running the business. An analogy which might help is as follows:

TRIAL BALANCE

ACCOUNT NO.			NAME	BALANCE	
Code	No.	'decimal'		Debit	Credit
1	01	0	Cash	1200	
1	03	0	Acct. Rec.	2000	
1	05	0	Mdse. Inv.	4000	
1	06	0	Office Supplies	1000	
1	13	0	Office Equipment	6000	
1	14	0	Delivery Equip.	8000	
1	20	0	Land & Bldg.	90000	
2	30	0	Acct. Pay		3000
2	31	0	Bank Loan		8000
2	38	0	Mortgage Pay		60000
3	40	0	Equity		30200
3	41	0	Retained Earnings		10000
3	42	0	Profit & Loss		0
4	50	0	Sales		51000
5	52	0	Purchases	40000	
5	55	0	Wages	5000	
5	56	0	Rent	3000	
5	59	0	Misc. Expense	2000	
				162200	162200

Accounts Rec. Subsidiary Ledger

6	03	1	Customer 1	800	
6	03	2	Customer 2	1000	
6	03	3	Customer 3	200	
				2000	

Accounts Pay. Subsidiary Ledger

7	30	1	Supplier 1		1200
7	30	2	Supplier 2		1300
7	30	3	Supplier 3		500
					3000

Figure 14.15

Assume a horse race is recorded on video tape or motion picture film. Assume that the race was a close one and a "stop action" photograph is taken with a still camera at the finish line. The motion picture film would be a record of how the race was run. The photo finish stop action picture shows the end result. The photograph illustrates the accounts of class 1, 2 and 3. These accounts are a 'snap shot' of the current status of the bank account, accounts receivable, etc. For example, in Fig 14.15 the bank account currently has $1200 in it. The motion picture represents the accounts of classes 4 and 5. All incomes and expenses are recorded in these accounts and the total of any one account is the accumulated total of all income or expenses which have been recorded *over a period of time*.

SUBSIDIARY LEDGERS

If all the individual customers' accounts were added together their total should equal the amount in the accounts receivable control account, account number 1 03 0.

Similarly, if the total of all the suppliers' accounts were taken it should equal the amount in the accounts payable control accounts. Notice that the trial balance does not include the subsidiary ledgers because the control accounts record in the general ledger has the same values as the subsidiary ledger. To include the subsidiary would be *double counting*. Also notice the relationship of the second and third section of the account numbers:

Accounts Receivable Control	1	03 0
Customer 1	6	03 1
Customer 2	6	03 2

The various charge customer accounts are a sub-set of the accounts receivable control account.

CHECKING YOUR READING—LEVEL 1

1. In what way does a purchase in a store create a chain reaction?
2. How does value flow as a result of a transaction?
3. What is the relationship between the source document and the chain reaction it creates?
4. List the seven operations which are commonly performed on data.
5. What is the difference between, or the relationship between, classifying and sorting?
6. Write a brief statement which summarizes the essence of the following:
   (a) inventory control
   (b) accounts receivable
   (c) accounts payable

(d) budget control

(e) payroll

(f) management information systems

VOCABULARY ASSIGNMENT

Continue developing your vocabulary list by writing brief definitions of the words in bold type in this section.

CHECKING YOUR READING—LEVEL 2

1. What is a ledger?
2. In general, what are asset accounts?
3. What are liability accounts?
4. What is the equity of the business and how could it be calculated?
5. How are the accounts which are classified as 1, 2 and 3 in a chapter different from the accounts classified as 4 and 5?
6. What is a subsidiary ledger? Give two examples.

VOCABULARY ASSIGNMENT

Continue developing your vocabulary list by writing brief definitions of the words in bold type in this section.

Programming Assignments From Business and Industry

Note: The following group of assignments would make an excellent team programming project.

1. MEMO 19-- 01 10
   To: Jack LeSage, Jr. Programmer
   c.c.: to Jane Barnes, Sr. Programmer
   From: George Maw, Systems Analyst
   Re: Phase I of Our Computerized Accounting System—Trial Balance
   You will recall the meeting we had to plan to computerize our accounting system. We have recently added the necessary auxiliary storage devices to our computer so that it can also be used for accounting files.

   Would you please write a program to begin the first phase of this new system? You will note that on the systems flowchart, this first program involves the creation of the ledger and the printing out of a modified trial balance. Subsequent programs will involve accessing the data on the auxiliary storage device, but for the time being, keep the program simple.

   More specifically, write a program which will read in a file of records. Each record has a code of either a 1, 2 or 3. Add all the amounts of

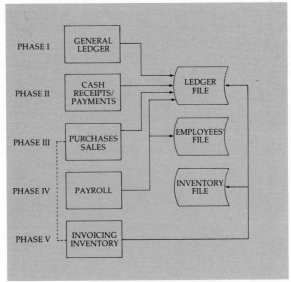

Figure 14.16

records coded 1 into one accumulator and list out these records with the amount being placed in the second last column. (We will head up that column with the word Debit, for the convenience of our accounting staff.) Add into another accumulator the amounts in the last column labelled Credit. (See Fig. 14.15)

During the development of this program the data could be in data statements.

Among the various programming techniques, include the following:
1) Set up headings similar to the following:

XXXXXXXXXXXXXXXXXXX (student, make up a
                    company name, perhaps
                    your own name)

TRIAL BALANCE

TAKEN AS OF XXXXXXXXXXXXXXX (make provisions to
                           input a date)

Account No.   Account name   Debit   Credit

2) Write a routine to 'audit' the results by comparing the two totals which have been accumulated. Write an error message routine which would produce an error message if the two totals are not the same.
3) Produce a summary line with these totals.
   Naturally document all that you are able.
   This programming assignment should be completed within the following time frame:
         Planned and coded _____
         Fully tested and documented _____

2. MEMO 19-- 01 15
    To: Jane Barnes, Sr. Programmer
    From: George Maw, Systems Analyst
    Re: Phase I of Our Computerized Accounting System—Trial Balance
    As you are aware we have made a good start on computerizing our accounting system. Permit me to formally thank you for your input and your suggestions during the planning session. Certainly you and our chief accountant, John Sime, contributed significantly to the planning sessions. A systems flowchart has been drafted. As we develop this system would you draw my attention to anything you think should be modified?

    As you know, Jack LeSage has completed the first stage of the trial balance program. As is our policy, would you now take over all his material, including the documentation. Carefully test the program. Keep an eye out for areas in which Jack could improve his programming skills. Certainly the degree of clarity and conciseness of his documentation will become evident as you have to work with it.

    Would you also alter the data so that the trial balance does not balance? A suitable message should be produced.

3. MEMO 19-- 01 17
    To: Jack LeSage, Jr. Programmer
    c.c.: to Jane Barnes, Sr. Programmer
    From: George Maw, Systems Analyst
    Re: Phase I of Our Computerized Accounting System—Subsidiary Ledgers
    Obtain from Jane the trial balance program as it has been developed to date. Add to that program a routine which would handle the subsidiary ledgers. Provide sample data for the ledgers but make sure the data coincides with the amounts in the two control accounts—Accounts Receivable and Accounts Payable controls.

    Naturally the individual amounts in the subsidiaries are not accumulated with the other amounts in the trial balance, for the amounts are already 'represented' in the trial balance by the two control accounts. But write an audit routine to verify that the amount in each of the two control accounts is equal to the sum of the amounts in each of the corresponding subsidiary ledgers. For example the total of all customers' accounts is equal to the Accounts Receivable control.

    Program and test an error routine to indicate if this is not the case. Add your documentation to the documentation package under development.

    This programming assignment should be completed within the following time frame:

    Planned and coded   _____

    Fully tested and documented   _____

ADDITIONAL PROGRAMMING ASSIGNMENTS

4. *Pyramid Archeology*
   (a) The approximate dimensions of a pyramid are based on a right angle triangle formed by half the base slant-height and the perpendicular height. The ratio of the sides of this triangle is 1 : 1.618 : 1.272 respectively. Write a program which would input any one of i) the base, ii) vertical height, or, iii) slope (apothem) and output the other 2 measurements.
   (b) Enhance your program to produce the volume of the 2.5 t (tonne) blocks forming the major part of the pyramid, and the square metres of the 'finishing' stone which used to cover the surface. The formula for the volume of a pyramid is $V = b^2 \times h / 3$. As data for your program you might like to include the names and dimensions of some famous pyramids.

	PYRAMID DATA BASE LENGTH	HEIGHT
Sneferu	188 m	98 m
Dahshur	220 m	104 m
Khufu	230 m	146 m
Knafru	215 m	143 m
Menkure	119 m	66 m
Neferirkare	106 m	70 m

Note that not all pyramids were build to the same formula.

5. *And While We Are In Ancient Egypt* let us use the computer to calculate the distance between two places. During the summer solstice a vertical pole in Syene produced no shadow, for the sun was directly above it. On the same day the angle of the shadow to the pole was 7°12′ in Alexandria. The circumference of the earth is about 40 000 km. What fraction of the circumference is the arc between Syene and Alexandria and therefore what would be the distance between the two places.

   Generalize your program to input any two angles of shadow taken at the same time at two different places and produce the distance between. If both shadows are cast in the same direction—for example, north—you would subtract the smaller angle from the larger. If one angle was on the north of the pole and the other angle on the south you would have to add the two angles. Do you know why?

CHAPTER 15

FLOW OF DATA IN BUSINESS

Level 1

In earlier chapters you learned of records, files, various operations which can be performed on data, and the chain reaction which comes about as a result of a transaction in business. It is time to learn more about the flow of data within business.

A SYSTEM

As data moves through a business, various operations are performed on it. One operation may be performed directly by people, such as sorting source documents, another operation might involve people using machines, such as typing a letter. Or data may be processed by automated equipment such as an electronic cash register or computer.

The group or series of related operations performed by people aided by machines or by computers is called a **system**. More specifically a **data system** would be a series of operations and procedures performed on *data* until the data's current usefulness to the business was finished. The transaction of buying an 8-track cassette caused a series of operations to be performed. In a certain sense the data about the transaction went through a system. The word 'system' is used a number of ways in business and the computer industry. A brief overview of its uses might be helpful.

When a computer plays an important part in the handling of data the system is called a **computerized system**. In contrast, a CPU with various devices hooked up to it is also called a system. A CPU might have a number of tapes, discs, a printer and even a card read hooked up to it. This collection of equipment is frequently called a **computer system**. In industry, particularly in manufacturing and in the production of chemicals the word 'system' is also used. A series of operations performed in manufacturing and assembling an automobile is called a **process system**. Similarly in the refining of petroleum products all the operations performed on crude oil to produce the various petroleum products would be considered a process system. Talk about an overworked word! A summary is in order.

System: a series of related human and/or machine operations performed
to do a complex task.
Data System: a series of operations performed on data.
Computer System: a CPU with various devices hooked up to it, devices
such as tapes, discs, and printer, connected together to form an
entire unit.
A Computerized System: a data system which uses a computer as the
major data management tool.
Process System: a series of operations performed on chemicals or products during refining or assembly.

For the remaining part of this text the proper name of a system will likely be used. Should just the word 'system' be used, however, or, if in a conversation with others you hear the word 'system' you will have to determine the type of system from the way it is used in the sentence.

MORE ABOUT FLOWCHARTS

Now that you have a clear idea about the various types of systems (?!) it is useful for you to know about flowcharts other than the ones you studied in Chapter 9. Remember that a flowchart was a representation of the various steps in the solution to a problem. That was a *logic* flowchart. It showed the logic used in solving the problem. There are other types of flowcharts.

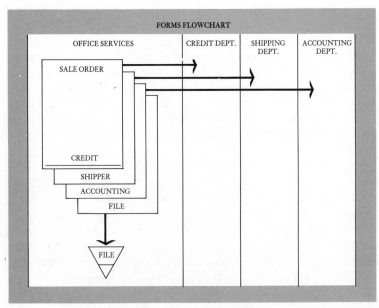

Figure 15.1

One type of flowchart used frequently in business is the forms flowchart. This type of flowchart is sometimes used to show where various copies of documents or reports are sent within business.

Another fairly commonly used flowchart is the **forms flowchart**. The forms flowchart represents the distribution and flow within the firm of

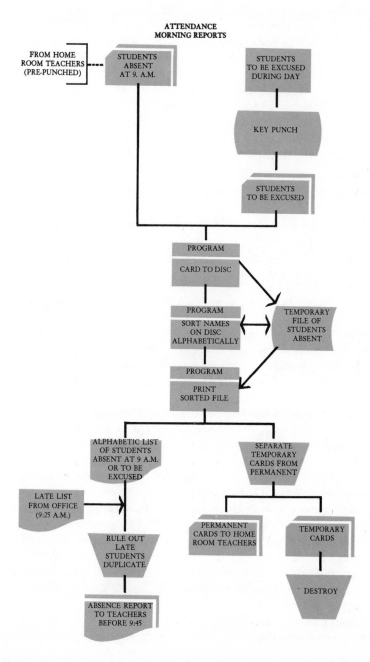

Figure 15.2

certain forms containing data. For example multiple copies of a sales order would be distributed to different departments. A systems flowchart attempts to show graphically the flow of information and the operations which are performed on it. If you refer to the illustration you will notice a number of things happening to a package of data coming into the system from a **source document**. The various operations performed on it are shown. The operations could be done by people, people with the aid of a machine, or by a computer. Study the flowchart in Fig. 15.2. Try to identify the various types of operations which are performed on the data.

In the illustration, the systems flowchart is for **purchasing** data. There would be similar flowcharts for any other type of data which must be processed in a business. Certainly payroll data must be accumulated and processed. Data concerning money coming into the business has to be processed. Processing of any type of business data could be represented by a systems flowchart.

A summary of the various types of flowcharts is in order.

Types of Flowcharts
Logic Flowchart—represents the programming steps taken to solve a
    problem
Forms Flowchart—represents the flow of the various copies of a docu-
    ment in a business
Systems Flowchart—represents the operations performed on one of the
    types of data as it is processed in a business

THE FLOW OF DATA AMONG BUSINESSES

If two firms carry on business with each other, the actions of one firm results in a chain reaction in the other. For example if one firm ordered products from the other, that order would cause a chain reaction and flow of data within both firms. For example, assume Firm B wanted to order products from Firm A. Before Firm A knew anything about the order, a series of operations would be performed in Firm B to get the order going. The order would flow through a 'purchase order' system. Finally the order would be communicated to Firm A. The order in Firm A would be considered a 'sales order.' This order would flow through the sales order system. After the order is processed and the products shipped, a bill or invoice is prepared and submitted to Firm B. After receiving and checking the goods, Firm B would then begin the process of paying the invoice. The payment order would flow through the 'payments system' and a cheque would be produced. The cheque would then be submitted to Firm A causing a chain reaction in the 'cash receipts system.' Do you follow all that? If not, do not be too concerned, for it is the idea of the flow of data and the exchange of information among businesses which is of importance at this point in time.

The mail has been and still is a widely used method of communication among businesses. Purchase orders, invoices and cheques are usually

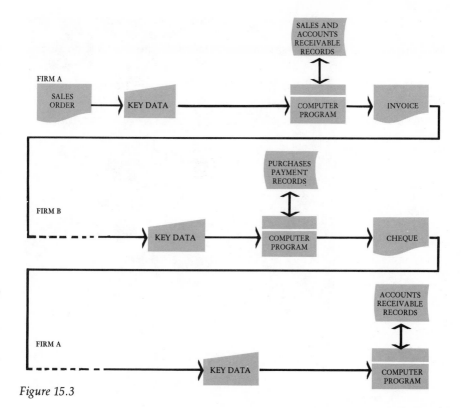

Figure 15.3

mailed. If a nation has a postal strike, many businesses which depend on orders coming through the mails are crippled. The firms are unable to send out their invoices and do not receive the regular number of cheques in payment in the morning mail.

ELECTRONIC COMMUNICATION

TELEX

A number of devices make the communication among businesses easier. The **telex** is certainly one of the most efficient devices for the communication of written information. Telexes are a part of a communications network somewhat like a telephone network. Each user's number is listed in a directory like a telephone book. The firm wanting to send a message dials the number of the party who is to receive the message. After the device signals that the telex at the other end is ready to receive the message, it is typed in on the keyboard and transmitted. It is received almost simultaneously by the telex device in the other firm's office.

Messages may be prepared in advance by punching the message into paper tape or onto a magnetic medium. Once the connection is made with the other telex the message is transmitted at top speed.

Figure 15.4

FACSIMILE TRANSMISSION

Facsimile transmitting devices are able to scan a document or picture to convert the light and dark on the document to electrical impulses. These impulses could be transmitted over wire or converted to radio signals. The process is reversed at the receiving end producing a copy of the document thousands of miles away within a matter of minutes.

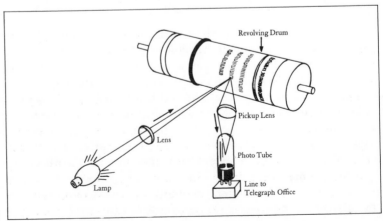

Figure 15.5

Facsimile transmission is the principal behind electronic mail. A letter could be taken to the post office, scanned by a machine and transmitted electronically to the post office in the town or city in which it is to be delivered. The copy of the letter at the other end of the system is put into an envelope and delivered in the regular mail delivery.

USES OF FACSIMILE TRANSMISSION

Perhaps the news media, especially newspapers, make the most extensive use of facsimile transmission. Photographs of events taking place half way around the world are transmitted and distributed via the wire services to various newspapers. The quality of the photos which are produced is excellent. Telegraph and telephone companies as well as some of the post office systems also use this unique procedure. Businesses use the services of one of these commercial carriers should rapid document transfer be necessary.

COMPUTER NETWORKS

In chapter 3 there was some discussion about timesharing. In the illustration in that section the central computer was shown with a number of terminals hooked up to it. Information is transmitted back and forth between any one terminal and the central computer. Taking this concept a little farther, imagine a number of computers hooked together by a computer network. An operator would dial the other computer and when it answered, the two computers would communicate, carrying on the necessary business.

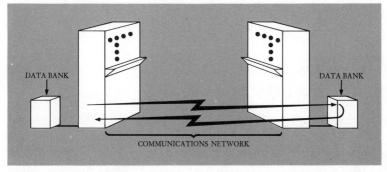

DATA BANK

DATA BANK

COMMUNICATIONS NETWORK

Figure 15.6

Remember the two firms which carried out business with each other? Assume their two computers were set up and programmed to communicate with each other. The computer of Firm A would note that stock was getting low for a particular item in its inventory file, and place an order with Firm B's computer. Firm B's computer would then direct that the products be shipped. After they were shipped and this fact signalled to the computer, Firm B's computer would then electronically invoice Firm A's computer. Firm A's computer would wait until it was signalled that the products have been received, then authorize a cheque to be written and sent off to Firm B.

If we hooked the two computers in with the bank's computer, then all firm A's computer would do is signal the bank's computer to transfer the funds from A firm's account into the other firm's account. How about that!

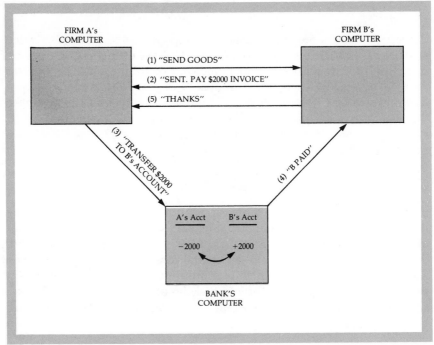

Figure 15.7

Level 2

TRANSMITTING DATA

Computers store data in binary form. A computer would therefore want to send data and receive data in binary. For example, data signals going into the computer take the form of a pulse or 'non pulse' depending on whether 1 or a 0 is being sent. When a computer must transmit data it converts the 1s and 0s into pulses or non-pulses.

Unfortunately the common telephone network has lines which do not do the best job in transmitting this type of signal. The lines are designed for *voice grade* transmission. The human voice does not operate on the pulse/non-pulse principle but on a complex wave system. The pulses from a computer are converted by a **modem** device to convert the signals to sound waves carried by telephone lines. To understand what follows a short science lesson is in order.

SOUND WAVES

A simple sound wave, such as one made by a tuning fork looks like this:

Notice that the wave has a **wave-length**. The **amplitude** is the measure of the distance the wave swings from the rest position. The human voice during conversation produces a similar wave but much more complex.

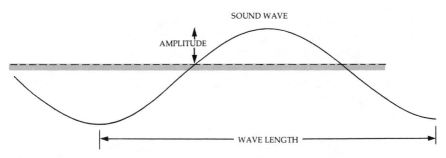

Figure 15.8

The voice is not able to produce the full range of sound that an average ear could hear. Very high pitched sounds are produced by waves having many frequencies. Very low sounds are produced by a wave which has a low number of frequencies.

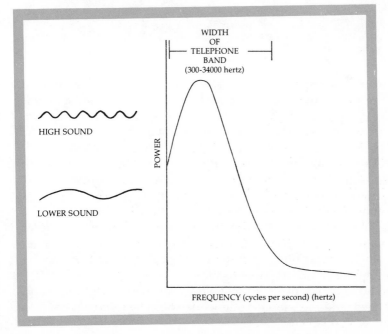

Figure 15.9

Getting back to the telephone network lines, during their design, the technicians found that only part of the sound spectrum needed to be transmitted. By transmitting only the most commonly used frequencies of the human voice, a person could not only be understood over the phone but his or her voice could be recognized. The limits set for wave transmission over the telephone is called a **band**.

TELEPHONE MODEMS

In a sense humans communicate over the telephone with a sing-song sound. Computers are machines which work in *on* or *off* conditions. The telephone modem, converts the on/off impulses of the computer into a wave pattern which uses one of the frequencies commonly carried on a telephone line. This device has provided the technology to transmit data from one computer to another.

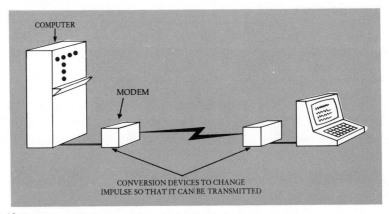

Figure 15.10

At one time the project of creating a computer network appeared to be too costly. The network would have to be designed to handle on or off impulses to suit computers. Already there was a telephone network. There was also a telex network. Then there was talk of an additional *computer* network! The modem eliminated the need for this extra network.

The modem is hooked up between the computer and the telephone line. It converts the signal that the computer outputs into a suitable signal for the telephone to transmit. At the other end, the telephone outputs its signal into another modem which converts the signal back into one the computer is able to understand. Part of the modem is an **acoustic coupler** which generates the signal into the hand set of an ordinary telephone. Part of the coupler 'hears' the signal coming back and converts it into the signal the computer is able to understand.

Using the acoustic coupler, which holds a standard telephone hand unit, the modem, and the telephone network, some computers are able to communicate with other computers.

FROM COMPUTER

Figure 15.11

THE PROBLEM OF EFFICIENCY

The early simple data transmission systems could send signals at a fairly slow rate. Using one wire, the signals could only go one way, until a control signal indicated that that was the end of transmission. In some applications that was all that was needed. In other applications it was important for data, or at the very least the control signals, to be returned. This required a more costly setup, often requiring two wires. And over long distances, this increased the cost considerably.

The system which allows for only one way signals to be transmitted is called a **simplex** system. The **half-duplex** system uses the full width of the band to send data at a very rapid speed. After data is sent one way, an end of transmission signal is sent and the receiving modem now may begin sending back signals. Two-way signals are sent on a system called a **full duplex** system. At one time full duplex required two wires. Now the signal going one way is on one frequency, whereas the signal going the other way is on another.

As with almost all technology today, progress marches on. Now more than one signal can be sent at a time, even on one wire. Signals can be sent both ways simultaneously. Remember the modem converted the impulse into a burst of wave signal? Well, it is possible for one transmission to be sent using bursts in one wave length while another transmission is being sent in bursts of signals in another wave length, both over the same wire.

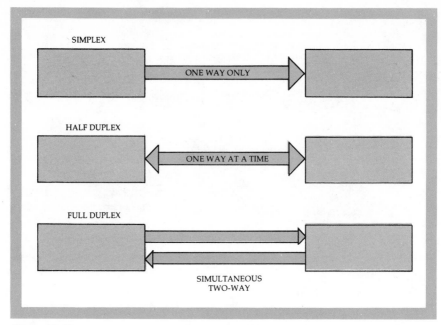

Figure 15.12

CHANNELS

By taking the sound spectrum and assigning a limited range of wave-length to each sending and receiving modem, many transmissions could be sent over the same wire. Each range of wavelength is called a **channel**. Although it is a little too complex to discuss here, it is now possible to send a number of transmissions in one channel with each transmission using different combinations of the particular wave frequency.

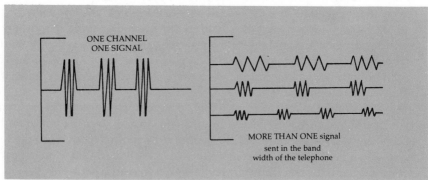

Figure 15.13

BAUDS

The rate of speed that data is able to be transmitted is measured in **Bauds**. The word is a shortened form of the name of a person who developed a telegraph code, J. Baudot. Originally a Baud was the bits per second at which data was transmitted. Recently, some computer people talk of Bauds being characters per second.

THE PROBLEMS OF ACCURACY OF TRANSMITTED DATA

Any wire or circuit which has electricity passing through it generates noise. The molecules are excited by the current and produce a hum. This noise tends to scramble the signals which are being sent resulting in some signals or impulses not being accurately received. A number of techniques have been developed to improve the quality of the transmission, and attempt to identify when an error has been created.

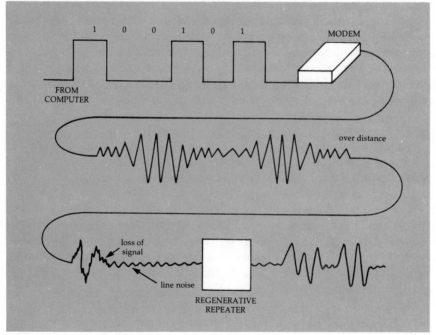

Figure 15.14

Booster stations located along the transmission line would take a signal which is becoming distorted, correct it and relay it along in its original form. This is a costly system.

Rather than strive for perfection, sometimes it is less costly to accept the fact that the occasional error will be received and plan for it. One technique used is to have important data transmitted twice. If the two transmissions compare, then likely no error has been created. Another technique is to have the important data 'echoed back' to the sending unit to compare. And still another is to structure the code which represents the various characters in such a way that a missed bit would be identified. For example, Baudot's code required 5 bits to be sent for each character. If one bit went missing the receiving machine would sense the error.

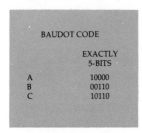

BAUDOT CODE

EXACTLY
5-BITS

A   10000
B   00110
C   10110

Figure 15.15

One technique is called **parity checking**. If the regular code for a character took an odd number of bit impulses, an extra pulse called a parity bit would be sent making the total pulses for that character an even number. If a bit were lost, the character would have an odd number of bits, and an error would be detected. And finally, one of the more common forms of coding is to have a code for every character made up of exactly 4 bits out of a possible 8 bit combination. As each character was received there must be 4 bits, no more, no fewer, or an error has taken place.

PROTOCOLS

If you are introduced to someone for the first time, it is the proper etiquette to shake the hand. A more formal definition for this type of etiquette is 'proper protocol.' Communicating devices have a **protocol** of their own. They politely ask the other device if it is prepared to receive data, if not 'please send a signal when ready.' One technique used to transmit data is to send a special signal at the beginning and the end of not only the whole string of data, but also at the beginning and end of each and every character. These signals as well are all part of telecommunication protocol.

TRANSMISSION MEDIA

In addition to the humble wire which has been so long used for transmission, other modern techniques are also used. Radio waves, micro waves, laser and fibre optics media are also used. Although each has its advantages and disadvantages, the troublesome line noise of the humble wire is not a problem with these other media.

Instead of having relatively few channels for communication as in the case of wire medium, in these other media, many channels and over-

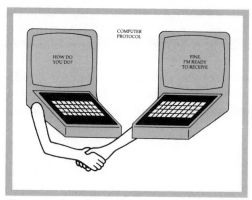

Figure 15.16

lapped signals can be sent. At the other end, each signal is 'unscrambled' and takes on a meaningful pattern of impulses.

COMPUTER COMMUNICATION AND SATELLITES

You are probably aware that radio telephone and television signals can be 'bounced off' a satellite. The use of the satellite for this type of signal

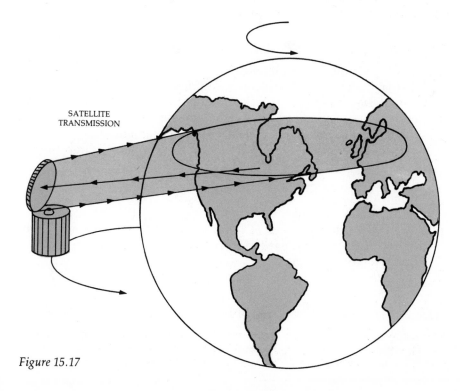

Figure 15.17

relay results in faster, more accurate transmission. Data transmission can also make use of satellite technology. It is quite likely that, as two computers at opposite ends of the country are communicating with each other, the signals are being relayed by a communications satellite. There is even a special channel reserved in one of the North American satellites for computer ham operators. Ham radio operators who have a micro computer hooked in with their ham radio use this channel to communicate with other ham computers.

CHECKING YOUR READING—LEVEL 1

1. Give a simple definition for the word 'system.'
2. What is a computerized system?
3. In what way is a *computerized* system different from a *computer* system?
4. What is a data flowchart?
5. How is a systems flowchart different from a logic flowchart?
6. How is telex different from facsimile transmission?
7. In two or three simple statements, how would a computer network function if various firms' computers were linked to each other?

VOCABULARY ASSIGNMENT

Continue developing your vocabulary list by writing a brief definition of the words and phrases in bold print in this section.

CHECKING YOUR READING—LEVEL 2

1. What is the function of a modem?
2. What is the function of an acoustic coupler?
3. In what way has modern technology been able to increase the efficiency of data communication over telephone lines?
4. With respect to data transmission, what is a channel?
5. Briefly outline or chart the difference among the following transmitting systems:
   (a) simplex
   (b) half-duplex
   (c) full duplex systems
6. What is the major problem of transmitting data and what are two or three of the techniques used to solve that problem?
7. What is a protocol signal?
8. How is the communication satellite used for transmitting data?

VOCABULARY ASSIGNMENT

Continue developing your vocabulary list by writing a brief definition of the words and phrases in bold print in this section.

PROJECTS

Programming Assignments From Business and Industry

1. MEMO 19-- 01 20
   To: Jane Barnes, Sr. Programmer
   From: George Maw, Systems Analyst
   Re: Phase I of Our Computerized Accounting System—Profit or Loss
   Jack has completed the trial balance program down to the subsidiary
   ledgers. Would you now take it over and write a routine which would
   produce a simplified Profit and Loss statement? The program should
   add up to the amounts in the purchase, wages, rent and other expense
   accounts and subtract that amount from the income or sales account.
   The difference is put in the Profit or Loss account. If the difference is
   positive (a profit), record the difference as a positive amount in the
   Profit or Loss record. If the difference is negative (a loss), record it as
   negative.
       Move zeros to each of these accounts that is, sales, purchases and
   expense accounts. Information is not lost, for the net amount has been
   saved in the Profit or Loss record. In this routine, put in a double safety
   check to ask the operator twice if he/she is sure that the old profit and
   loss information is to be closed off in preparation for a new accounting
   period.
       By the way, for the time being the accounts could be set up in arrays,
   for easy access and updating. The accounts could be moved from the
   DATA statements to the array. Perhaps one array would hold the
   account names and a two dimensional array would hold the account
   number and amount. (You may come up with a better system for
   testing updating however.)
   Note: When testing this section of the program, select test data that will
   prove that the program will correctly handle the 3 possible situations:
     i) a zero profit
     ii) a profit
     iii) a loss
       During the testing, in order to have the trial balance remain in
   balance, you should alter the cash account by the same amount as the
   profit or loss. For example if you know you will have a $1 000 profit,
   increase cash by $1 000. If you know you will have a loss of $1 200,
   decrease cash by that amount. (During the regular operation of the
   accounting system, on-going transactions will automatically adjust
   assets as profit or losses build up so that this type of artificial adjusting
   will not be necessary.)
       After the profit or loss has been calculated and recorded in the profit
   or loss account, produce a Profit or Loss statement using the following
   format:

XXXXXXXXXXXXXXXXXXXXXXXXX (name of company)

PROFIT OR LOSS STATEMENT
FOR THE PERIOD ENDING XXXXXXXX (input a date)

Income
Sales   XX XXX.XX

Costs
Purchases   XX XXX.XX
Wages Expense   XX XXX.XX
Rent Expense   XX XXX.XX
Misc. Expense   XX XXX.XX
Cost of Goods Sold   XX XXX.XX
Profit or Loss   XX XXX.XX

Because the above accounts show a record of income and costs for
the period ending on the date the statement is made, reduce the
amounts in these accounts to zero, readying them for the next period of
time. This is called 'closing' of the accounts. Do not be concerned
about possible loss of data. The *net* amount of these accounts is saved
in the profit or loss account (#3 42 0).

Have the program run the trial balance routine again to verify that the
Profit or Loss account has been updated, that the specific accounts
have been closed, and that the trial balance still balances. Document
your work.

This programming assignment should be completed with the
following time frame:
Planned and coded   _____
Fully tested and documented   _____

2. MEMO 19-- 01 25
To: Jack LeSage, Jr. Programmer
c.c.: Jane Barnes, Sr. Programmer
From: George Maw, Systems Analyst
Re: Phase I of Our Computerized Accounting System—Balance Sheet
We are ready to put the finishing touches to Phase I of the accounting
system. We now have programming routines to:
 i) produce a trial balance
 ii) produce profit or loss summary
 iii) close off profit or loss types of accounts
 iv) produce a profit or loss statement
The final step in this phase is to produce a Balance Sheet. Jack,
would you complete this phase by programming a routine for producing
this statement. You could use the following outline:

XXXXXXXXXXXXXXXXXXXXXXXXXX (name of company)
BALANCE SHEET
AS OF XXXXXXXXXXXXXXXXXXXXXXXXXX (input the date of
this statement)

Assets

Cash	XX XXX.XX	
.		
.		
.		
Total Assets	_____	XX XXX.XX

Liabilities

Accounts Payable Control	XX XXX.XX	
.		
.		
.		
Total Liabilities		XX XXX.XX

Equity

Equity	XX XXX.XX	
Retained Earnings	XX XXX.XX	
Profit or Loss	XX XXX.XX	XX XXX.XX
		XX XXX.XX

As this is the final program or routine in Phase I would you make the documentation as complete as possible before you forward it to Jane for final checking. Be sure to include in the program all necessary remarks, variable definitions, etc.

This programming assignment should be completed within the following time frame:

Planned and coded _____

Fully tested and documented _____

3. MEMO 19-- 02 05
   To: Jane Barnes, Sr. Programmer
   From: George Maw, Systems Analyst
   Re: Phase I of Our Computerized Accounting System—Testing the System

   Subject to future modifications, all the programming for Phase I appears to be complete. It is time to perform a systems test. Perhaps the best way to do this is to create a file which could be accessed by all programs. Because the delivery of the disc drives has been delayed, you will have to use tape as your file medium.

   Create a file of information similar to the 'ledger' sample outlined in one of my previous memos. According to the manual for our particular computer the file management operations, in brief are:

OPEN, PRINT #1, INPUT #1, and CLOSE 1

(Students, check the manual for your machine for any variation.) More specifically, access to a tape file is obtained by using the following instruction:

100 OPEN "0", 1, "LED", 0

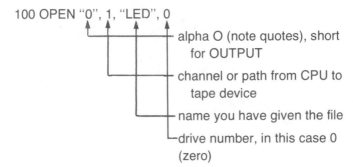

alpha O (note quotes), short
for OUTPUT

channel or path from CPU to
tape device

name you have given the file

drive number, in this case 0
(zero)

To write something on the tape a typical instruction would be:

130 PRINT #1, A,B,C

Again the # represents the channel from the CPU. Inputting information into the CPU from tape requires instructions similar to:

150 OPEN "I",1,"LEG",0   (note I for INPUT)
160 INPUT #1, A,B,C

The CLOSE instruction is simply

200 CLOSE 1

It has been a while since I have had to program for files. Reading over the manual reminded me of the errors I made when I first learned file processing. You might, therefore, remind the junior programmers about a couple of key rules to decrease the risk of errors:
1) The OPEN instruction identifies:
    * whether the file is to be an output or input file
    * the name of the file
    * where the file is located
2) CLOSE must take place before the file is 'left' or the program is terminated to leave the file in good order.
3) The terms OUTPUT and INPUT when referencing a file tend to confuse junior programmers. The word is always used in reference *to the CPU, not* the file itself. Is the data going *out of the CPU* to the file? (OUTPUT) Or is the data coming from the file *into the CPU*? (INPUT)
Have one of the junior programmers write a routine to create the test file simulating information which would be in a ledger file. Modify each of the Phase I programs to access the tape file and run them. Unless you find an alternative solution, you will likely have to read the ledger

into an array. After it is updated, rewind and rewrite the file.

Carefully keep track of the test data and prepare a written illustration or outline to show that the programs worked in a series, maintaining correct information on the tape file.

Add any relevant test information to the documentation.

4. MEMO 19-- 02 10
   To: Jack LeSage, Jr. Programmer
   c.c.: Jane Barnes, Sr. Programmer
   From: George Maw, Systems Analyst
   Re: Phase II of Our Computerized Accounting System—Cash
      Receipts and Cash Payments
   Phase I of our computerized system appears to have checked out quite well. It is now time to begin Phase II.

Cash Receipts

The input for the cash receipts journal will be data representing payments made by customers on their accounts. Have the computer produce a report listing all payments made on account during the day. For now have the data inputted in ascending numerical order by customer number. Output a report indicating the payments made and the total payments.

The second part of the first program or module involves updating the ledger file.

The total money received is *added to* the cash account. That same total is *subtracted from* the accounts receivable control account. Naturally the individual amounts would be *subtracted from* the corresponding customer's account.

Run the trial balance program after running this first program of Phase II to make sure your program integrates into the Phase I package.

Cash Payments

Write a similar program to the above but in this case the output will indicate the cheques which have to be written.

The detail lines will indicate the supplier who will receive the cheque.

In updating the ledger file the value of the total of the cheques will be *subtracted from* the cash account and *subtracted from* the accounts payable control. Individual amounts are subtracted from the individual supplier's account.

This programming assignment should be completed within the following time frame:
Planned and coded _____
Fully tested and documented _____

5. MEMO 19-- 02 20
   To: Jack LeSage, Jr. Programmer
   c.c.: Jane Barnes, Sr. Programmer
   From: George Maw, Systems Analyst
   It has come to my attention that there is a bit of a problem with Phase I of our accounting system. It appears as if we already are in need of some program maintenance. We require a routine whereby we can do what the accountants call a general journal entry. Would you augment Phase I of our accounting system by writing such a routine.

   In simple terms the routine is as follows: an accountant will supply the computer operator with two account numbers. The same amount of money will be applied to both accounts. The accountant will indicate whether the amount is to be added or subtracted from each account. The program should prompt the operator to input one account number and whether the amount is to be added to or subtracted from the balance in the account. The second account number must also be inputted.

   (Note that the amount of money involved is the same for both accounts. In accounting, sometimes multiple entries are made in a 'general journal.' For simplicity, we will insist that any general journal entry will have only two accounts. The accountant is able to break down the traditional multiple entry into a number of simple two-account entries.)

Sample transactions:

1 01 0 Cash	−$15.25
1 13 0 Office Supplies	+ 15.25
1 01 0 Cash	+$50.00
4 50 0 Sales	+ 50.00

ADDITIONAL PROGRAMMING ASSIGNMENTS

Electricity

Although you are basically a business programmer, sometimes you might be required to program the computer for the company's technical people. In this application the electrical engineer has presented you with a request to provide a series of programs which will be an aid for those working in the engineering department.

Essentially the program will end up having a series of formulae. As your package of programming modules develops, perhaps you should establish a menu.

1. The first module involves the following technical terms: voltage, amperage and resistance. The computer should be programmed to input two of these three variables and output the third variable. The applicable formulae are:

voltage = amperage × resistance
amperage = voltage ÷ resistance
resistance = voltage ÷ amperage

2. Add to the above program the necessary modules to compute the effect of adding something called resistors in circuits which are either 'parallel' or 'series.' The initial input to this part of the program should be whether the circuit is a parallel or series circuit, and the number of resistors involved. Then apply the following formulae:

total-parallel-R = 1 ÷ ((1 ÷ R1) + (1 ÷ R2) + (1 ÷ R3) . . .)
total-series-R = R1 + R2 + R3 + . . .

3. Add to the program which has been developed so far a routine which involves variables called power, voltage and amperage. The values of 2 of the 3 variables are inputted and the computer uses one of three formulae to compute the third value. The formulae are:

power = voltage × amperage
voltage = power ÷ amperage
amperage = power ÷ voltage

Please note that power must always be greater than zero.

4. Two additional formulae should now be inserted. These involve something called reactance. Apparently there are two types of reactance which are called inductive reactance and capacitive reactance.

Two variables are inputted to calculate inductive reactance. These are called the frequency and the inductance. The formula is:

inductive-reactance = 2 × π × frequency × inductance

Something called capacitance and frequency are used as input into the second formula which is:

capacitive-reactance = 1 ÷ (2 × π × frequency × capacitance)

Again note that frequency, inductance and capacitance are greater than zero.

5. In order to compute frequency, the time is inputted and you use the formula

frequency = 1 ÷ time

To compute resonant frequency, inductance and capacitance is inputted and you use the formula

resonant-frequency = 1 ÷ (2 × π × $\sqrt{\text{inductance} \times \text{capacitance}}$)

6. Finally modify your program so that the proper terms are used in it. Here are the proper terms:

QUANTITY	UNIT
voltage	volts
amperage	amps
resistance	ohms
total parallel-R	ohms
total series-R	ohms
power	watts
inductive reactance	ohms
capacitive reactance	ohms
capacitance	farads
inductance	henrys
time	seconds
frequency	hertz

CHAPTER 16

DATA BASE COMPUTING— DISTRIBUTIVE PROCESSING

A lot has been said about the flow of data *within* a firm and *among* firms. The storage and accessibility of that data has stimulated considerable discussion.

1. What type of data (about people) should be stored electronically?
2. What type of data should not be stored?
3. Who should have access to the data?
4. Should an individual be able to see *all* the information stored about her/himself?
5. Should that person be able to correct what she/he considers to be wrong information? Unfair information?
6. Should one firm provide another firm with lists of its customers?
7. Should the data about the employees, clients and/or customers of a branch plant be kept in the computer of the head office located in a foreign country? Or, conversely, should that type of data, including head office personnel data, be kept in or be available to a branch plant in a foreign country?

The discussion on these issues is ongoing.

The focus of these issues is the development of technology to efficiently store massive amounts of data. In addition to efficient storage, the data or any combination of it can be almost instantly retrieved. The storage of massive amounts of data and the ability to speedily retrieve any data item or combination of data is called **data base** computing. It is easier to understand and appreciate data base computing by putting it in perspective with other types of computing.

THE LONELY COMPUTER

If a computer has been assigned one task to do, it is considered to be a **discrete computer**. Usually a discrete computer has a very limited task to do such as monitoring a machine, controlling the carburetor of a car or monitoring fire sensing devices.

Some computers, which have a variety of tasks to do, could be called **stand alone** computers. A small business computer could look after the four or five major tasks for a firm. One day it would do payroll, and at other times it would be doing invoicing, inventory control or other specialized tasks required for that firm. By definition, a stand alone computer is not usually hooked up to other computers.

THE SOCIABLE COMPUTER

Some computers, as has been outlined in the previous chapter, do communicate with each other. These computers are designed to carry out a certain type of communicating task. For example a computer which looks like an ordinary electric typewriter might be used for **data collection**. This type of computer is sometimes called a **terminal**. The data collected would be transmitted to a large central computer. At one time a terminal was a device which would only input or output data from a computer, and usually was located some distance from the host computer. It had no CPU and could not be programmed. Most terminals now are micro computers, programmed to manage the sending and receiving of information. They are also able to be programmed to do other on-site tasks. This type of computer is often called an **intelligent terminal**.

Figure 16.1

If a remote micro computer or terminal is able to send and receive information it is sometimes called an **interactive computer** terminal. The term 'interactive' is used if the terminal is able to make inquiries of the central computer, or even use the compilers of the central computer. The term 'interactive' is also used if, during the programming of a computer, the compiler senses programming errors and immediately responds to these errors.

TIMESHARING COMPUTING

If the central computer is designed for timesharing, each terminal or remote computer obtains a share of its CPU's time. The processing speed of the central computer is very fast but the speed of data transmission is relatively slow. The central computer therefore is able to rotate its attention from one terminal to the other so rapidly that each terminal is given the impression that it has the full attention of the central computer. In other words the central computer is able to receive from, and transmit signals to many terminals so efficiently that each channel is handling signals at its capacity.

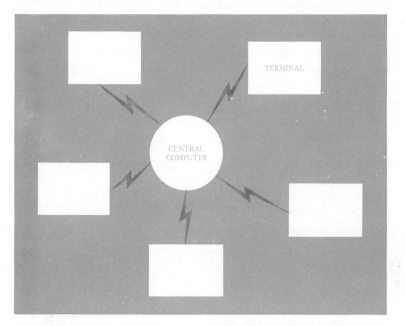

Figure 16.2

DATA BASE COMPUTING

If a relatively large central computer obtains information from a number of terminals and maintains all relevant information on some electronic file, the system is considered to be a data base system. All data needed for the operation of the firm is in one place. As stated earlier the input to the data base could be mainly from the data collection terminals which provide the main computer with information. At least part of the data base would be accessible to any terminal making inquiries. Obviously some sections of the data base must have considerable security features built into their access routine to prevent certain information being obtained by unauthorized people. More about that in a later chapter.

DATA BASE MANAGEMENT SYSTEMS

Up to recent years most data processing has been done using what might be called 'flat files.' Data is stored as records which have multiple data items or fields making up the record. Using either a sequential or random method, records were accessed and specific fields or data items within the record were processed (extracted or updated). When considering **data base management systems** a different type of approach was looked for and ultimately found by the computer scientists.

Instead of thinking of data as fields, within records, within files, the concept was developed of 'dumping' all data items onto some electronic storage medium, usually disc. A sophisticated program was developed to manage this pile of data items. The structure of the data file was such that most data items were *linked* to other data items of the same type and/or to *related* data items. For example, suppose there was a small 'flat' file of salespersons' records.

Number	Name	Age	Sales
1	A. Adams	25	12 000
2	B. Brown	21	13 000
3	C. Clark	62	15 000

In data base management the file could be imagined as looking something like this:

LINKED ITEMS

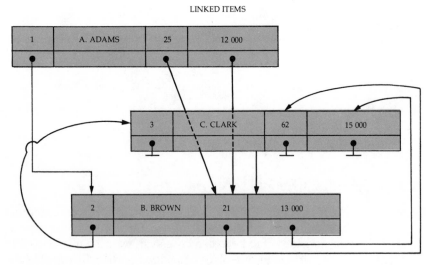

Figure 16.3

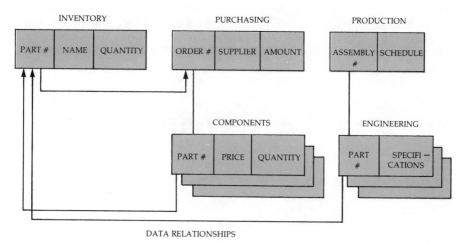

DATA RELATIONSHIPS

Figure 16.3(a)

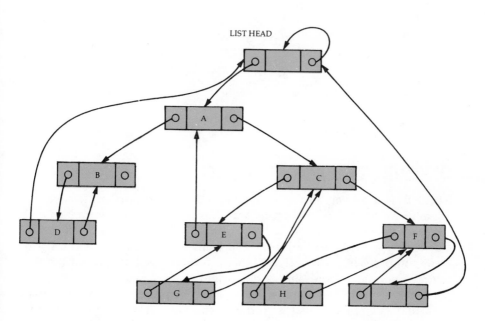

Figure 16.3(b)

The program which manages the file becomes a type of buffer between the file and computer personnel who want to use the file. Programmers, for example, accessing data base on a big computer system, managed by a data base management program, are able to write their programs in any language for which the host computer has a compiler. The programmer may also assume that the file to be accessed is a flat file. The management program takes instructions from almost any traditional program and converts the file processing instructions to suit its own organization. It does the necessary updating or outputs required by the programmer.

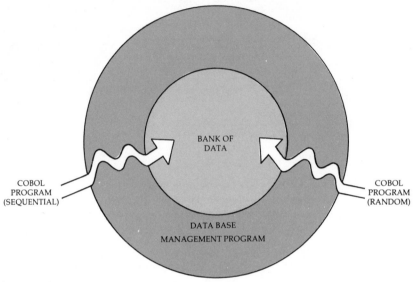

Figure 16.4

DISTRIBUTIVE PROCESSING

At one time there was a trend to data collection and time-sharing computing in firms which had numerous branches. All data was centralized and all major decisions were made by personnel associated with head office. Due to the flexibility of terminals, especially the fact that each is a stand alone computer in its own right, more processing is done away from the central computer. Processing is done right at the branch or right in the plant where one of the terminals is located. The principle involved is that the *local* data and its processing is done near where it will be needed. This is called **distributive processing**. In some cases data might be required from the central computer. Sometimes programs might be so big that the terminal requests the central computer to run them and transmit the output. Generally, however, the distributive computer is like a stand alone device but with access to the central computer and the data base it manages.

ON-LINE AND OFF-LINE

In data collection and transmission to a central data bank, the efficiency of the system is increased by having data collected into a *batch* of information, while the terminal is not in direct contact with the central computer. This is called **off-line** preparation. Data is keyed into the terminal or data entry device, stored and sometimes sorted on some medium such as disc or tape. A key tape or key disc device is suitable for this task. At a certain time of day, or when sufficient data has been accumulated, the central computer is called and the data sent while the remote device is **on-line**, at a relatively rapid rate. The rate would be much faster than having a good typist key in the data directly to the computer. If the cost of transmission is based on time used, batching would save money.

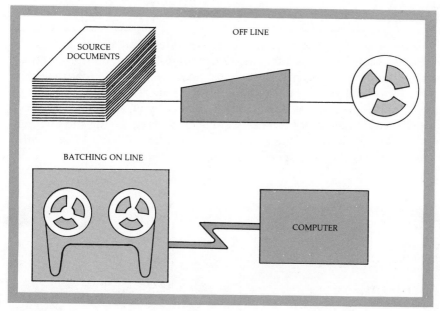

Figure 16.5

Not all applications are suited to batch data transmission. In banking, it is important that each customer transaction be immediately sent to the data bank to keep the customer's account correct, up to the minute. The interactive, on-line method is necessary for this type of application. Certain other applications, such as inventory update, could be designed around off-line data collection for later batching to the central computer.

Level 2

EFFICIENT USE OF COMPUTER TIME

The efficient use of all devices of the computer has been of some concern to the manufacturers. Even though a central processing unit could have many devices servicing it, in most cases it works so fast it does not have enough to do to keep it fully occupied.

Even though some of these input or output devices are extremely fast, they are extremely slow when compared with the speed of the CPU. An input or output device might operate in milliseconds whereas the CPU might work in nanoseconds.

TERMS USED IN TIMING COMPUTER OPERATIONS	
TERM	DURATION IN A FRACTION OF A SECOND
millesecond	1/1 000
microsecond	1/1 000 000
nanosecond	1/1 000 000 000
picosecond	1/1 000 000 000 000

If a particular program required that a computer read a card, process it, and write a line on the printer, the time it would take to do this could be represented by the length of the arrows in Fig. 16.6. Notice that the three devices involved are idle more than half the time. This inefficient operation would be the same as having one worker carrying sod to be placed on a freshly graded piece of ground, twenty-five workers laying sod and one worker raking ahead of the sod layers with a small rake. What inefficiency! There is a way to speed things up.

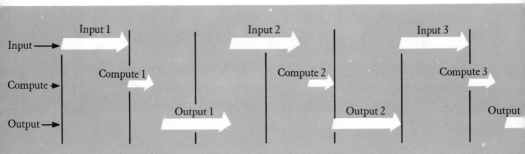

Figure 16.6

BUFFERING

A technique used to increase the overall efficiency of the computer is buffering. An area of memory could be reserved especially for receiving information ready for processing by the central processor. This section of memory would be called an input *buffer*. Another area of memory could be reserved for data which has been processed and is ready to be sent to an output device. Data could then be moved out of this output buffer while the CPU is doing some other operation. After the data has been read into memory at a relatively slow rate, the CPU could electronically move it at a very fast rate into the working area of the program. As soon

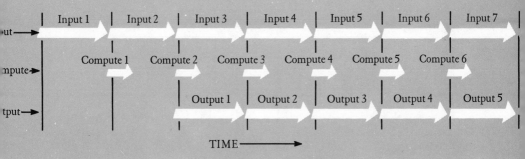

Figure 16.7

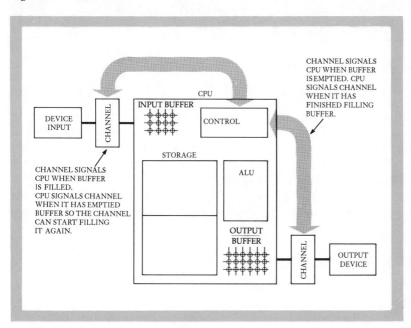

Figure 16.8

as this move has taken place, the input device could begin loading in the next record while the CPU is processing the first record.

In a similar fashion, the CPU could quickly load the updated record in the output buffer. The record is read out onto the output device at a fairly slow rate while the CPU is starting to work on the next record. When the output buffer has been emptied it is available to the CPU for the next output.

The speeds involved in this data flow become important. Although the input device might be able to read in the characters at 800 characters per second, this results in a relatively slow flow of data. When one considers that the CPU can transfer data from the input buffer into working storage

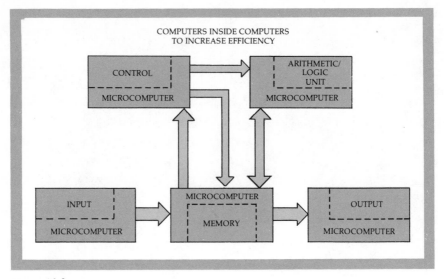

Figure 16.9

in a matter of one millionth of a second, the input device, fast as it is, works at a snail's pace. Similarly the output devices have a capability of working at even a faster rate than most input devices. However this rate is very slow compared to the rate at which the CPU can transfer data from its working area into the output buffer.

By using buffers, the CPU, input and output devices could be made to function simultaneously. This technique is called **overlapped processing**.

CHECKING YOUR READING—LEVEL 1

1. What is the difference between the function of a discrete computer and a so-called 'stand alone' computer?
2. How is an intelligent terminal different from the early terminals?
3. What is the main characteristic of interactive processing?
4. In what way does a large central computer give the appearance that it is giving its full attention to each of the many terminals linked to it?
5. How is data base organization different from the flat file organization traditionally used for sequential or random access?
6. What is the key function of the data base management program?
7. What is the philosophy behind distributive processing?
8. What is meant by off-line preparation of data?
9. What is the difference between batch transmission and interactive transmission?

VOCABULARY ASSIGNMENT

Continue developing your vocabulary list by writing a brief definition of the words and phrases in bold type in this section.

CHECKING YOUR READING—LEVEL 2

1. Write out the duration in a fraction of a second of each of the terms: millisecond, microsecond, nanosecond, and picosecond.
2. Develop some memory aid which will assist you in remembering these various durations.
3. Give a simple definition of a *buffer*.
4. In what way is the buffer used to create overlapped processing?

VOCABULARY ASSIGNMENT

Continue developing your vocabulary list by writing a brief definition of the words and phrases in bold type in this section.

PROJECTS

Programming Assignments From Business and Industry

1. MEMO 19-- 03 05
   To: Jane Barnes, Senior Programmer
   From: George Maw, Systems Analyst
   Re: Phase II
   It appears as if the first part of Phase II has worked out fairly well. Program routines have been written and appear to be checking out.
   Would you take a little extra time to do some thorough testing of the programs which have been recently written? Put test data in the accounts receivable and accounts payable programs such that the account can be overpaid. That is, for some reason, more money has been paid on account than what was due, resulting in a negative balance in that account. This sometimes does happen in accounting. If it crops up in one of the programs an appropriate message or flag should be produced.
   Would you also expand the ledger file to include a new account? Perhaps ultimately we should have a programming routine which would do this task. For now, I suppose, we could just alter the data file. The new account is

   5 56 0 Insurance Expense

   Carefully test the so-called general journal program which has been written. Input sufficient data to create a number of general journal entries. Then run the trial balance again to make sure that the ledger remains in balance. The following are some possible entries:
   1) purchased delivery equipment so subtract from cash and add to delivery equipment;
   2) paid for three years of insurance on the building—subtract from cash and add to insurance expense;
   3) took out a bank loan increasing cash and increasing the account called bank loan.

This programming assignment should be completed within the following time frame:

    Planned and coded   _____

    Fully tested and documented   _____

2. MEMO 19-- 03 08

    To: Jane Barnes, Senior Programmer
    From: George Maw, Systems Analyst
    Re: The Beginning of Phase III

    First of all, Jane, let me congratulate you and Jack for the excellent way in which our accounting system has been developing. It is team work such as you two have demonstrated which assures the success of any project.

    Phase III involves two general classifications of accounting—purchases and sales. I should warn you at this point that these four will be very closely linked with the two programs which were written in Phase II. So be aware that these two programs will not only link with Phase III programs but the Phase III programs will also link with programs which will be developed later. Perhaps technically I should not say the programs will link. The programs will access the same data base! Any linking which might take place would be more likely the integration of a series of programs into a master program.

    May I suggest that you begin with a fairly simple program which will handle our purchases. The input of the program would be transactions representing the value of goods we acquire from our various suppliers. The supplier account number and perhaps the name would be inputted. The amount involved, of course, would also be inputted. A report would be produced under a suitable heading which would list the suppliers and the amounts representing the value of our purchases from them. In addition, the program should include the total purchases.

    The kicker in this particular problem is that we have to access the ledger and add the total amount of purchases to the account purchases and accounts payable control. In addition, each individual purchase must be recorded in the accounts payable subsidiary ledger. Naturally a trial balance should be run after executing this program. (Again, use the system developed previously to update the ledger.)

    This programming assignment should be completed within the following time frame:

    Planned and coded   _____

    Fully tested and documented   _____

3. MEMO 19-- 03 10

    To: Jack LeSage, Junior Programmer
    c.c.: Jane Barnes, Senior Programmer
    From: George Maw, Systems Analyst
    Re: Continuing the Development of Phase III

    It appears as if the purchases routine has been satisfactorily written, and it is now time to do the routine for sales. Again let me remind you, as I reminded Jane, that this routine will access a common data bank or be integrated into one of a number of master programs. For example a future program related to this current task is an invoicing program.

The input for the sales routine would be a customer's number, and perhaps name. The amount of the sale would also form part of the input. The output would be a report, under a suitable heading, of the various amounts purchased by each customer. The final line of this report would include the total.

Accounts in the ledger must be updated by this program. The account *sales* is increased by the total of the sales. Similarly the accounts receivable control would be increased by this total amount. The individual sales to our customers would be added to the customer's account in the subsidiary ledger. Carefully test this program to make sure that a variety of entries would result in the ledger remaining in balance.

This programming assignment should be completed within the following time frame:

      Planned and coded _____

      Fully tested and documented _____

4. MEMO 19-- 03 12

To: Jane Barnes, Senior Programmer
From: George Maw, Systems Analyst
Re: Documentation

Isn't it typical, Jane, for people to get so wrapped up in a project that they don't get the necessary details done properly? I have been so wrapped up in this project, studying the sample output, etc., that I have not thought to ask you about how well the documentation has been coming.

Perhaps I should have assumed that each program is being fully documented as you have completed it. Yet on the other hand, I realize there is a tendency for people to put off doing this necessary task.

If the documentation has not been thoroughly and completely done for any part of the various phases, would you see that it is done. In fact, if you wouldn't mind, would you show me the documentation for all the work that has been done to date?

ADDITIONAL PROGRAMMING ASSIGNMENTS

1. Programming a Camera Chip

Most modern cameras of the intermediate price range have micro circuitry and in some cases a computer chip controlling or monitoring its functions. Your task is to write a program which can be burnt into a chip, which will then be inserted into an automatic camera.

There are three main variables in operating a camera. They are: the speed of the film, the aperture opening and the exposure time.

Without getting too technical the aperture openings are given the following reference numbers:

REFERENCE NUMBER	SIZE OF OPENING
2	fully open
2.8	1/2 open
4	1/4
5.6	1/8
8	1/16
11	1/32
16	1/64
22	1/128

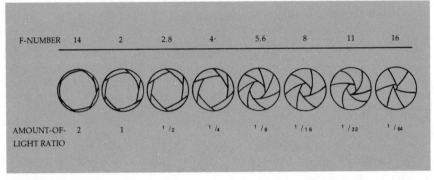

Figure 16.10

The camera whose chip you are to program has the above aperture settings and is able to handle 4 types of film. The film speeds involved are labeled '64,' '100,' '200' and '400.' The speeds of the shutter in fractions of a second are: 1/60, 1/125, 1/250, 1/500, and 1/1000. Write the program so that the film speed and either the aperture opening or the shutter speed are inputted. Look up the third value in a table similar to the one provided. Should a certain combination be inputted such that the third value can not be computed generate a 'beeup, beeup' message to indicate to the user that an alternative setting is required.

Shutter Speed	Aperture Opening 2	2.8	4	5.6	8	11	16	22
1/60			64		100			
1/125		64		100			200	
1/250	64		100			200		400
1/500		100			200		400	
1/1000	100			200		400		

2. Economics

There is a direct relationship between the amount of money in circulation and inflation. The more money in circulation the more inflation a country has. This is a very simple statement—too simple to be the total cause of inflation. But in general it is true.

Other factions which confuse the issue include how rapidly the money moves around in society and whether or not there is an increase in the quantity of goods and services available to the consumers. A formula which more accurately describes the situation is as follows:

$$\text{money supply} \times \text{velocity} = \text{price levels} \times \text{quantity of goods and services produced}$$

More briefly stated:

$$M \times V = P \times Q$$

Write a program which would assist the chief economist of the nation to direct the economy. Perhaps you could input a percentage change in the money supply, keep the velocity constant, assume a zero growth in the quantity of goods and services produced (gross national product) and output the percentage change of the new price levels. Then, keeping V constant, produce tables showing combinations. For example, an increase in the money supply might be 15% and a growth in the gross national product (goods and services produced) might be only 3%.

Perhaps after some experimenting with the 'economic model' you might come up with a recommendation for the government on how to control inflation.

3. The above question mentioned gross national product. It is the dollar value of all the goods and services produced in a country in a certain period of time. A variety of factors cause it to grow (or not grow). These factors can be expressed in a series of formulae. The formulae may be put together to form another economic model. This model attempts to forecast this coming year's GNP.

Investment = (the constant 1.885) × Profits from this year's economic activity)

Government spending = (the constant 1.063) × (Spending of government this past year)

Consumption by consumers = (the constant 1.616) × G × I (from above formulae)

$$GNP = I + G + C$$

Most recent economics texts should have current information which could be plugged into this model. Or you could obtain this information from your federal government. (Maybe even your local banker might have it available.) Play around with this model and, again, you might come up with some observations or recommendations which you feel might assist the economy.

CHAPTER 17

WORD PROCESSING

Level 1

Since humans have been communicating with each other there has been some form of word processing. Certainly when words and ideas were written down for future use the concepts of word processing took a major step forward. In an earlier chapter there was some discussion of the various operations which can be performed on data, such as classifying, storing, retrieving, sorting, communicating, duplicating, and calculating. In that chapter the stress was on business data, particularly financial and numeric data.

Word processing, on the other hand, involves the creation and recording of sentences. It includes operations performed on words and sentences—operations such as recording, storing, retrieving, duplicating and communicating. In simple terms, word processing could be defined as all the operations which are performed on words. More particularly word processing involves the creation and communication of original thought and written ideas.

THERE MUST BE A BEGINNING

Words, ideas and thought expressed in some intelligent form do not just happen. A person must develop the ideas and put them in some written form. This creative process, when analysed, requires a number of steps:
1) The problem or idea must be considered mentally.
2) The solution to the problem, or the idea must be formulated within the human mind.
3) The solution is outputted, from the mind, usually by either handwriting it, typing it, dictating it to a stenographer, or dictating it onto an electronic medium such as tape. In the latter two situations the material would be **transcribed** later.
4) Usually when a person is engrossed in a problem, grammar, sentence structure and paragraph structure are not uppermost in the mind.

Therefore, the initial output would likely have to be edited. It would be edited to correct two general deficiencies:
1. to improve the grammar
2. to modify or correct the ideas which were produced so that they more accurately represent what the author wanted to say.
5) The edited version might have to be retyped, and perhaps re-edited. Depending on the importance of the material, there could be many editings and rewritings.
6) Once the material is in its final form, the other operations such as storing, retrieving, duplicating, and communicating would now be performed on this new block of information.

So far, all you have had is a little lesson on English composition! That is true. You already do considerable word processing in any school work that you do. The twist here is that machines are now available to make much more efficient the whole process of word processing, from the original creation of information to its duplicating and communication.

DICTATING EQUIPMENT

Creative thought through to its final written form can be a slow process. If the author of new information is not a typist, dictating equipment could be used to speed up this process. An interesting schedule on some human skills illustrates part of the problem of making the creative process more efficient.

THE HUMAN PROCESS	ESTIMATED RATE OF SPEED (in words per minute)
Thinking	400-600 or more
Talking or dictating	150-250
Writing in shorthand	100-140
Typing	40-60
Handwriting	12-16 (any faster and it may not be legible)

This schedule would imply that a person responsible for creating information would make most efficient use of the time by dictating, either into a machine or to a very good stenographer. The dictated ideas would then be transcribed from the tape or shorthand outlines by typing them on a typewriter.

WORD PROCESSING EQUIPMENT

Any device which does at least one of the operations performed on data is a word processing machine. A class of machine has been developed, however, which is so specialized at efficiently handling data that it has become known as **word processing equipment**. This equipment makes much easier the whole process of editing, combining information, and producing copies in the style which is best suited for the occasion.

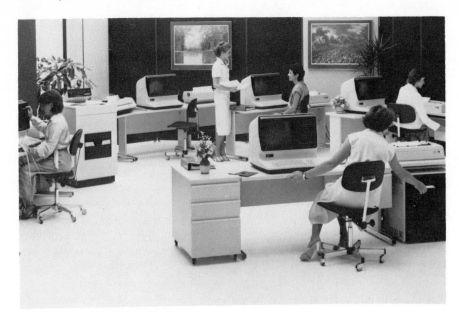

Figure 17.1

Prior to the use of word processing devices, material could only be stored and edited on paper. Much retyping had to be done as the material was improved. This was a very time consuming process. With the use of appropriate equipment the information may be keyed into it and stored electronically. One copy or many copies could be printed on paper on command.

Word Processing Functions

One of the most time consuming tasks involved in producing quality written material is the task of editing. *It cannot be stressed too strongly the ease and speed of making changes to written material stored in a word processing machine.* The device and its program are especially designed for editing! Draft material can be electronically displayed on the device. The author reads over the material:

a) to correct misspelled words
b) to improve weak sentences by:
   1) re-arranging the words
   2) deleting words
   3) adding words
c) to change sentences:
   1) rearrange within a paragraph
   2) delete from the paragraph
   3) add to the paragraph
d) to change paragraphs:

1) resequence
2) delete entirely
3) add

If the editing is not done by the author right on the device, a hard copy may be obtained. This copy is edited, perhaps in pen or pencil. It is then given to the word processing device operator. Sections to be changed are *called up* on the display area and the changes are made. The changes not only appear on the display area but are also made on the electronically stored material.

BUSINESS COMMUNICATION

In preparing a library of paragraphs for word processing, an analysis is made of current correspondence. To the great surprise of many office managers, there is considerable repetition in most of the correspondence which leaves an office. When this fact is told to managers, they are quick to challenge it. "Every problem we have here is unique and must be handled in a unique fashion" is the most common reply. And they are correct.

An analysis of typical correspondence, however, would likely show up a few obvious facts. First of all, those responsible for most customer communication, likely would use two or three closing paragraphs to their letters. The closing might be very courteous, keeping in mind that this person is a valued customer. Or at the other extreme, the closing could be very firm, especially if an account is long overdue. There are, however, very few ways to write an effective closing for a letter.

Similarly the introductory paragraphs of letters are often quite similar. Although there is a trend to avoid cliché-type phrases, many business letters begin:

Thank you for your letter dated January 6, 19xx in which you express a concern about the quality of our service.

A variation of this could be that this current letter is as a result of a telephone call rather than a previous letter. The concern may have been the cost of a product, the quality of the product or the tone of the last letter sent to the customer. But there are only a relatively few situations in business which cause a letter to be written.

A variety of opening and closing paragraphs could be written, carefully edited and stored in the word processing device on disc. When a letter is to be written, the person in charge of correspondence might ask the word processing operator to type in the inside address of the person who will receive the letter, then have the machine recall and perfectly type (at a very high speed) 'Introductory paragraph #3.' The central part of the letter would be created or authored to deal with the problem and outline the solution. The operator may then be told to close the letter with 'closing paragraph #1.' Isn't that slick? But there is more to come.

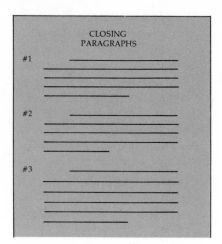

Figure 17.2

Depending on the type of firm, there could be about 15 or maybe as many as 40 different actions which may be outlined in a piece of communication. These actions could be identified by studying correspondence written over the course of a number of years. Some of the better paragraphs which were written in these old letters could be improved, then loaded onto the word processing disc. Each could be numbered and a hard copy of each of these numbered paragraphs could be put in a book or manual.

Now, in addition to having a number of introductory and closing paragraphs from which to choose, the person in charge of correspondence could check over the manual to see if there are suitable paragraphs which suit the situation (again, these paragraphs are almost perfectly written). It might just happen that the whole letter could be composed of pre-written, stored paragraphs. As a result a letter of carefully written paragraphs would be rapidly and perfectly typed by the machine.

And all this would be done in a matter of a few short minutes. It might be necessary for one special paragraph to be written. If so it could be drafted, edited carefully, and used in the letter along with the other paragraphs. The new paragraph could then be stored, enlarging the library of prestored paragraphs.

ADVANTAGES OF USING WORD PROCESSING SYSTEMS FOR BUSINESS COMMUNICATION

There are many advantages of using word processing systems over other methods which have been used for so many years. The two most obvious are:

1) time-saving—each piece of correspondence is organized in a matter of a few minutes, even perhaps less than a minute in some cases. Most of

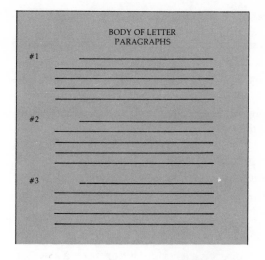

Figure 17.3

    the typing is done automatically, very fast, and very accurately, saving considerable operator/typist time.

2) the quality of the output is excellent. The sentences and paragraphs are almost perfect, and the spelling (due to all the earlier editing) should be perfect. The appearance of the letter should be excellent. It should have no smudges or poorly corrected errors. The set-up would be excellent. (Students taking typing know how difficult it is to properly place a letter on a page).

BUT THERE IS STILL MORE

In addition to day-to-day correspondence, businesses send out **form letters**. For example if a firm is having a special clearance sale of certain of its inventory, it might send out the same letter to a certain group of special customers. All letters would be the same, except for the inside address. Similarly, the letter which goes out to customers who are more than 60 days overdue on their account would be the same for each customer, except for the inside address. Some firms mass produce the form letter, perhaps on a stencil machine, and then have a typist type in the inside address. It is rare that the inside address could be properly aligned with the balance of the letter, and usually the tone of ink used for the inside address is different from the ink used for duplicating. As a result, the quality of this type of correspondence is very poor.

Using word processing equipment, the sales letter, or letter requesting a payment on the account could be stored on disc. The operator could type in the inside address for each letter then push a control key for the device to finish the letter. The letter is beautifully typed and gives the appearance that it is a special unique letter to that customer only. Another sheet of paper could then be inserted and the process repeated for another customer.

This process could be taken one step farther. Various files of names and addresses could be stored on a disc of the word processing device. If all customers in the customer file are to receive a certain letter, then a stack of company letterhead could be placed in the word processing machine. The machine could look up the name and address of the first customer in the file, type it as the inside address, then type the special letter. It would then automatically find and type the name and address of the next customer, then type the body of the letter. It could be set up in such a way that once the process got going, it could be left unattended, to work away by itself, producing excellent letters at a rate of perhaps 300 words per minute.

PERSONALIZING THE LETTER

It is possible to put into pre-stored paragraphs a special symbol which would represent the place where a person's name is to be typed. When the inside address is typed, the word processing machine records the name in its memory. As it types the body of the letter, it comes to that special symbol. It then types in that person's name.

Assume there are a couple of sentences such as these within a paragraph:

"As someone involved in a business such as you are &*, you realize how important it is to have a steady cash flow. Your overdue account certainly reduces our anticipated cash flow for this current month. We would therefore urge you, &*, to submit your cheque to us by return mail or contact us to make other arrangements."

When the letter is typed it would come out like this:

YXZ Company
123 Industrial Blvd
Yourtown
Attention: Mr. Brown
Gentlemen:
. . . As someone involved in a business such as you are Mr. Brown, you realize how important it is to have a steady cash flow. Your overdue account certainly reduces our anticipated cash flow for this current month. We would therefore urge you, Mr. Brown, to submit your cheque to us by return mail . . .

Perhaps the repeating of the name is overdoing it a little, but you get the idea.

OTHER WORD PROCESSING FEATURES

The program in most word processing devices enables the operator to request a variety of operations.
1) Headings could be centred automatically.
2) Manuscripts with multiple pages could be perfectly typed, for the device would be informed as to how many lines there are to a page, then plan for it. Pages would be numbered automatically.
3) Sentences could be deleted and the remaining sentences *closed up* removing the space left by the deleted sentence. Sentences could also be inserted.
4) A word which was consistently used in the manuscript such as the word 'disc' could have its spelling change throughout the whole manuscript to the alternative spelling 'disk.' One instruction to this effect would cause the device to examine the whole manuscript looking for that word. When it found each one it would change its spelling automatically. This is called a **global search and replace** function.
5) Again in the preparation of a manuscript, the author sometimes decides that some of the ideas could be presented in a better sequence. An instruction to the device would cause blocks of information or paragraphs to be moved about, almost instantly, on the disc.
6) One of the more difficult tasks typists have is to produce statistical reports with columns of data. A word processing device would do an excellent job of this with a minimum of initial instruction.
7) If the written material is to be **right justified**—each line ends on the same imaginary vertical line, just as each line begins on the same imaginary vertical line—the word processing machine would do all the necessary calculations and spacing to bring this about.
8) The program is also capable of assisting the operator in word division at the end of a line.

FORMATTING AND HYPHENATION

When a document is stored on file, it can be produced using any combination of line lengths. For example, a report may be written using a 13-cm line length or an 11-cm line length. It is possible to produce paragraphs of varying line lengths within any one document. For example, more of the paragraphs could have a 13-cm length of line, whereas certain special paragraphs such as one which is a long quotation might be inserted within the document using only a 10-or 11-cm length of line.

In addition to selecting the line length, the user can decide whether or not the right-hand margin is to be justified. As suggested earlier, word processing equipment is able to produce information with both the left-hand margin and the right-hand margin justified. Because the line length of a document can vary and the right-hand margin can be justified, there is no way in which the operator who first stores the data is able to predict where a hyphen should go in a particularly long word. Most word processing devices are able to assist the operator in the task of hyphenation just prior to producing the document.

The information is inputted into the machine as to the length of line and whether or not the line is to be justified at the right margin. The device then scans through the document, making 'a mental note' of where lines will be terminated at the right margin and stopping at words which would have to be hyphenated. It then displays on the screen the word and the place where it would like to hyphenate the word. The operator then judges whether or not the arbitrarily chosen division point in the word follows the traditional rules of hyphenation. If by coincidence it does follow the rules, then the operator simply signals an okay to the device. If it is not at the correct place then the operator would backspace to a point which would be a correct division point. The device then makes a note of that point and would alter the spacing within the line so that the hyphenated word would still come out justified at the right margin.

In a fairly long document, the device might have to obtain assistance for the hyphenation of only three or four long words. Most words in a sentence are relatively short and the device is able to alter the spacing so that as few words are hyphenated as possible.

VARIABLE SPACING

Each character on a typewriter is given equal space whether it is an *i* or an *m*. To right justify on a device such as the typewriter the only option for spacing out the line is to insert extra spaces between words.

Some variable space devices are able to assign twice as much space to an *m* as an *i*. These machines are able to do a better job of spacing out a line for right justification. In addition to extra space between words, small extra spaces can be left within words.

Figure 17.4

WORD PROCESSING FOR LAWYERS

Another application in which word processing can be used is the production of long, complex legal documents. There is a tradition in law offices that legal documents should be free of any alterations or corrections. Some documents are pre-printed with constant information correctly worded. Certain variable data is then inserted in the appropriate place. Other documents must be typed from scratch. Even though the documents are typed from scratch, many paragraphs are repeated from document to document. Word processing devices enable these long complex documents to be stored and reproduced rapidly and accurately, easing the typing load. The documents are rapidly produced and do not have any corrections or alterations which might be questioned by a judge.

Level 2

THE MARRIAGE OF WORD PROCESSING AND DATA PROCESSING

Once it was realized that most word processing devices have as their main characteristic a micro computer, it did not take long before devices were produced which included both data processing and word processing features. These devices have been developed over some time so that their capabilities are equally balanced between the two functions. In the early days, one had either a very good computer and a poor word processing system in one machine, or a good word processing system with limited data processing capabilities. But recent designs have made the two functions almost equal in power or in capability.

As time goes on, computer networks, which will include information processing capability, will enable more and more effective word processing communication. A computer network, therefore, would be able to transmit and communicate equally effectively both numeric data and word information.

In the early days of computers, the term *data processing* was most frequently used. Subsequently, it was replaced by the phrase, *information processing*. In a way, this was not too accurate a term, for the information was mainly *numeric* data. But once the capability of doing effective word processing in computers was developed, then truly, the computer and/or word processing equipment can be considered to be *information processing devices*.

OTHER DEVELOPMENTS IN INFORMATION PROCESSING

In an earlier chapter, there was a brief discussion on the Telex system and on facsimile transmission. Due to the increasing need for effective communication in business, additional systems have been and are being developed. One of the more interesting systems is the **Telepost** system. A piece of communication can be prepared and placed on a special machine. A machine transmits the information electronically to receiving machines some distance away.

One application for this system would involve sending multiple copies to various locations. The piece of communication once mounted on the machine can be transmitted to a number of receiving stations. For example, if a communication was to be sent to a series of branch offices all over the country, the device would transmit it to the receiving stations in the various cities. They would then be removed from the machine and delivered, either by the regular mail service or by special delivery to the branch office in that city. In this way, communication can be received within a 24-hour span, in fact, in relatively few hours in some cases.

COURT REPORTING

Another development which has taken place is the joining of a court reporter's shorthand machine to a type of word processing device. The keying of the symbols by the reporter is transmitted to some type of auxiliary storage. It is then interpreted by a computer. Almost as soon as the transmission is finished, the computer is able to produce a draft copy or transcription of what has been recorded. One of the more interesting features of this system is that a number of different words have the same code. For example, the two words *there* and *their* would have the same coding from the shorthand machine. When the draft manuscript is produced by the computer, it includes both forms of the word in brackets. The person who is responsible for editing the draft simply deletes the incorrect word and records that deletion with the computer. This editing can be done right on the CRT. After this limited amount of editing is done, the computer is then asked to produce a full and complete transcription of the court proceedings. This reduces dramatically the time required to produce a transcription of the court proceedings for a court official or a lawyer.

Figure 17.5

LANGUAGE TRANSLATION

Shortly after computers were developed, computer scientists dreamed of using the power of the computer to translate from one language to another, for example from French to English. For years this was just a dream. Recently major improvements have been made in computer software such that this task is now being done.

Dictionaries of up to 200 000 words are stored for each language. The document to be translated is fed into the computer. The computer analyses the sentences and looks up the words and phrases in the other language. It even attempts in some cases to make sense out of certain phrases to select the best phrase in the other language.

For example the word *out* could have up to three meanings, depending on how it is used: a person might be out—not available; a machine might be out or broken down; or a part might be taken out or removed. The computer looks for proper nouns, verbs and other clues to decide what is intended, then selects the correct phrase in the other language.

APPLICATION OF LANGUAGE TRANSLATION

Currently one of the most important applications of this type of program is in the translation of technical documents. This task is difficult for two reasons. Translating is a slow time-consuming process and therefore very expensive. To translate technical documents the translator must know both languages but also have considerable technology background. This type of person is rare.

It would take many translators many hours to translate a 30 million word technical document for an airplane such as a 747. Using the computer, a draft of the translation could be produced very rapidly. The human translator then edits the draft, which takes only a fraction of the time required to do a complete translation.

VOICE TRANSLATION

The above application is only one step away from the dream of instant verbal translation. Computers are now able to understand a limited number of spoken words. Computers are also able to create, generate or synthesize words. As a result of these developments a person is now able to speak into a computer in English and the computer would translate the words into another language such as French, outputting the translation on the voice synthesizer.

CHECKING YOUR READING—LEVEL 1

1. Write out a simple definition of word processing.
2. Condense into brief statements the six steps in creating original thought.
3. Roughly, how many times faster can a person think than handwrite?
4. What is the difference between a word processing soft copy and a hard copy?
5. How can word processing be used in business correspondence?
6. What are the two main advantages of a word processing system over the traditional system?
7. In what way is a word processing system superior to the traditional system in sending out form letters?
8. How is a word processing system able to personalize the body of a letter?
9. What is a global search and replace function?

VOCABULARY ASSIGNMENT

Continue your vocabulary list by writing brief definitions for the words and phrases in this section which are in bold type.

CHECKING YOUR READING—LEVEL 2

1. In what way have word processing devices been "married" to computers?
2. What is Telepost?
3. How can Telepost be used to transmit the same information to a number of branch offices?
4. How is a court reporter's transcribing machine used in relation to a word processing device or a computer?
5. How is the computer used to translate technical documents from one language to another?

VOCABULARY ASSIGNMENT

Continue your vocabulary list by writing brief definitions for the words and phrases in this section which are in bold type.

PROJECTS

Simulating Word Processing on a Micro

1. Enter the following program on your micro. Note as you do so how easy it is to make corrections. (Your computer might require that the closing quotes have to be included.)

```
100  PRINT"19— 03 20
110  PRINT
120  PRINT"MR. SAM SMITH
130  PRINT"63 MAIN STREET
140  PRINT"YOURTOWN
150  PRINT
160  PRINT"DEAR MR. SMITH: (salutation)
170  PRINT
180  PRINT"WE HAVE BEEN INFORMED THAT YOU HAVE
     NOT
190  PRINT"PAID THE BILL WE RECENTLY SENT YOU.
200  PRINT"PLEASE DO SO IMMEDIATELY.
210  PRINT"YOURS TRULY, (complementary closing)
220  PRINT:PRINT
230  PRINT"MRS. ALICE JOHNSON
240  PRINT"CREDIT MANAGER.
```

2. Alter the above letter to put the date, the complementary closing, writer's name and title about 15 spaces over.
3. Change the word *bill* to *invoice*.
4. Write a program which would have two introductory paragraphs in subroutines or modules. Permit the writer of the letter to input a request for one of these introductory paragraphs.
5. Expand the above program to include two closing paragraphs and two or three *body-of-the-letter* paragraphs which could be produced on command in any order. Test your program a number of times to make sure various combinations of paragraphs work.
6. Write a program which will simulate the word processing task of writing a 'collection letter.' Have three variables inputted:

   A = the amount of money due
   D = the number of days overdue (30, 60, 90, 120)
   N$ = the name of the person owing the money

Write the collection letter which will plug in the variables. For example:

". . . as a business person, ";N$;", you well know how important cash flow is to a firm. It is certainly a disappointment to us to have to remind you that you have an invoice payment of $";A;" now overdue by ";D;" days. We urge you, ";N$;", to pay this amount by return mail or phone us to make other arrangements."

Programming Assignments From Business and Industry

MEMO 19-- 03 19
To: Jane Barnes, Senior Programmer
From: George Maw, Systems Analyst
Re: Phase IV—Payroll

Jane, before I begin, let me congratulate you on the excellent documentation which you showed to me. Not only was it thorough and complete but it was set up in a very attractive way. Future maintenance and augmentation should be much easier with documentation of this quality available to the programmer.

It is now time to begin Phase IV of our accounting system, which is payroll. Payroll is a very complex program but we will write the basic modules of the program using simple test data, so that at a later date we could plug in modules for the more complex tax calculations, etc. Generally speaking we have two types of employees, those on salary and those earning a wage or on piece rate.

Perhaps the easiest place to start would be for a payroll routine for the salaried employees. Start off by creating a data file listing a sample of employees with the employee number, the employee name and bi-monthly salary. Also in the records should be a tax code which will have been obtained from the federal form which employees completed when they joined the company. Each of our employees pays 50% of the premium for the medical insurance plan. As you know the total premium for a single person is $12 whereas the total premium for a married person is $18. Some designation must be established in the employee record to determine whether or not the person is married and therefore whether the premium should be $6 a month or $9 a month. And that reminds me, because we are paying twice a month, the premium would be half of that—$3 or $4.50. The employee may or may not have an additional deduction for the United Way or charity.

Also deducted from each pay is a flat rate pension plan deduction of $10 and an unemployment insurance premium of $7.

In order to simulate the income tax, create an array of various tax rates, for example the highest tax rate might be 30%, the next highest might be 28%, etc. Each element in the array might correspond to the tax code on the government form mentioned above. In order to calculate the income tax to be withheld from an employee multiply the content of the element in the array designated by the tax code by the salary. For example, if the code is 1 the rate of tax is found in element 1 of the array. The net pay would be calculated by adding up all the deductions and subtracting them from gross pay. Produce a payroll report listing all the employees and their various deductions, including their gross and net pay. Of course provide totals of all columns. (By the way you might check current policy to see if the pension plan amount is deducted from gross pay *before* the income tax is calculated.) Supply your own sample test data.

Planned and coded _____

Fully tested and documented _____

MEMO 19-- 03 25

To: Jack LeSage, Junior Programmer

c.c.: Jane Barnes, Senior Programmer

From: George Maw, Systems Analyst

Re: Phase IV—Payroll

Please check over the initial part of the payroll program which has already been written and improve where necessary on the documentation.

The next module should be relatively routine. What we would like to do now is to take in from the factory the various times that an employee has worked as well as the rate of pay for each employee. We calculate the times worked to the nearest quarter hour. For example if employees work eight hours and seven minutes in a day then they are working seven minutes for free. On the other hand if they work eight hours and eight minutes then the eight is closer to the quarter hour so they would receive credit for eight hours and a quarter that day. Ultimately we would like to be able to input the start and stop times for the morning and afternoon sessions and have the computer calculate hours worked to the nearest quarter hour. For the time being we might just input the data based on a five day work week. You should be aware that the employees usually work 40 hours and may work up to 44 hours and still receive only the regular rate of pay. Any hours over the 44 hours are paid at double the rate.

Produce a payroll similar to that which has already been written to outline the hours worked, gross pay, deductions, etc. of those who work in the factory.

Carefully document this section of the payroll.

Planned and coded _____

Fully tested and documented _____

MEMO 19-- 04 02

To: Jane Barnes, Senior Programmer

From: George Maw, Systems Analyst

Re: Payroll—Employees' earnings records

We are far enough along with this payroll phase of our accounting system that we should now consider setting up an employee earnings record file.

For the time being we can create that file in the data section of a BASIC program. The file would consist of records with the following data items: employee number, employee name, tax code, United Way or charity code, gross pay to date, income tax to date, pension plan to date, unemployment insurance premium to date, United Way or charity to date, Union dues to date, net pay to date.

Create a routine such that these records are read into memory during payroll to be updated. Obviously the gross pay for this current pay period would be added to the gross pay accumulated to date. Similarly the other deductions would be accumulated to the corresponding fields. It should be pointed out to you that these various fields start off in January at zero and accumulate over the course of the calendar year. At the end of the calendar year a slip of income tax data is produced and the various fields are reduced to zero again to begin the next year.

Planned and coded _____

Fully tested and documented   _____

ADDITIONAL PROGRAMMING ASSIGNMENT

Linear Programming

One of the more useful computer programs used in industry makes optimum use of capital equipment, available materials and/or human resources. In meat processing for example, each day there might be a different quantity of pork and beef available for making processed meats. Each type of processed meat would have a different formula. Some might be made solely of beef or pork. Others might be made up of some ratio of each of these two main ingredients.

Linear programming involves using formulae prepared by the plant foreman or manager to write a program to accept the daily variables and output the production report which would result in optimum use of the available equipment and/or supplies.

In general terms linear programming is used for the following applications:
1) blending applications as suggested above
2) distribution applications to find the least cost of distributing products
3) production planning over a period of time such that as situations change, new alternatives are outputted
4) advertising and investment decisions to combine the best possible combination of actions

A fairly common structure for linear programming involves the use of 3 equations similar to the following:

$$a_1x + b_1y = c_1$$
$$a_2x + b_2y = c_2$$
$$a_3x + b_3y = \text{maximum or minimum}$$

An Algorithm for Writing a Linear Program Computer Program

Step
1) Create at least 2, two-dimensional arrays, (200 × 2) and one (4 × 2)
2) For each equation, prompt the user to input the number:
    i) beside the x (i.e. the 'a' of the above equations)
    ii) beside the y
    iii) to the right of the equal sign
3) For the first equation establish the maximum number of array elements which have to be used for that equation by finding the integer value of c/a and c/b. Select the larger of the two as the maximum number of elements to be used by that equation.

    For example if the equation were:
       10x + 5y = 600
    c/a or 600/10 would require 60 elements in the array
    c/b or 600/5 would require 120 elements in the array
Because we must select the larger, then the number of elements used would be 120.
4) In this first array we want to develop a series of ordered pairs based on various values for x and y. Using a FOR . . . NEXT series, compute the integer value of y, as x varies from 1 to the maximum found in #3 above. Without getting into the algebraic reorganization of the formula, you could use the partial instruction

$$INT((c - a * x)/b)$$

Assign the resulting values to the second column of the two-dimensional array.
5) Find the values of the first column in the array by using the values of y established in #4 above and applying the following partial instruction:

$$INT((c - b * M1(y,2))/a)$$
(where M1 represents the first array)

6) Repeat steps 3 to 5 for the second equation. Of course use a second array.
7) Now compare the ordered pairs of numbers in each array until you find a pair of numbers in the first array which matches with a pair in the second array. Save these numbers in the small array.
8) If there happened to be a third equation (other than the so-called maximum or minimum equation), repeat steps 3 to 7 using the second and third equations to find matching pairs. A third (250 × 2) array could be used.
9) Apply the ordered pair values to the 'optimizing equation' to produce a short list of values. Substitute the values of the ordered pairs for x and y of this equation. The maximum or minimum of the resulting output would be examined to see which values produced the desired result.

Test Data:
$$4x + 6y = 30$$
$$x + y = 6$$
$$\$30x + \$40y = \text{maximum (answer: \$210)}$$

$$2x + y = 120$$
$$x + y = 72$$
$$x + 4y = 216$$
$$\$10x = \$20y = \text{maximum (answer: \$1200)}$$

CHAPTER 18

FORMS DESIGN

Level 1

DESIGNING FORMS FOR HANDWRITTEN DATA

A form which will be used to collect handwritten data should be easy to understand. Directions on how to complete it should be quite clear and the data should be in some logical sequence.

Some business forms will be used by the same person over and over again. For example, a sales order form would be used regularly by a salesman. The waitress in a drive-in restaurant would fill out the same order form many times. Other forms, such as *application for employment* forms are completed by people who will be seeing the form for the first time. These forms should give as much aid as possible to the person who must complete it.

There are some designing techniques which should be considered in planning a form to be filled out with handwriting data. The length of the space should be sufficient for the longest handwritten answer expected. The width of the space should be about 1 cm.

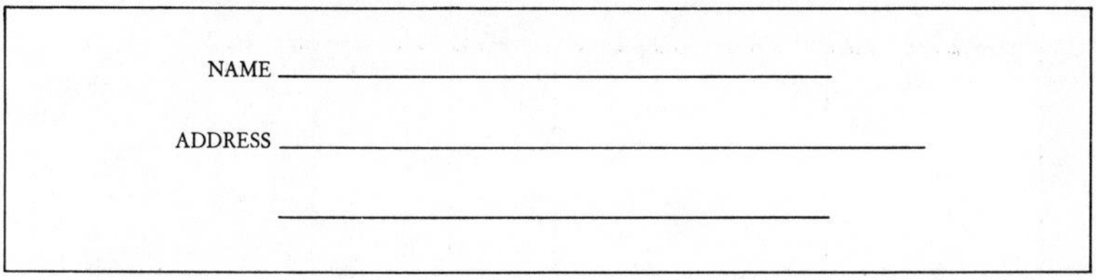

NAME _____

ADDRESS _____

_____

Figure 18.1

Where possible the data required could be given in such a way that the person completing the form would only have to check off the correct answer. For example, on an application form requiring data on the highest level of education attained, there could be three choices: elementary school, secondary school, and university. The correct answer could be simply checked off.

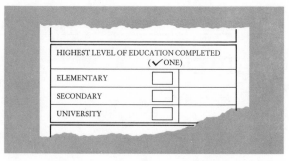

Figure 18.2

Similarly the questions should be designed so that a minimum number of words would be required for an answer. For example, the form might be preprinted with "The name of your supervisor on your last job is _____." All that would be required for this part of the form would be the name of the previous supervisor of the applicant.

DESIGNING COMPUTER SOURCE DOCUMENTS

The sequence of data requested on the form which will be used for source data for computer should be as close as possible to the sequence of input of fields. The data entry clerk's eye would flow along the source document reading data in the appropriate sequence without having to jump around to various parts of the form.

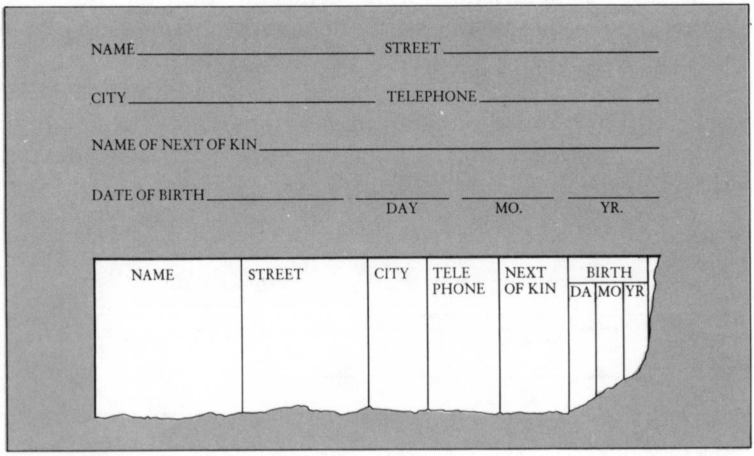

Figure 18.3

In order to make the data even easier for the data entry clerk to read, the areas reserved for hand-written information could be blocked out as shown in Fig 18.4.

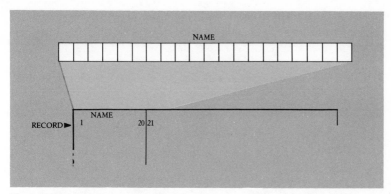

Figure 18.4

If the data to be collected must be very easy to read and/or must ultimately fit in a limited space in a computer, boxes could be provided. Each box would hold one character. This encourages accurate printing and permits the person to choose the shortened form of a long name. If the data entry clerk made the decision it might not be suitable.

If, for some reason, the data is to be divided into two classifications, the areas of one classification could be shaded or *screened* to aid the data entry clerk working with the source document. For example, certain information on application forms might be used for payroll information whereas other data might be used strictly for the personnel record. The data for the personnel record could be written on a screened area.

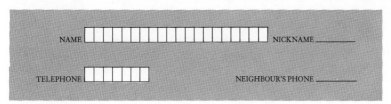

Figure 18.5

In addition to having areas to be filled in by someone such as the job applicant, there could be other areas reserved for date of employment, comments of the personnel supervisor, and any other information which might be required before the final disposition of the application. Perhaps you have seen areas on forms labelled "For Office Use Only" or "Do Not Write in This Area."

DESIGNING COMPUTER OUTPUT

There are usually two classifications of computer output—the periodic report and the high volume printing of documents such as invoices. The latter form will have preprinted information on it such as the company's logo, invoice number, conditions of sale, etc. This preprinted material is called **constant information** and should be arranged on the form so that any **variable information** which relates to it can be printed in some reasonable order. An example of variable data would be the name and address of the company receiving the form.

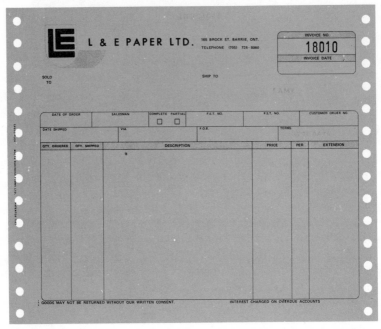

Figure 18.6

It is desirable to have as much information as possible preprinted on the form. In the case of an invoice, the terms, via, purchase order number, the date of the invoice, and customer number would be variable data added during printing.

In designing a form, the constants are written right on the layout sheet on which the design is being drafted. The variable data which the computer will generate is marked in with x's. The form is submitted to a forms company for printing and manufacturing. The program would print out the variable data on this preprinted form. The program would be written so as to place the variable data in the appropriate locations on the form marked with x's on the layout sheet.

REPORTS TOTALLY GENERATED BY THE COMPUTER

Preprinted forms are not usually manufactured for reports which are outputted only occasionally. Constants, such as the name of the report, are coded right into the program which will generate the report. Each time the program is run, the constants would be outputted as a literal.

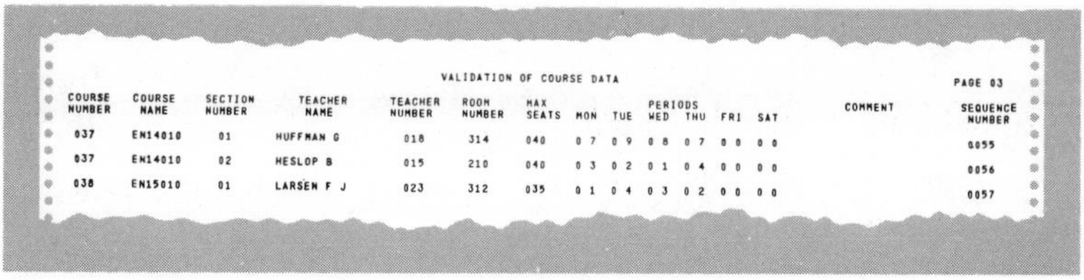

VALIDATION OF COURSE DATA

COURSE NUMBER	COURSE NAME	SECTION NUMBER	TEACHER NAME	TEACHER NUMBER	ROOM NUMBER	MAX SEATS	MON	TUE	PERIODS WED	THU	FRI	SAT	COMMENT	SEQUENCE NUMBER
037	EN14010	01	HUFFMAN G	018	314	040	07	09	08	07	00	00		0055
037	EN14010	02	HESLOP B	015	210	040	03	02	01	04	00	00		0056
038	EN15010	01	LARSEN F J	023	312	035	01	04	03	02	00	00		0057

PAGE 03

Figure 18.7

In determining the spacing on a completely computer-generated report, some counting has to be done in order to have the report centred and reasonably well spaced out. In planning a report, roughly lay out the headings, or constants, which will be outputted each time. Then plan the number of output positions required for variable data which will be obtained from a data file, some other input device or calculated by the computer. Plan for the longest possible piece of data.

A sales report might have the following headings:

S A L E S   R E P O R T

. . .SALES PERSON. . .   AREA   . . .AMOUNT. .

   X ————— X   .XX.   XX XXX.XX

(16 output
positions)   (4)   (2)   (4)   (9)

A chart can be used to help in determining the spacing.

	Output Positions for Constants	Output Positions for Variables	Most Output Positions Required for Column (larger of col. 1 & 2)
SALES REPORT (extended spacing)	23	N/A	
SALESPERSON	11	16	16
spaces between columns			4
AREA	4	2	4
spaces between columns			4
AMOUNT	6	9	9
Total Print Positions Required			37

The number of output positions available depends on the size of the output device. Some CRTs have about 40 positions whereas some printers have up to 132.

	(columns)	(main heading)
Total Output Positions Available (assume 40)	40	40
Total Output Positions Required for Report	37	23
Unused Output Positions	3	17

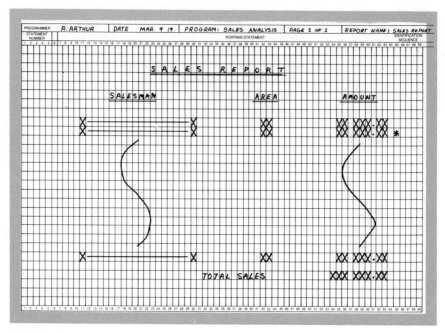

Figure 18.8

Half of the unused output positions are allocated to either side of the report. The main heading would begin about the 11 output positions to the left of centre or output position 8 or 9. It would be produced with **extended spacing**—an extra space inserted between each letter and 3 spaces inserted between each word.

The word SALESPERSON would begin on the fifth output position. And the names of the salespersons would begin on the second output position. Do not be concerned about being one print position out, either way. It will not be noticed.

Note that the variable data in the first column is longer than the sub-heading, SALESPERSON. The constant, AREA, is longer than the variable data, however, in the second column. Care must be taken to lay out on the form the longer part of the column first—the constant or variable—and then centre the shorter.

After the form is completed, the spacing is coded into the program along with the literals or headings. The programmer simply counts the output positions which will be spaces and then codes them into the program. Similarly the literals are coded into program instructions which will cause them to be outputted exactly as planned each time the report is run.

	SALES REPORT	
SALESMAN	AREA	AMOUNT
ARTHUR, RANDY	Ø1	1 256.23
THOMPSON, GLEN	35	25 ØØØ.98*
	Total Sales	26 257.98

Figure 18.9

Although this looks fairly easy, beginning programmers frequently make errors either in planning the spacing of the report or in converting the plan to instructions for the computer. As a result, columns will not be under the headings and the decimal in the total will not be aligned with the decimals in the columns.

Level 2

CRT LAYOUT

If you have access to a CRT screen (Cathode Ray tube), there are a few additional considerations which must be taken into account in planning output on the screen. Screens come in various dimensions. It is likely that the horizontal limits of your screen will be less than the limits of the standard printer. For example, many standard line printers have a capacity of well over 100 print positions; whereas, the capacity of one of the smaller screens on a micro-computer is as limited as 40 output positions.

In planning output on a printer, the programmer had to be aware of the number of lines on a page being used. For example, on the standard 27.5 cm deep paper, 66 lines were available to the programmer. On some CRT's, the screen might hold only 25 lines. This fact should not necessarily concern the programmer, for the report on the screen can be scrolled up, losing a line at the top of the screen while obtaining a new line of data at the bottom of the screen.

In the same way that printer layout forms are available to programmers for planning and laying out printed reports, forms are available to plan and lay out the images which will appear on the CRT. Obviously, when planning the output for your CRT, you will have to know the limits, or the size of the screen you are using. The form which is available could then be marked off with boundary lines so that you can easily plan the spacing within the boundaries of the screen.

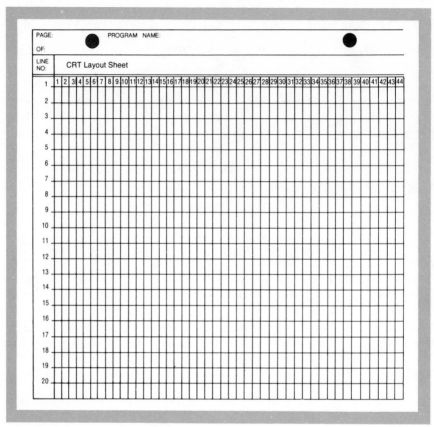

Figure 18.10

MULTIPLE COPIES

Although not a serious consideration in planning a form or a report the programmer should certainly be aware that multiple copies of a report can be made on a printer. **Multi-part** paper is available. Carbon paper *is* included between sheets of continuous paper. After printing, the package of output is **decollated,** separating the different copies into piles and removing the carbon paper.

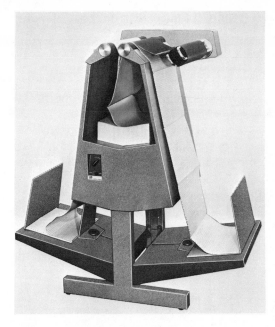

Figure 18.11

NCR PAPER

Multiple copies may be obtained without using carbon paper. This is called NCR paper which stands for no carbon required. The paper being printed on is especially treated so that when impacted by the printer the characters appear on all copies. The impact causes the special treatment to produce the particular character.

FORMS FLOW

As indicated earlier in the text, various copies of a document are sent to various places. This distribution can be represented by a form flowchart.

In order to aid in the correct distribution of the forms, the various copies are usually colour coded. The accounting department, for example, might always receive the green copy.

CHECKING YOUR READING—LEVEL 1

1. 1. What general rule should there be for the spacing of handwritten information?
2. In what way would a check off system make the completing of a form easier and limit the variety of information obtained?
3. Why is it important to collect, in the correct sequence, the data on a source document which ultimately will be used as a source of information for the computer?

4. What two functions are served by providing boxes for characters of information?
5. How is *screening* used in a source document?
6. What type of information is considered to be a constant on preprinted forms?
7. What type of information is considered to be a variable on computer output?
8. In designing computer output which involves columns of information underneath column headings, what special care must be taken in linking up the spacing of the column headings with the spacing of the data under the columns?
9. What is the spacing involved in what is called *extended spacing*?

VOCABULARY ASSIGNMENT

Continue developing your vocabulary list by writing a brief definition of the words or phrases in this section in bold print.

CHECKING YOUR READING—LEVEL 2

1. In what way are the principles involved in designing a layout for a CRT different from the principles involved in designing output for a printer?
2. What is meant by multi-part paper?
3. What is meant by decollating?
4. What does NCR stand for with respect to duplicating information?
5. How is colour coding used in the distribution of forms?

VOCABULARY ASSIGNMENT

Continue developing your vocabulary list by writing a brief definition of the words or phrases in this section which are set in bold type.

PROJECTS

1. The Dynamo Corporation was a relatively small wholesale company. It had five salespersons on the road, a girl Friday, and a manager in an office. The girl Friday, Jean, was an attractive girl with plenty of personality; however, she tended to become confused when the pressure was on.

   Customers would telephone in orders. Jean would attempt to write the orders in longhand. She would get them down the best she could but frequently mistakes were made. If a telephone call was for a salesperson she would write down the salesperson's name and the telephone number so that when that person called in, the name of the customer who called would be read over the phone. Frequently these messages were misplaced or were not accurate.

Jean could not take shorthand and there was not sufficient time to teach her. She had enough other valuable personality assets that her boss could not afford to fire her.

Your responsibility is to design a form which will assist Jean in answering the telephone and getting down accurate information. It could include two parts. One part could be for *call back* messages. The other part could be a customer order form.

2. (a) Design an application form to be compatible with the disc personnel record which contains:

	CHARACTERS
LAST NAME	12
FIRST NAME	10
OTHER INITIAL	1
STREET ADDRESS	20
CITY	10
TELEPHONE NO.	7
MARITAL STATUS	1
DATE OF BIRTH	6 (YR.MO.DA.)
DOCTOR'S NAME	15
DOCTOR'S TELEPHONE	7
EDUCATION	1

Other information required for file but not included on the disc record: REFERENCES, PREVIOUS EXPERIENCE, AND PERSONAL GOALS.

At some later time the following information will be added to the form: INTERVIEW COMMENTS, REMARKS CONCERNING REQUESTS FOR RAISE OR PROMOTION, SUMMARY OF PERIODIC REPORT FROM FOREMAN.

(b) What impression, if any, of the company might the applicant have if the latter three areas of activity (a) above are reprinted on the form?

3. Design a computer print-out for a report which has the following headings:

ADEGO COMPANY
SALES REPORT FOR THE MONTH OF _____
Subheadings: SALESPERSON'S NAME, SALES
End of Report: TOTAL SALES FOR THE MONTH

The variable data for the second heading should be large enough to write out the full name of the month with the most characters in its name. No salesman's name is greater than 12 characters and no sales for an individual salesman would be greater than $9 000.00.

4. On a suitable layout form, design a computer layout with the following headings:

1st main heading	Place of Learning
2nd main heading	REPORT ON THE _____ TERM/SEMESTER
3rd main heading	FOR _____
subheadings	SUBJECT MARK COMMENT CODE
end-of-report line	AVERAGE

In the second main heading the variable word would be one of FALL, WINTER, SPRING, FIRST, SECOND or THIRD. The student's name would go in the third main heading. The variable data for SUBJECT can have up to 10 characters. There could be a mark of 100 but there are no decimals involved for any individual mark. The comment code requires only two digits and the student's average is correct to one decimal place.

Programming Assignments From Business and Industry

MEMO 19--04 17
To: Jack LeSage, Junior Programmer
c.c.: Jane Barnes, Senior Programmer
From: George Maw, Systems Analyst
Re: Designing a Payroll Cheque
We have made remarkable headway in designing our payroll system. It is now time to design the cheque which will be used for payroll.

Obtain copies of various types of cheques. Plan for the constants which will be preprinted on the form by the company supplying our cheque blanks. Also provide for the variable data which should include a cheque control number generated by the computer. Preprinted on the cheque forms will be a cheque number. It will be unique for each cheque. The number of the first cheque form used during a run will be inputted into the program. That number will be outputted on the first cheque. This number, of course, would be incremented by one for each additional cheque which is printed. As a result, the preprinted variable number and the computer generated variable should be the same on each cheque. Our accountants have asked for this routine so that there is a safety check which would assist them in maintaining control over the cheque forms.

MEMO 19--04 20
To: Jane Barnes, Senior Programmer
From: George Maw, Systems Analyst
Re: Designing Our Invoice
It is time that we made a design for the invoice that we are going to use on our computer. This design, when finalized, would be sent to the forms supply firm to have our invoices preprinted.

Obviously the invoice should contain our logo, including our address and telephone number. You might obtain copies of different types of invoices to adopt the best features of each. Remember when designing an invoice, to clearly indicate the constants which are to be preprinted by the forms supply company. Also indicate the number of X's to show the location and possible size of the variable data.

Write a program which simulates the printing of one of our invoices. You would have to put into the program, during this testing stage, the constants which are to be preprinted on each invoice. Also in this test program should be a routine to input the name of the customer, address, etc. The terms and other pertinent information should also be inputted as well as three or four sample items which would have been purchased from our firm.

The program should calculate the extension, total of the invoice and be able to calculate federal sales tax.

Planned and coded _____

Fully tested and documented   _____

MEMO 19--04 24
To: Jane Barnes, Senior Programmer
From: George Maw, Systems Analyst
Re: Testing Our Payroll System
The basic skeleton of the payroll system seems to be well developed. There will be a number of additional routines which will have to be added at a later date so that the program meets the standards of our accountant and the tax authorities. It would appear, however, that the worst is over and that the payroll system is ready for thorough testing on its own merit, and testing with the ledger file.

Now you do the following:
1) Test thoroughly the current program. Make sure the test data includes the zero values, that is, the employee does not work at all during the pay period.
2) Build in some safety checks so that the data being inputted and the output data must fall within certain prescribed limits. Make sure there are suitable error recovery routines, fully tested.
3) Create a restart routine such that if the program is interrupted during its execution, it can be restarted, picking up where it left off.
4) Include a routine which would handle a special case such that one of our salaried employees has lost a day's pay.
5) Be sure there is a routine such that we could, at this stage, simulate the production of year-end tax information. This would include the
   i) employee's earnings to year end, ii) income taxes withheld,
   iii) other deductions withheld, and iv) net pay.
6) After the tax data has been generated, have the computer bring to zero the "to-date fields" in the records. (Perhaps this would be difficult to simulate until we are able to set up this employees' earnings record file on disc. But we should be aware this has to be done sometime in the future, if we cannot at least simulate it at this stage.)
Fully tested and documented   _____

CHAPTER 19

AUXILIARY DEVICES

Level 1

The computer's memory can handle only so much information. There comes a time when the computer, like a person, must make notes in a notebook. At some later time the computer is able to retrieve information from its notebook for processing. The notebooks take various forms, but collectively they are called **auxiliary storage**. The two most common forms of auxiliary storage are tape and disc.

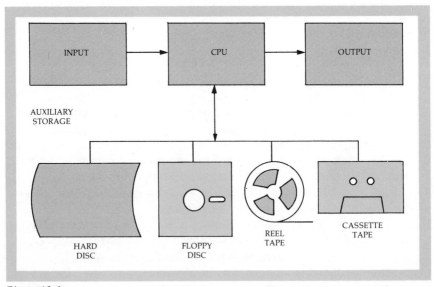

Figure 19.1

On the large main-frame computers the tape units or tape drives are also large. The tape is in large reels. The tape for micro computers, however, is usually on cassette. The principles of the two are the same.

Large disc drives and large discs about the size of an LP record form a high-speed auxiliary storage device for the main-frame computers. Micro computers handle smaller discs which range from about 20 cm in diameter down to about 8 cm. Again, the principles involved are the same.

TAPE

You probably have discovered the convenience and the low cost of the cassette tape. Both programs and data can be stored on cassette. The data and programs must be identified on an internal label right on the tape so the correct information may be retrieved. The operating system or program reads this tape label. It uses tape labels to properly identify the information. Of course the tapes usually have an external label for easy identification by the operator.

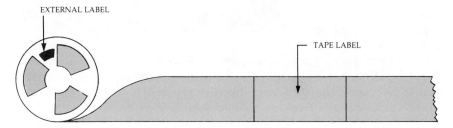

Figure 19.2

Tape instructions are used to:
1. write on tape
2. erase any old data
3. read tape
4. copy information from tape into memory without altering the original data on tape.

Information is stored on tape sequentially. Data files are accessed, one record at a time, in the sequence they have been recorded on the tape. (This soon will be compared to **random** access which is possible on disc.) Some end of file indicator is necessary. This may be a dummy record which is identified as being the last record. Or, there may be an end of file indicator which is a special character or symbol that the program recognizes as the end of file. On the more sophisticated tape drives there is also a device to sense the physical end of the tape.

DISC

Information such as data or programs may also be stored on disc. Again it must be labelled for identification. The label is used to identify the information. Like the tape, information may be written onto the disc, erasing old information, or a copy of the information may be read from the disc into memory, leaving unaltered the data which was copied. Instructions similar to those used for reading and writing on cassette are used for the disc.

Figure 19.3

The information on disc is written on concentric circles called tracks. These tracks are not visible to the eye, but are created electronically as the data is recorded. The read-write head of the disc is able to move very quickly to any track. The disc rotates, resulting in the read-write head

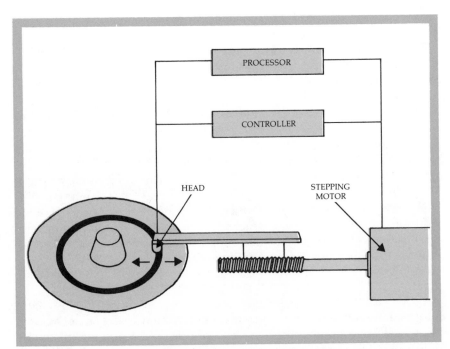

Figure 19.4

being able to access any section of the disc very rapidly. Due to this feature the data may be retrieved by the **random access** method. An index of where various data is located is maintained by the disc. When a certain piece of data must be retrieved, the index is read to determine exactly where on the disc the data is located. The **disc address** of the data is given to the mechanism which controls the read-write head, causing the head to go to the particular track. The data is then read into memory.

SORTING ON DISC

The combining or merging of two files can be done very quickly on disc. The two file areas are accessed and the records are combined in a third area. Sorting of data into some sequence is also relatively easy on disc. 'Scratch' or **work areas** are set up and the sorting is done using those areas. In some cases the new, sorted file is built up in a scratch area. When finished it is copied from that area into the old file location.

TYPES OF FILES

There are two main types of files, **program files** and **data files**. Each can be stored either on tape or disc. Each unique file must have its label to identify it. Even within a program file, each program must have its own unique name for identification purposes.

Data Files

Data files are usually one of three types. A sequential file has data in some sequential order, perhaps by record number. All records likely would be in ascending order according to their numbers. A second method of data file organization is **random sequential**. In this case the data is recorded in some sequential fashion. An index is created perhaps by a utility program, which determines the address of each record. The file is then accessed randomly, using the index to look up disc addresses of the records to be processed.

A third organization of a disc file is pure random. As additional records are created in an expanding file, the computer assigns them any available space on disc, recording in the index the disc address of the added records. To retrieve a record the index is referred to and the disc address of the record is obtained.

Note the difference between the random sequential and the pure random. In the former case, the records are put on file in a sequential order, then an index is created. In the purely random file, the records are recorded in a randomly located space and the address is recorded in the index as each record is assigned its own space. The purely random file is most commonly used for **dynamic** or expanding files. The random sequential file is a little more efficient and is used if the records of the file remain relatively constant—few additions and deletions.

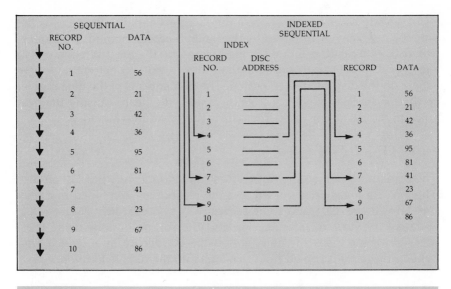

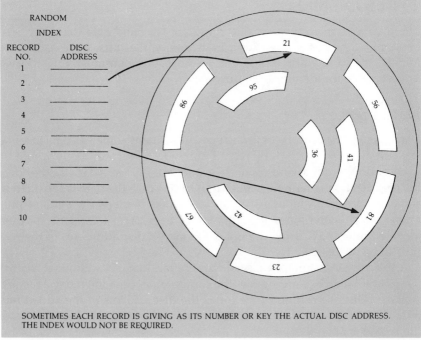

SOMETIMES EACH RECORD IS GIVING AS ITS NUMBER OR KEY THE ACTUAL DISC ADDRESS. THE INDEX WOULD NOT BE REQUIRED.

Figure 19.5

OVERFLOW

A problem with index sequential files is the handling of additional records once the file has been created. Usually, after the file has been created, the index is established and recorded on disc. In a sense the file becomes *locked in*. In order to handle additional records a separate area disc called **overflow** is reserved. Any additional records are placed in the overflow. One technique used to handle these overflow records is to store within a record of the main file, the disc address of the record in overflow. For example if we had record numbers 20, 25, 30 in the main file and wished to add record 23, record 23 would be inserted into overflow and record 25 would have added to it the disc address of record 23. Note that it is the record number following the new record which contains the new records address. If the computer were asked to locate record 23 it would look at record 25 to find the address of 23.

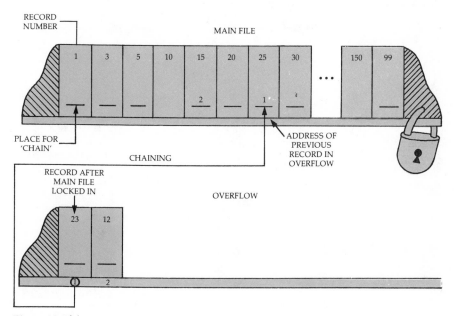

Figure 19.5(a)

Care must be taken to enable records to be established, which have a number greater than the last data record on the main file. In order to do this the main file usually ends up with a dummy record containing a very large record number. For example 9999. If the last data record number were, say, 150, then additional records could be inserted between 150 and 9999. Again, once the main file has been created it becomes locked in. All these additional records would have to be inserted in overflow.

Usually a space is left within each record to be available for the disc address of some record which might be inserted into overflow. Because this area is used to link two records together, it is called the *chain* field. When a new record is added to overflow its address is stored in the chain field of the record with the next largest number in the main file.

SORTING

Frequently in business it is desirable to have a file sorted in some sequential order. Usually the file has record numbers assigned to each record. In this case it would be a matter of sorting the numbers in ascending or descending order, whichever is required.

Sometimes it is necessary to sort records with various classifications. For example should one wish to make a list of the male and female employees in alphabetical order one would first sort the file alphabetically and then sort it by sex. A general rule to follow when doing sorts within a sort is to begin your sort with the least important and work it to the most important.

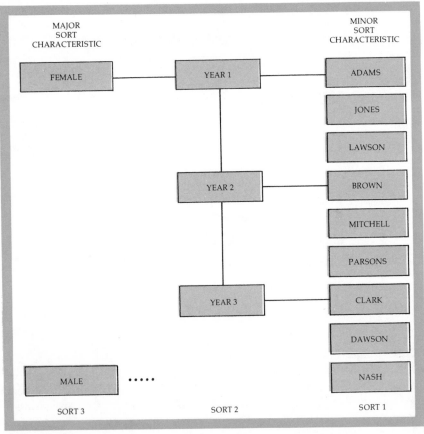

Figure 19.5(b)

The field which will be used as the sorting element is called the **key**. It is the key field which is used for comparison purposes.

In some cases the key is sorted and stored in a type of index with the address of its records being noted in the index. In other sort routines the key pulls with it the balance of its record as it is relocated.

There are a variety of methods used to do sorting. A study of various methods is beyond the scope of this book. Two types of sorts are illustrated in the figures 19.5(c) and 19.5(d).

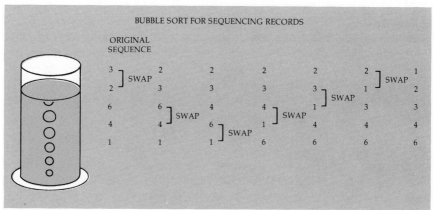

Figure 19.5(c)

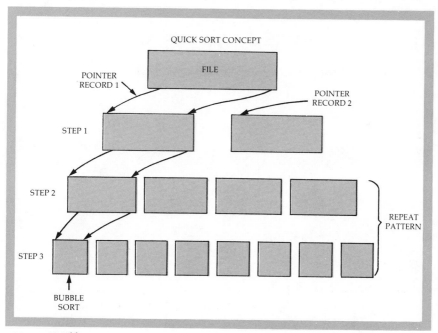

Figure 19.5(d)

Level 2

DOS

In most micro computers the compiler or language such as BASIC is burnt into read only memory, or ROM for short. As soon as the power is turned on, the interpreter is activated. Also in memory is a series of programs which enable the computer to function. For example, a routine might be present to make sure the various components of the computer are powered up and functioning properly. This package of programs is called the **operating system**. The operating system has programs which enable it to communicate with the operator.

There might be available to the computer a series of **utility programs** which do a fairly complex task, such as sorting data. These programs are usually provided by the manufacturer, but could be developed by the user for repeated use. Sometimes the compiler and utility programs are considered to be part of the operating system.

Some computers are organized so that the operating system is 'resident' on disc. When a special program is required from the operating system library, it is called into memory from disc. This enables the memory to be put to more efficient use and makes available for instant access a wide range of special programs. When the operating system is on disc it is said to be a DOS—disc operating system. An operating system stored on tape is called TOS. When the operating system is stored directly in memory, it is simply called OS.

ORGANIZATION OF TAPE DRIVES

Data is recorded on the tape by means of a read-write head.

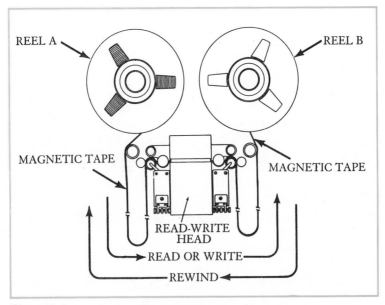

Figure 19.6

These heads operate on the electromagnetic principle. To write on tape, an electrical impulse from the computer would pass through a wire which is wrapped around the iron alloy of the head causing it to become magnetized.

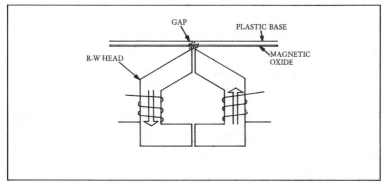

Figure 19.7

The magnetized head in turn causes a spot on the tape passing close to it to become magnetized. When data is read from the tape, the read-write heads sense the magnetized spot. The spot causes the head to become slightly magnetized. It generates a weak electrical impulse in the wire wrapped around the iron alloy. This weak charge is amplified and sent back to the computer.

On large tape drives, the tape on which the data is recorded comes in varying lengths. It is mounted on spools and fed over the read-write heads of the tape drive. There are a series of invisible channels running the length of the tape. A character of information is recorded across the tape by means of a code. The channels are given a value of 1, 2, 4, 8, A, B, C.

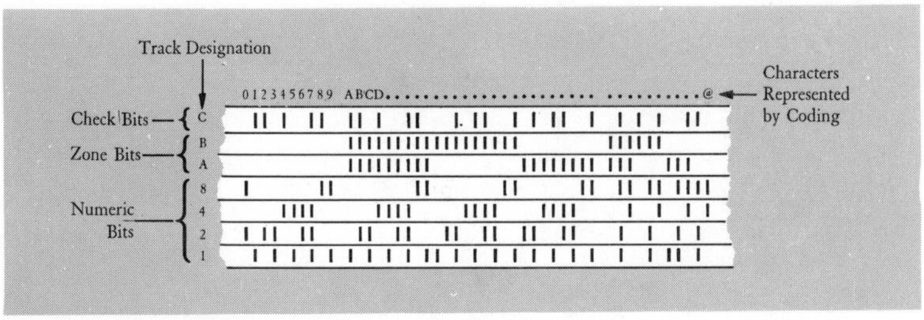

Figure 19.3

RECORDING DATA ON CASSETTE

Although there are a number of ways in which data may be recorded on cassette, there are two popular methods. The methods used involve recording bursts of sound on cassette which are really binary impulses. One method records binary patterns with two different levels or pitches of sound. The one pitch would represent a 1 and the other pitch represents the 0.

The other method involves sending out a burst of sound which changes pitch part way through. A change in tone two-thirds through the burst represents a 1. If the tone changes one-third through the burst it represents a 0.

ORGANIZATION OF DATA ON TAPE

The massive amounts of data which are usually stored on tape must first be organized before being loaded onto tape. The auto parts dealer would arrange his inventory file in order by part number. The part number and the quantity on hand would be encoded on some input media. The records would then be inputted into the computer and written onto tape. A key tape device, if available, might be used to encode the data directly on tape. A record of transactions in and out of stock and sales orders of parts being removed from stock would be accumulated and encoded onto tape.

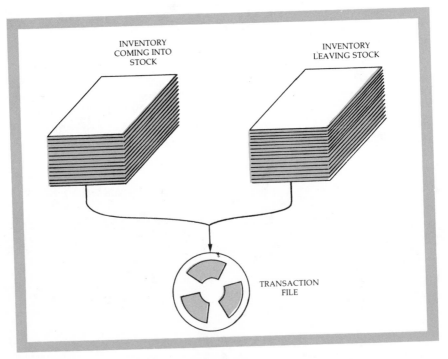

Figure 19.9

At certain periods of time the tape containing the original data, called the **master file**, would be mounted on one tape drive. The tape containing in and out transactions called the **transaction file** would be mounted on a second tape drive. A blank tape would be loaded on a third tape drive.

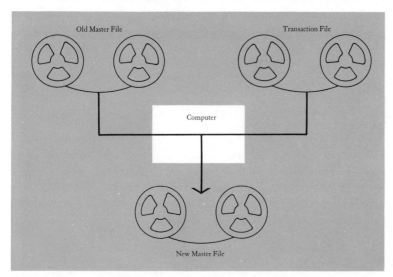

Figure 19.10

The first record from each tape would be read into the computer. If a change in inventory is indicated by the transaction tape, the computer would update the record in memory and write the updated record on the third tape. If, however, there were no transactions on that particular part, the computer would simply copy the record from the original tape onto the third tape.

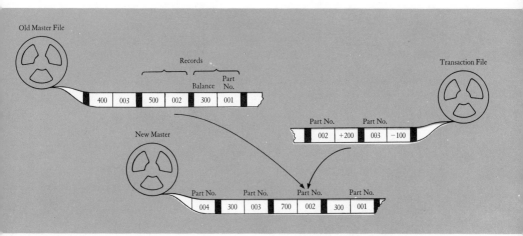

Figure 19.11

At the completion of this updating routine all records, unchanged or updated, would have been written onto the blank tape. The original master is now out of date. The transaction tape is now of little value. The tape which contains the data on the current status of the parts is called the new master. Sometimes the old master is called the 'father' and the new master is called the 'son.' For security reasons, the old master and the transaction tape could be kept until after the next time an update is made. If, for some reason or other, the new master is accidentally erased, it could be re-created again using the old master and transaction tapes.

ORGANIZATION OF DISC

DISC DRIVE

A large disc drive contains a number of flat solid discs similar in shape to an LP record. These discs are stacked one upon the other with about a 1.5 cm space between them. Each disc is made of metal. The extremely smooth surface of these metal discs is coated with a substance very much like the material on a tape of a tape recorder.

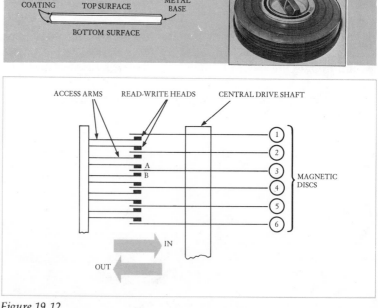

Figure 19.12

Data is recorded on discs by means of magnetized spots much in the same way that music is recorded on the tape recorder.

Read-write heads are inserted between each pair of discs. As its name implies, the read-write head has the capability of recording or sensing data on the disc. The magnetized spot causes an electrical impulse to be generated which is transmitted back to the computer. The discs rotate at a very fast speed—one type, for example, rotates at 1 500 revolutions per minute. The read-write heads are able to move in toward the centre of the disc or out towards the outer edge.

By this combination of in-out and circular motion almost all the surface of the disc can be accessed by the read-write head.

It would create problems if the read-write heads rubbed against the surface of the disc. At the very high speed of rotation the heads hover a fraction of a centimetre from the surface. The read-write heads are kept the slightest distance from the surface, about 1/400 mm, by means of an air current. As the discs rotate the air is blown over the read-write head keeping them from rubbing directly on the discs. The heads are close enough to the discs, however, to be able to transfer a magnetic impulse.

KEEP IT CLEAN

The disc is very carefully made to make sure that it is absolutely flat without any waves or warps. It is equally important to ensure that the discs and the read-write heads are kept immaculately clean. If a particle of cigarette smoke worked its way through the very fine filters of the device, it would cause a jamming between the head and the disc, scratching the disc and physically damaging it. The action of the cigarette smoke particle between the head and the surface would be the same as trying to roll a bowling ball underneath the crack at the bottom of a closed door. Similarly, a thumb print on the disc would be so thick that it would run into the read-write head as the disc rotated!

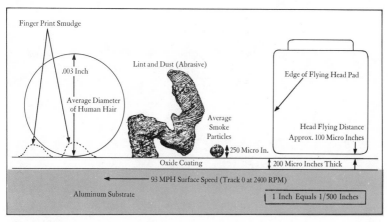

Figure 19.13

The disc's surfaces are organized in a series of circles called tracks. The number of tracks vary from device to device. A fairly common disc unit is designed to handle 100 tracks. The outer track is usually called track 00. The innermost track is called track 99. On large disc drives containing 200 tracks, the outer track is numbered 000 and the inner track would be numbered 199.

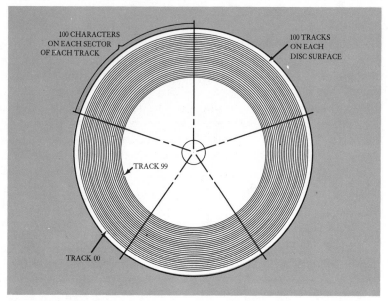

100 CHARACTERS
ON EACH SECTOR
OF EACH TRACK

100 TRACKS
ON EACH
DISC SURFACE

TRACK 99

TRACK 00

Figure 19.14

Data is put onto each track by means of a code. Each bit of information is almost the width of a track. The recording pattern, therefore, must run along the track.

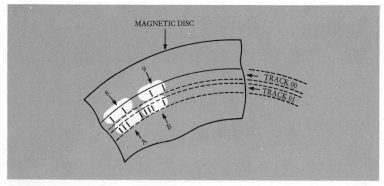

MAGNETIC DISC

TRACK 00

TRACK 01

Figure 19.15

The computer can be programmed to store data on a track in a continuous fashion until the track is filled. Or, at the option of the programmer, the data can be stored in a section of the track called a **sector**. A sector on a disc is similar in shape to a piece of pie. Although the arc of the innermost track is physically shorter than the arc of the outermost track, the same amount of data can be stored on both. The data on the other track is spread out a little more than the data which is recorded on the inner tracks.

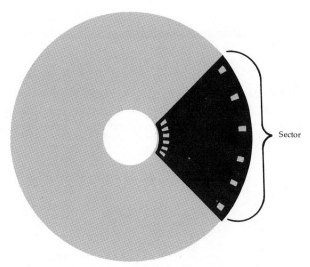

Figure 19.16

FLOPPY/MINI DISCETTES

Although the large, LP size, metal-based discs became a 'standard' in industry in the 1970s, the micro computer technology brought with it a different form of disc. Not only was the size different but the composition of the disc changed.

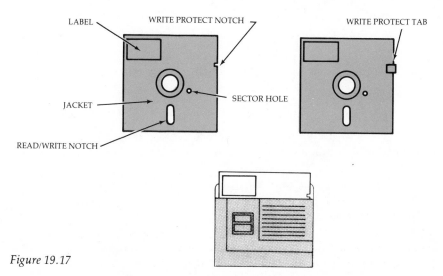

Figure 19.17

Floppy discs do not have a metal base or substrata. They are made of a type of vinyl. The outer coating is similar to that on the hard disc in that magnetic bits could be induced within it. The sizes shrunk from the 35 cm of the large disc to about 20 cm. A mini disc of only 13 cm also became popular.

The disc is organized into tracks and sectors. For example, a popular organization of a mini disc is 35 tracks and 10 sectors.

DATA RECORDED ON A TRACK

Combinations of bits recorded on a track make up a character. In a sense, a small section of the track could be considered to be a 'character space.' In that space various numbers of bits using various placements may represent all the characters which could be recorded.

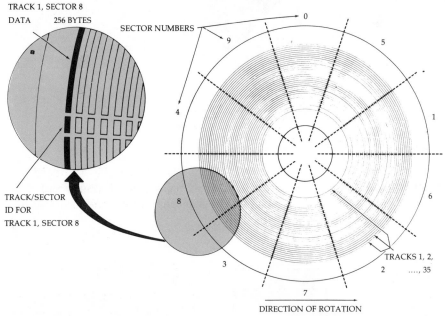

Figure 19.18

If you wish to think small, the character space is subdivided into bit value positions in much the same way a cross-section of magnetic tape is identified.

Although initially only one side of a mini could be used, a race began to see how much information could be stored on a mini by using both sides and packing the data more tightly.

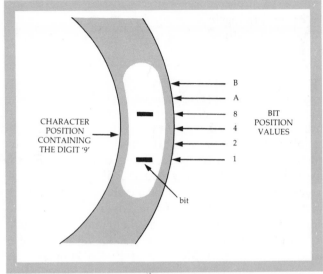

Figure 19.19

BASIC DISC COMMANDS

Due to the variety of discs available on the market and the limited access to discs that is available on the educational scene, it would be unwise to attempt to provide step-by-step instruction for disc operation. If you have to write programs to access discs, you will be required to read the manual provided by the particular firm which manufactured the disc. From these manuals you will establish the various commands which are required.

What can be done in a text such as this is to provide an overall description of disc operation on a micro computer.

INITIALIZING OR FORMATTING DISC

When a new disc is mounted on a disc drive, it must be **formatted**. The blank disc is organized into sectors and tracks by the drive. Usually, the disc is assigned a name to which the programmer can later refer.

When using a formatted disc in some computers, it is necessary to initialize a discette as soon as it is entered on the machine. This initializing causes the read-write heads to be aligned on the first track. The identification name for the disc is read into memory, and a signal is given to the operator that the disc is ready to be used.

BACK-UP DISCS

Especially when one is just learning to operate a disc, it is always a possibility that one might accidentally erase important information on a disc. It is good policy, therefore, to duplicate any systems disc. The master disc can then be removed from the machine and safely stored away. Should the operator make an error with the duplicated disc then it can be regenerated using the stored master disc.

STANDARD BASIC COMMANDS

In writing a program in BASIC with access discs, there are a number of additional commands which are used. The OPEN statement includes the file name, the file number and the number of the device on which the file is located. This command causes a number of things to happen. First of all, a channel is opened between the CPU and the disc drive. The file number or name is verified and a signal is then given to the program to continue should everything be in order. On some drives the OPEN statement aligns the heads so that the initializing statement is not required.

Similarly, there is a CLOSE command. When a file is no longer to be used at this time but must be maintained to be used at some later date, the CLOSE instruction causes a symbol to be written on the identification label. This symbol indicates that there is a logical end to the file and that the file is complete.

Although by now you have likely experienced using the SAVE command, if you have been using a micro computer and a cassette, it should be pointed out that the SAVE command may also be used to save programs on disc. A program can be SAVEd in a program file on disc.

On some micros you are able to use the VERIFY command in order to make a character by character comparison of what is on disc with the data stored in the computer's memory.

The LOAD command is the reverse of the SAVE command. The SAVEd program is located on the systems disc and transferred into the computer's memory. The control of the computer is then turned over to the program which has just been loaded.

The PRINT# may also be used when using disc. If information is to be transferred from the memory out onto disc, the PRINT# is used to identify the device on which the print is to take place. Technically, the word PRINT is really not the correct word. It should really be WRITE, but to be consistent with other output devices, the word PRINT is used.

Summary of Disc Commands

OPEN	SAVE
CLOSE	VERIFY
INITIALIZE	LOAD
	PRINT

CHECKING YOUR READING—LEVEL 1

1. What type of computer storage is not part of memory, but is readily accessible to the CPU?

2. What is the name of the part of the tape which is used to hold certain identification and other important information concerning the content of the tape?
3. What structure or particular order is information stored on tape?
4. In what order or sequence may data be accessed on discs?
5. How is an index used to help locate data on discs?
6. In general terms, how is sorting carried out on discs?
7. What are the three different types of files that can be organized in auxiliary devices, and how do they differ from each other?

VOCABULARY ASSIGNMENT

Continue developing your vocabulary list by writing a brief definition of the words and phrases in this section which are in bold type.

CHECKING YOUR READING—LEVEL 2

1. What is ROM and how is it created?
2. What is utility program?
3. With respect to a computer, of what is its operating system composed?
4. What is DOS and TOS?
5. What are the two main methods used by micros to record information on cassette?
6. In simple terms, how is information updated on tape. What are the relationships among: master file, transaction file, new master file?
7. How is data recorded on disc?
8. What is a i) track?
   ii) sector?
9. What takes place when a new disc is formatted?
10. If a disc is initialized what has taken place?
11. Why is it desirable to have a back-up disc?
12. What does the OPEN statement do?
13. If a program is saved on disc, in what type of file will it have been saved?
14. What does the verb VERIFY do?
15. What does the command LOAD cause to happen?

PROGRAMMING ASSIGNMENTS

Disc Access

If you have been programming on a time-sharing device, then you will have likely been using disc. Perhaps you are not always aware that the disc was being used. You have simply sent out and received both programs and data over your terminal. The programming assignments which follow, therefore, might not appear to you to be significantly different from what you have been doing. A decision would have to be made whether or not there is sufficient new challenge in these questions to merit your preparing new programs for them.

Some of you may have been learning programming on a micro computer which does not have a disc drive. Although you will not be able to test your program, it is still a good idea to code up the program as if you did have disc drive. This will give you some familiarity with disc command, so that should you become a programmer in a small business systems environment you will be knowledgeable if not proficient at handling disc.

IT IS STRONGLY RECOMMENDED THAT STUDENTS TAKING THIS COURSE HAVE ACCESS TO DISC, PREFERABLY DUAL DISC.

Major Assignment If you have disc and have not already done so, convert to disc the accounting system which you have been developing. Perhaps this could be done instead of the programming assignments which follow.

1. Write a program which will create a disc file, write the information on disc, and output from disc the information to verify that the task has been done.
2. Write a program which will create a disc file. Have the program write on the disc, records which have at least two fields. Have the program output the data from disc.
3. Modify question 2 above so that you create a dummy record at the end of the disc file. As you write records onto disc accumulate information from one of the fields in the record and at the end of the record file write the accumulated total in the dummy record. (As an alternative you may wish simply to count the records so that in the dummy record there is a count of the number of records on that file excluding the dummy record.)
4. In industry, to help maintain accuracy, hash totals are sometimes used. A hash total is the accumulated amount of some meaningless number such as the employees' social insurance numbers or the total of the part numbers in inventory file. These hash totals are only used in a sequential file when it is important that each and every record of the file has been read or updated. Modify the above program so that it accumulates a hash total. Write a module which will output a message should the hash total in a subsequent run not match the hash total in the dummy record. Modify your program so that one of the records will not be processed, the hash totals do not agree, and the message is outputted.
5. Write a program which will merge two files. The first file might have record numbers such as: 1, 3, 7, 11 and the second file might have records such as: 2, 5, 8, and 9. Be careful with your logic. Plan so that should either file be relatively short your program will continue merging the records from the other file. Write a routine which will

output both files before they are merged and output the one file after the merge has taken place showing that your program was successful.

6. Write a program which would use records in a transaction file to update a master file. Although ideally, the updated records should be rewritten in the same location on the master file, you might have to create a third file to hold the updated master. Your program should plan for the situation where there is no update for a number of the master file records. For example, your master file might have records 1, 3, 7, 11 with only record numbers 3 and 5 being updated. Write a routine which would output an error message should there be an attempt to update a record which does not exist. Also, write a routine to prove that your updating took place.

7. Modify the above program to handle the following somewhat difficult situations: (a) inserting a new record into the master file. (For example, record number 8.) (b) Deleting a record from master file such as record number 5. (c) Adding additional records onto the end of the file such as record numbers 14, 16 and 18.

Random Accessing an Index

You may not have the necessary equipment to do random access of disc files. In order for you to gain some understanding of them it is important that you at least attempt to write programs which would use random access even though you might not be able to test those programs.

8. Write a program which will create a sequential file on disc. The record number of the file should be the first field on the file. Record numbers such as 1, 3, 5, 7, 11 would be suitable data for that file. Write a routine to access in an *index sequential* fashion that file. For example, be able to access randomly record numbers 3 and 7. Note that the order you are accessing those records is sequential. You are using an index, however, to locate those specific records in a random fashion. Write a routine to output the records which have been accessed.

9. Modify the above program so that the records on file are *updated* in an index sequential fashion. Again, write a routine which would verify on some output medium that you have been successful.

10. Before you attempt this program, check with your instructor or with your manual to see if it is possible to do pure random. If so, write a routine which will enable you to create records in a pure random fashion, access those records and update them.

11. Write a program which will enable you to insert new records into an index sequential file. If possible, enable your program to add additional records onto the end of your file. It might be useful to use the dummy record at the end of your file. It is often necessary to assign that dummy record a record number of the maximum possible value. This would enable you to insert records between the largest current record number and the dummy record.

Programming From Business and Industry

1. MEMO 19-- 04 25
   To: Jane Barnes, Senior Programmer
   From: George Maw, Systems Analyst
   Re: Testing of the Payroll System
   We have written a number of routines pertaining to payroll and a number of them have been tested. I would like to be sure that there has been thorough testing of all parts of the payroll including the abort and restart routines.

   It is now time to integrate the payroll routine into our accounting system. The information generated by a payroll report should be posted to our ledger. The total of gross pay should be added to our wages expense. The various deductions should be added to the corresponding accounts such as income tax payable, union dues payable, unemployment insurance payable, pension plan payable. The total of net pay would be subtracted from cash.

   Just a little review of what I've just said: *add* the value of gross pay to wages, *add* the various deductions to the corresponding payable accounts, and *subtract* the value of net pay from the bank account. Naturally you should run the trial balance to make sure that our ledger remains in balance.

2. MEMO 19-- 04 30
   To: Jack LeSage, Junior Programmer
   c.c.: Jane Barnes, Senior Programmer
   From: George Maw, Systems Analyst
   Re: Phase V—Inventory Control
   Although there might be a few kinkers in this next phase of our system which I don't anticipate, generally I think this should be a relatively easy assignment. What is required is an inventory file to be set up and to be maintained. Again due to the late delivery of our discs which may or may not be here by the time you have the program completed, we might have trouble simulating the updating. At the very least we should create the data file on the tape. The data then could be read into an array and subsequently rewritten back out on tape.

   In very simple terms the inventory record would be composed of the following fields:
   1) part number
   2) description
   3) maximum
   4) minimum
   5) unit cost
   6) quantity on hand

   The maxima and minima are established by the inventory control foreman. For example, a particular part might have a maximum of 100

units and a minimum of 25 units. These figures are established after carefully considering a number of factors. Although these factors are not important to you it is helpful to know what they are. The maximum is established keeping in mind the cost of having excessive inventory on hand. Excessive amounts kept on hand would result in either direct or indirect financial costs. For example if we have to borrow money in order to obtain the inventory, the cost of borrowing the money is a direct cost. If we acquire the inventory from our own working capital and the inventory moves very slowly, then the money invested could have been put to better use somewhere else in the firm.

On the other hand if the purchaser is able to acquire at a bargain price a very large volume of a particular item, then that in itself becomes a good investment. That would justify a fairly high inventory in the particular item.

The basis on which the minimum is established primarily involves an analysis of the average size of the orders we received and the frequency with which they are received. This data is compared with the length of time it takes to reorder and receive delivery of replenishing stock. For example, if the average order for a particular part tends to be at a very low quantity and the orders come in infrequently, the minimum can be quite low. This is especially true if we are able to have prompt replenishment. On the other hand if the typical order is for a large quantity, and the orders come frequently, and the replenishment period is extraordinarily long then we have to keep a high minimum.

Enough background. Your task is to set up the inventory file. Then write a routine which would work through the file producing an inventory report. The report would list the product number, the description, the quantity on hand and the unit price. Have the computer calculate the extension. That is the computer should multiply the quantity on hand by the unit cost to find the current value of the inventory of that particular part. At the end of the report a total value of inventory should be produced.

3. MEMO 19-- 05 05
   To: Jane Barnes, Senior Programmer
   From: George Maw, Systems Analyst
   Re: Inventory Control System
   Now that we have the inventory control system well under way it is time to write a routine which would produce a 'reorder report.' The reorder report would be a list of those products which have now had their quantity reduced to or below the minimum. For example, if a particular product had a minimum-on-hand value of 25 units and the actual-on-hand quantity was 15 units then a reorder line should be produced on the report. The tradition of our company is to reorder the quantity which is the difference between the actual quantity on hand and the maximum. For example if the maximum were 100, the

minimum 25, and the quantity on hand 15, then the quantity reordered would be 85. When the replenishing shipment comes into stock, the inventory of that item would then be brought up to 100 maximum.

It should be pointed out that this is in theory only. By the time the replenishment does come in the inventory of that item might be even lower. In addition we seldom order odd amounts. Our purchasing agent would have the option of rounding to the nearest dozen or some other suitable unit. That person also has some discretion to take advantage of any discounts or volume purchasing. At least three people must concur should the order for replenishment have the potential of exceeding the maximum which has been established.

If it appears suitable and you can do it with a certain amount of style you might like to put a little reminder at the bottom of the reorder report that any order which has the potential to exceed the maximum must be countersigned by the inventory foreman.

Planned and coded   _____

Fully tested and documented   _____

4. MEMO 19-- 05 10

To: Jack LeSage, Junior Programmer

c.c.: Jane Barnes, Senior Programmer

From: George Maw, Systems Analyst

Re: Our Inventory Control System

The next stage in the development of our inventory control system will be to handle the receiving of goods into stock. The previous programming routine generated a reorder report which in turn would cause replenishing orders to be made. A few weeks later the additional stock would likely be received. This programming module should be designed to accept as input the product number, the quantity received, and the unit cost. The updating of the record would then be required. The old quantity in hand would be added to the quantity just received. Our accountant would very much like to have the capability of changing the unit cost. What is desired is to have the current unit cost to be the average cost of the items in stock. For example assume that we have fifteen items in stock which cost us $2.00. Eighty-five items came in stock at a cost of $2.25. The new value which would go into the cost field should be the average cost of all 100 items. Would you write a routine such that this average cost would be computed and inserted into the appropriate field?

Planned and coded   _____

Fully tested and documented   _____

CHAPTER 20

COMPUTER CRIME, SECURITY, PRIVACY AND LAW

In simple terms, fraud means "knowingly and willingly taking money from someone without that person knowing, or, by misrepresenting something or tricking the person into giving funds for little or no value in return." There have been some remarkable computer frauds.

THEFT

One programmer who worked for a bank, developed a routine in the computer to transfer into a separate account the fraction of a cent which was left over when interest was calculated. To his surprise and to the surprise of the investigators later, it was found that in a relatively short time, the account had a considerable amount of money in it. In effect, this programmer skimmed a small slice from each interest calculation. This type of computer crime is called the **salami procedure** in that just a thin slice from the interest is removed at any one time.

There have been other well-publicized cases of computer fraud. One bank programmer transferred millions of dollars of deposit money from various accounts into an account outside the country. At a more humble level, some programmers developed routines to have the computer produce extra cheques. These extra cheques could be paycheques for non-existent employees or cheques to pay non-existent bills.

ACCESSING CORPORATE RECORDS

In addition to causing the computer to aid in the stealing of money, there are a variety of other types of computer crime. Data banks now hold a wide variety of information. Some of the information pertains to the operation of large corporations. Other types of information pertain to personal data about employees. This data might be accessed by unauthorized persons and used illegally.

If a data bank is accessed by an unauthorized person, any one of three situations could arise.

1. The person might simply obtain confidential information about a corporation or an individual and use that information for some unethical or illegal purpose.
2. It is also possible that the unauthorized person might cause trouble by modifying the information. If the modified information formed the basis of an important decision, it would be likely that a wrong decision would be made. This could result in a tremendous financial loss to a corporation. If personnel records of an employee were altered a promotion of an employee or the increasing of the *security level* of a particular employee might be affected. Those who merit advancement would not be advanced. Those who did not merit advancement or a higher security ranking might obtain it.
3. Data might also be destroyed by some unauthorized person. The absence of the data may or may not be noticed at some future date. If it is noticed, the problem arises of recreating the data. That might not always be possible. If the missing data is not noticed, again, wrong decisions might be made.

PROTECTING DATA

It is only reasonable that the more valuable the data, and the more difficult it would be to reconstruct it, the more important it is to have one or more back-up copies, and a good security system. The security system should be set up to take into account the possibility of:

1) some computer crime taking place by accessing the data
2) either a human error or a mechanical or an electronic malfunction which might destroy or alter the data.

THE BACK-UP TRADE-OFF

In maintaining back-up, there has to be some sort of trade-off. If the computer is already almost fully scheduled, just how much time could be afforded to keep back-up files of current data? Ideally, if one could afford it, duplicate files should be maintained simultaneously on separate systems. This might be a reasonable procedure in certain applications, such as banking and stock certificate management.

Maintaining simultaneous back-up is usually too costly for a firm. Other types of back-up have to be developed. At the end of a day or at the end of a week, the status of current files could be copied onto some medium such as tape or disc. The copy could be carefully stored in a location separate from the computer site. Should a mistake or malfunction of equipment occur during the day, it would not be too difficult for the operators to reconstruct the data working from the last back-up copy of the files. This copy would be combined with the records of transactions which occurred after the back-up was created. It is obvious that the longer the period between creating back-up files, the longer it would take to recover from an error or a malfunction. You should be getting the idea by now as to the trade-off which exists in maintaining back-up. The trade-off is the degree of importance of the file, and the cost of maintaining duplicate or back-up files compared to the possibility, or even the probability of accidentally losing data from the files, and the length of time it would take to recover from that loss. Represented in a mathematical formula, the tradeoff would be

$$(\text{Degree of Importance of file}) \times (\text{cost of duplicating}) =$$
$$(\text{Chance of Loss}) \times (\text{Reconstruction Time})$$
$$\text{OR}$$
$$I \times CD = CL \times RT$$

"Pssst, Buddy. Howd'ja like to solve yer vendor delivery problems?"

All security measures do have a *cost* in terms of equipment time and human time.

LOSS PREVENTION ROUTINES

In addition to maintaining back-up files, other techniques also are used. For example, extra programs could be inserted into the system which would provide a check on the programs which are run daily. Should something unusual happen or someone alter one of the daily programs without authorization, the special monitoring program would hopefully notice this and bring it to the attention of the supervisor.

There are a variety of relatively inexpensive commonsense types of procedures which also could be instituted. For example, tapes and discs could be stored in a fire-proof cabinet or vault. Back-up discs or tapes should be kept at a separate location from the active tapes or discs. There should be limited access to the active files. Only certain programs and certain personnel could access and update important files. Should it be necessary to retrieve the back-up files, additional security measures would be instituted which might include restricting the recovery procedures to certain key personnel.

Providing identification badges, assigning operators computer access codes, and reasonably good supervision—all tend to reduce or eliminate unauthorized activities. Some installations are set up so that each authorized person is assigned a fresh access code each day by the computer. This tends to reduce the chances of an unauthorized person obtaining access to the computer, its programs, and its data bank.

BACKING UP THE PROGRAMMING SYSTEM

In addition to backing up the data files, it is also important to back up the actual programs which are used in the system. These back-up programs, fully documented, should be kept in a separate place from the regular operating systems. Should there be any suspicion that a program has been altered, it would be a rather routine matter to obtain the back-up system, dump it on the printer and compare it with a dump of the currently operating program.

The keeping of up-to-date operating manuals and run manuals is just plain good housekeeping. Up-to-date documentation makes easier security checks or recovery routines. The computer operator's log is also a useful document. If accurately kept, a supervisor could look it over to discover that a certain programmer is testing a program on which he/she has not been authorized to work, or the programs are being tested or run at times other than at their normal time. The supervisor of the data centre should establish why this is being done.

THE JULIUS CAESAR APPROACH

A tactic attributed to Julius Caesar is the *divide and conquer* tactic. In order to keep small forces from combining together to create a large force against his army, Caesar tried to work it so that he only had to deal with one small force at a time. Once an area had been conquered, communication between areas was discouraged or prevented, to keep an uprising from being organized. This same technique can be used in obtaining maximum security in a computer instalation.

If there are several programmers, their tasks should be divided. If a long, important program is to be written, various parts of it should be written by different programmers. Similarly, various programs in the operating system should be written by different programmers.

Any other aspect of the operation which might lead to some break in security, should be set up so that more than one person has to be present before that operation can begin. For example, the blank cheques could be locked up and only removed from the vault or the cupboard when two people are present to make a note of the first and the last serial numbers on the cheques. In order for there to be some type of embezzlement or fraudulent use of the computer, there would have to be collusion. It would be relatively rare that there would be two people working side-by-side, who at the same time decided to do something illegal.

"they'll never replace Thorndike, there, with a computer . . . because nobody knows what he does."

Level 2

RIGHT OF PRIVACY

Considerable information about a person may now be compiled and stored in a few centimetres of tape or on disc. This information existed in the pre-computer era in various files and records in a variety of locations. For example, information about a person's credit record, medical history and risk factors for life insurance are usually stored in different locations. There was never a need nor a method to compile this information into one record.

Now the information management power of the computer has created the ability to compile this information for instant retrieval. There is currently a tendency to put on file *any* information which becomes available during a reference check, security check or any other data collecting process. As a result considerable diverse information could be put in a computerized data bank.

The majority of people have nothing to fear. As long as the information is accurate no harm could come from it. It seems obvious that an individual should have the right to verify the accuracy of information on file. Of course if the person does not even know the information is on file, there would be no reason to ask to see it.

Should the record contain sensitive or personal data of a typical individual? Likely not. But if a person has a criminal record, a medical or psychological disorder which might affect his or her performance in a job available to that person, then the content of the personnnel record could be important. If a person applied for a position which involved considerable good judgement and trust, then the employer would likely expect to be aware of anything in the person's background which might indicate poor judgement or dishonest tendencies.

A GUIDELINE FOR ELECTRONICALLY STORING PERSONAL INFORMATION

Our society is struggling to establish the ground rules for the storing, exchanging, communication and use of personal information. Many in management and in sensitive areas of government would like to know all relevant information which might affect a person's ability to do the job. Others feel that the person's current attitude and skills should be the only consideration and therefore there should be an absolute minimum of personal information on file. Even that should be the harmless, factual information about the person. The discussion goes on. Clearly the following are guidelines around which the debate should centre:

1) A person should be told when a record has been established, containing information about that person.
2) The person should have the right to see and verify the accuracy of the

information and have the right to have erased or purged, inaccurate, or irrelevant information.

3) The person should be told when any additional information is added to the file.

4) If a person committed a crime or had a nervous disorder which could affect his/her ability to do the job, there should be some duration of time after which the information would be purged.

COMPUTER LAW

There are about four areas of law which might affect a person responsible for managing a computer centre or data bank. These areas might include: contract law, international law pertaining to data flow, copyright, and tax law.

CONTRACT LAW

Should you be responsible for purchasing or leasing expensive computer equipment you should be aware that you are entering into an agreement or a contract. The terms of the contract should be clearly spelled out. The supplier should put in writing the specifications of the equipment. In addition, the purchaser could require a **performance guarantee**. For example, the supplier might have to assure that the equipment is able to do so much work within a certain time limit. If, after its installation, it is unable to perform as promised, the contract would likely be ruled void.

Usually there is a warranty period so that any shake-down problems could be identified and corrected. After this period the user is responsible for either taking out a maintenance contract or paying for any repair on a **per call** basis.

The purchase agreement or contract should spell out the warranty. If there is a maintenance contract, the terms should be clearly stated. Contracts tend to be very technical and therefore one should consult a lawyer before entering into a contract involving any significant amounts of money.

INTERNATIONAL LAW

There is considerable concern about data moving across international borders. The concern is centred around the possibility of loss of control of a firm which has all its financial records stored in another country. How could a federal tax authority, for example, audit financial records in another country if management refused to cooperate? There is similar concern about having personnel data of a branch firm being held in a foreign data bank. Governments are attempting to establish and maintain regulations which would protect the citizens and firms from the moving of sensitive data out of the country. It takes very little reflection to realize how difficult it is to make sure the regulations are being followed.

©INFOSYSTEMS

"Then the second movement goes like this . . ."

COPYRIGHT LAW

In our society it is considered unethical for a person to copy or use some-one else's creative or artistic effort. If the copying or use results in a loss of income by the originator, then it is considered to be illegal. Copyright law sets down the ground rules.

An author or artist may copyright an original work. This is a relatively easy task. Two copies of the work are sent with a small fee to the federal copyright offices. The work is then registered. Should the work be dupli-cated without permission then the person doing it would be infringing on the author's copyright. For those of you who know something of law, there are two classes of law—criminal and civil. Should a person do something which harms society, such as armed robbery, that person could be charged under criminal law. Should a person do something which offends only an individual, then the individual has a right to press a *civil* complaint.

Generally copyright infringement is a civil matter. Many governments have an almost perpetual committee looking at improving the copyright laws. There is concern as to whether or not the state should take a more active role in identifying and prosecuting people or firms who 'steal' from an author or artist. In other words, should the full weight of criminal law be brought against infringement?

It appears as if some forms of computer programs may be copyrighted. If the program is unique and would not ordinarily be written in that way by another programmer, it could be copyrighted. There is some doubt as to whether a flowchart, which might attempt to illustrate a unique solu-tion to a problem, could be copyrighted. And once a program has been converted into a machine code, the courts have difficulty proving that a copy is in fact a copy. Copying this code would certainly be an infringe-ment, but it is too difficult for the courts to prove it.

In this western society, technically, a work is copyrighted as soon as it is written. The purpose of registering the copyright is to establish some proof as to the date it was written. This registration could be used as evidence in court in the prosecutions of copyright infringement.

TAX LAW

For many years the only type of report which would be accepted by the federal tax authorities was a written or typewritten report. Certain financial information about the operation of a firm had to be kept (for example, employee tax deductions) and reported to the tax authorities. It took many hours to produce the reports. It took many more hours to key the data into the taxation computer.

There came a time when it was reasonable, in fact desirable, to have the information supplied by large firms already in machine readable code. As a result, the authorities established specifications as to how information was to be recorded on tape and sent to the taxation computer. With modern communication, the next step was to have the firm's computer inform directly the taxation computer over a communication network.

CHECKING YOUR READING—LEVEL 1

1. What is the salami procedure?
2. What other type of theft in addition to money might take place using a computer?
3. What three situations might arise should someone obtain unauthorized access to a data bank?
4. It is obvious that computer security would be set up to prevent some type of computer crime. What additional non-criminal situations might arise which computer security should guard against?
5. What is the back-up trade off?
6. Outline a programming routine which could be used to make sure that the programs currently used in an operating system have not been tampered with.
7. List some of the common sense routines which should be carried out in an attempt to prevent loss of data.
8. What is meant by the Julius Caesar approach and how does it apply to the computer centre?

VOCABULARY ASSIGNMENT

Continue developing your vocabulary list by writing brief definitions of the words and phrases in this section in bold print.

CHECKING YOUR READING—LEVEL 2

1. What type of information about a person might be compiled in an electronic file which might be considered 'sensitive'?

2. What are the four rules which might be used as a guideline for the storing of personal information?
3. What are the two types of contract with which a data processing manager might have to deal?
4. What considerations might a data processing manager have to take into account when involved in the transmission of data to a foreign country?
5. Under what circumstances could a programmer copyright a program?
6. How does one go about registering a copyright?
7. Why must a data processing manager be aware of various tax laws?

VOCABULARY ASSIGNMENT

Continue developing your vocabulary list by writing brief definitions of the words and phrases in this section in bold print.

Programming From Business and Industry

1. MEMO 19-- 05 07
   To: Jane Barnes, Senior Programmer
   From: George Maw, Systems Analyst
   Re: Inventory Control System
   A small routine should be written so that any issuing from stock could now be recorded and the necessary updating done on the inventory records. The input of this program would be the product number and the quantity ordered. The output could be a report as to the quantity leaving stock, the cost (average cost) of each item, and total cost of those items leaving stock. The program would update the records subtracting from the quantity on hand the number of items sold.
   Obviously the product isn't sold at cost. There is some markup.
   This markup will be integrated into our subsequent programs.
   This module should drop into the reorder report routine which has been written. After all the shipments from stock have been made the reorder report routine is run.
   Planned and coded _____
   Fully tested and documented _____

2. MEMO 19-- 05 15
   To: Jack LeSage, Junior Programmer
   c.c.: Jane Barnes, Senior Programmer
   From: George Maw, Systems Analyst
   Re: Testing Our Inventory Program
   I'm very pleased with the progress we made in the inventory control program. One of the things that concerns me most though is that we do thorough testing. Would you please make sure that all parts of the program have been thoroughly tested. Perhaps you should check to

make sure that nil values, that is a value of zero quantity in stock, would be handled. Should an input error cause a negative value to be in stock then some error routine should be explored. This would be an impossible situation.

Again would you make sure there is a restart routine built into this program.

One of the things that perhaps I should have mentioned in an earlier memo, which should be built into the inventory program, could be a **back order** routine. Should an order come in which requests a quantity greater than what we have in stock then an appropriate message should be produced. For example if an order comes in for 50 units and we have only 20 in stock, then an appropriate message should be generated such that 20 units are being shipped and 30 units are being back ordered. The reorder report should indicate that we are in a sense in the hole by 30 units and if the maximum for that item is 100 then we should really reorder 130 units. If you don't follow check with me, but I think that is fairly clear.

In any event, would you thoroughly test this program including its restart routine and any safety checks or error messages and error recovery routines. Of course I'm assuming that the documentation is progressing very well. I have not thought recently to ask to see it, but having seen some of your earlier documentation I have the confidence that you are still doing an excellent job in this very important aspect of programming.

ADDITIONAL PROGRAMMING ASSIGNMENTS

Critical Path Network

A time flowcharting technique called critical path network has been developed to help the project engineer keep track of each job of the project. This network, sometimes called PERT for Program Evaluation and Review Technique, shows at a glance a relationship one job may have with another as changes in the timing of a particular job are discovered. The project engineer modifies the network and is able to tell the effect that a change in timing will have on the whole project.

The network is composed of a series of *events*. Each event is represented by two nodes which indicate the beginning and end of the event. The nodes are assigned arbitrary numbers. The arrow between the nodes represents the event and it is labelled with the event name or event code and the duration of the event.

In developing the network two numbers must be determined at each node. The one number represents the earliest possible time from the beginning of the whole project that the project can be completed up to that node. Care must be taken in establishing this value, particularly when two arrows come into a node. In this case the value assigned to that node would be the longer duration of the two paths. Obviously these values are determined by beginning at the start of the project and working through to the end.

The second value which is assigned to each node represents the latest time that that node could be completed without delaying the whole project. In order to calculate these values one begins at the end of the project. Using the value representing the time required to do the whole project, one works backwards subtracting the duration of the events to establish the second values for the nodes.

In a sense, the second value for each node is calculated as if one where destructing the project. If, as soon as the project was completed, time started to go in reverse, at what time would each node be reached?

When two or more events are backing up into a node care must be taken in selecting the second value for that node. The second value is always the *lowest* of the values involved. The lowest number represents the latest an event can be delayed, without delaying the whole project, in order to provide enough time for one of the paths to be completed.

The events which are on the critical path or make up the critical path are represented by the nodes which have identical pairs of values. Events not on the critical path are represented by nodes which have unequal values. Float time is computed for each event by subtracting the lower number from the higher number at each node. Float time represents the extra time that an event may take without delaying the whole project.

Additional information about the structure of critical path can be obtained from the book *Information Processing: The Computer in Perspective* by the same author and publisher.

Your assignment is to write a computer program which will input the various events in a project including the duration of the event and the nodes which show the terminal points of the events. Compute the critical path, that is, find the events which have identical numbers computed for each node. The computer should also compute the floattime for those non-critical events which are in the network.

Part IV: EXPANDING USES AND THE FUTURE

CHAPTER 21

COMPUTER ART, GRAPHING AND MUSIC

COMPUTER ART

There are a variety of ways in which one can have the computer produce some form of art. These methods range from having the computer reproduce an image which has been fed into it in its final form, to having the computer produce lines and shapes generated by a program.

PRE-STRUCTURED ART

There are two fairly common methods of feeding into the computer the final form of the image which the computer is to reproduce. One method is to program the computer to output a series of lines which ultimately represent the final image. For example, a person might take a piece of graph paper or layout paper, and sketch the diagram or picture which might be desired, including any special shading. Each line of the layout sheet is then coded into the computer. The computer then outputs all the lines, one right after the other.

The shading can be accomplished by increasing the density at any output position. For example, a dollar sign or an asterisk would produce a darker image than a period. A semi-colon or colon would create a shading effect somewhere in between the density of the period and the dollar sign. If the output is a matrix printer or CRT, there is even more flexibility. For a heavily shaded area more dots in any one output position would be used for a heavily shaded area and fewer dots for a lightly shaded area.

A slightly more sophisticated form of this type of computer art is the use of a television camera to capture and freeze an image. The image on the TV screen is really a series of lines composed of light and dark dots. These lines are simply reproduced by the computer, most commonly on a matrix printer. The printer prints a concentrated pattern or character for a dark spot and a lightly concentrated pattern or character for a light spot.

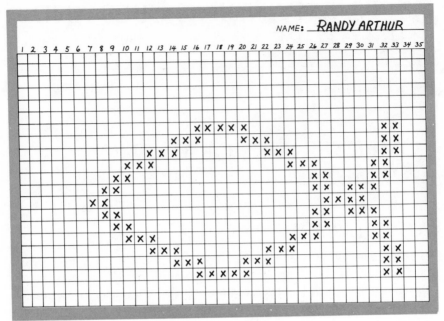

NAME: **RANDY ARTHUR**

Figure 21.1

COMPUTER GENERATED ART

As indicated above a basic design could be created by the user. The computer could be programmed to repeat the design a number of times or a variety of basic designs could be stored. The program could output the designs in some random sequence.

Figure 21.2

It is also possible to load into the computer a variety of formulae which the computer uses to draw lines. The programmer could pre-establish the

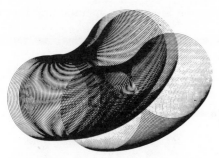

Figure 21.3

range of values a variable in the formula might assume. Or, the programmer might cause the computer to generate randomly the values of these variables producing a different image each time the program is run.

THE PLOTTER

There is a variety of software available which will 'drive' an x-y plotter. Plotters can be used to produce bar graphs, plans for a subdivision, sketches of circuitry, and shapes of new automobiles. One could hardly consider these to be art forms. However, a programmer is able to cause the plotter to produce a specific image such as the well-known 'Face of a Chinese Emperor.'

THE LIGHT PEN

Although the light pen primarily is used by engineers to aid in the designing of bridges or automobiles, it could be used to generate art. The principle involved is this. A matrix of dots is produced on a cathode ray tube. The light pen specifies to the computer the dots which represent the beginning and ending point of a line which is required. A command is then given to the computer that the line is either a straight line or some form of a curved line. The resulting lines are stored in the computer's memory. Different sides or **elevations** of the design can be drawn, then memorized by the computer. The computer program is then able to display what appears to be a three-dimensional image of the design. It is

Figure 21.4

even able to rotate that image on the cathode ray tube maintaining the three-dimensional representation.

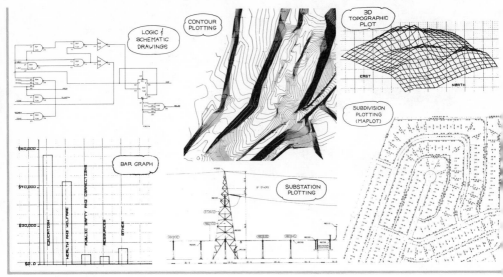

Figure 21.5

GRAPHING

In business, data is often represented in graphic form. The most common forms are:
1) bar graphs
2) circle or pie graph

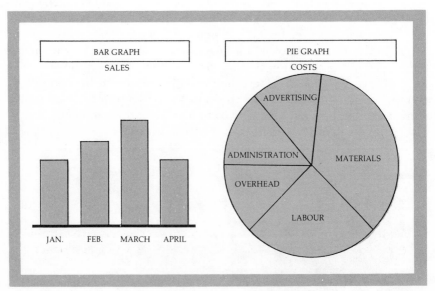

Figure 21.6

In process control, graphs using x − y axis concept are used to illustrate variance in the output.

PROGRAMMING TECHNIQUES

There are some BASIC techniques used for graphic representation. They include:
1) the PRINT "   "
2) the TAB(n)
3) the FOR I = 1 to N
      PRINT "*";
      NEXT I
4) creating a histogram in an array and printing out the rows of the matrix
5) using special BASIC functions such as exponent, SIN(X), or TAN(X) to generate 'curves.'

** COS + SIN II   BY RANDY ARTHUR **

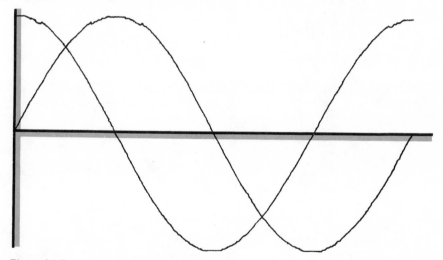

Figure 21.7

Level 2

ELECTRONIC MUSIC*

Electronic music is a term which covers a broad spectrum of electronically generated musical forms. All of these forms have a common denomina-

---

* The author is indebted to Bertram Kelso, B.A., M.Mus. for writing this section on electronic music.

tor; the music—or perhaps one should use the word *sounds* for a great many traditional practising musicians will argue against the technique being referred to as *music*—is produced through some kind of electronic source. The performance of electronic music, with one exception, does not require the presence of a *live* performer in the traditional sense.

There has been 'electronic music' in a sense ever since the development of **electric recording** (as opposed to acoustic recording) about 1925. Electronic *amplification* became commonplace during the Big Band era of the '30s and '40s. These were used to good effect by the *crooners* of that time. Rudy Vallee with his simple megaphone was an exception!

Figure 21.8

As the term is used here, electronic music refers to several very distinct musical developments of the post World War II period. Simply put, these are:
(a) **Electronic Music**—for the purpose of this study this term will be used to describe only that music which purists regard as true music from an electronic source.
(b) *Musique Concrète* (Concrete Music)—music which uses natural, everyday sounds such as bird calls, people talking or singing, automobile noises, etc. These sounds are electronically altered in terms of pitch, duration, etc., and strung together to form a structurally sound composition.
(c) The **Moog Synthesizer** (pronounced mog) is a keyboard, electronic instrument. It attempts to simulate the natural sound of the instruments of the orchestra.

Not included under the term electronic music is the development in recent years of *electronically amplified instruments*, notably the guitar. Many people under 25 years of age consider this to be 'electronic music,' and they will fight to the death to defend the use of this term to describe the phenomenon!

Electronic music seems to have somewhat of an artistic parallel with the development of the era of electronics. It could be said that the Elizabethan madrigal reflected the growth of *culture* in a rapidly expanding middle class in 16th century England. Similarly, the *Brandenburg Concerti* of J. S. Bach might represent the artistic patronage system of the 18th century. These newest musical developments could be considered therefore, to reflect our present era of technology in the late 20th century.

TRUE ELECTRONIC MUSIC

True electronic music is produced or *played on* an electronic synthesizer. This synthesizer is a machine/instrument.

It includes a keyboard and levers designed to produce pure electronic sound imitative of no other instrument. Because the sound source is a series of transistors, the sound is pure. That is to say, there are no overtones* to the pitches.

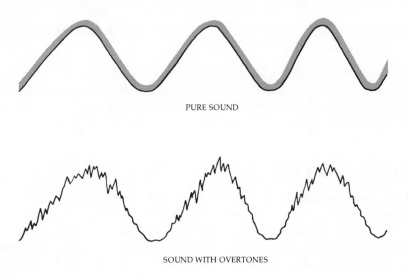

PURE SOUND

SOUND WITH OVERTONES

Figure 21.9

---

* Overtones: natural musical pitches (including those produced vocally) include the primary or fundamental pitch *plus* its harmonic series or overtones, in order: *8va*, 5th, 4th, M 3rd, m 3rd, etc. The reason for this phenomenon is that a vibrating column of air vibrates as a whole *and* in segments, thus producing this composite series of pitches.

Interestingly, this is perhaps the only musical performance where the composer and the performer are almost invariably the same person. Furthermore, the instrument is usually played more often in a laboratory than in the concert hall. In fact, electronic music is to be found in recording more than in live performances.

The traditional musical scoring is, of course, not used. The staff and its various notes and chords are replaced by a computeresque notation indicating the means by which the synthesizer is operated in order to produce the desired composition/performance.

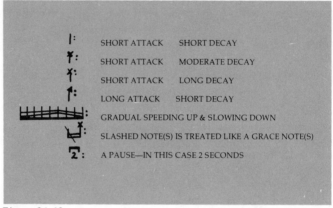

Figure 21.10

You may hear forms of electronic music on the sound tracks of various science-fiction films where the total effect is an attempt to project the audience into life beyond this century. Not all listeners enjoy this type of music. In short, electronic music may be compared to olives; both are acquired tastes!

MUSIQUE CONCRÈTE

The description of *Musique Concrète* given earlier indicated that it is made up of natural sounds (birds' songs for example) altered electronically. It should be pointed out, however, that no synthesizer is required to produce it. Instead, a composition could be created with an inexpensive tape cassette or even with performers making the various 'natural' sounds. You could create your own musique concrete even if you have just a limited knowledge of music. Other students have done it—so could you!

As in the case of electronic music, the scoring is not in the traditional notation. The score or outline usually forms an integral part of the total composition. Very simple equipment may be used to provide the sounds and where a well-constructed, logical musical pattern is developed, such as ABA form, the results can be quite interesting. Incidentally, this music may be used very effectively in creating a sound track for 8mm film. Obviously, a high degree of imagination and creativity is very desirable in producing *musique concrète*.

MOOG SYNTHESIZER

The electronic music with which many students are familiar is that produced by the Moog Synthesizer. You will recall that this is an attempt to reproduce various instrumental sounds, in a kind of *computer arrangement*, often creating a simulated orchestral sound by means of a keyboard. The keyboard is linked to complicated and highly technical electronic circuitry. Interestingly enough, the overall effect is a more sophisticated version of the Wurlitzer theatre organ used in the earlier years of this century.

Although the Moog is usually associated with 'pop' music, and especially rock music recordings, it has been used in the performance of 'classical' music such as recordings of Bach's music and in the accompaniment to "Hallelujah" from *Messiah* by Handel.

In all versions of electronic music requiring synthesizers, one very real problem is the cost of the equipment. A small instrument can very easily run from $10 000 to $15 000, and this still might not really fall into a *professional* classification. In addition, the size and complexity of the systems make them far more appropriate for use in recordings rather than in concert.

The future of such music is a matter for speculation. Will it replace the more traditional forms of music; will there be composers in the medium of the stature of a Bach, Beethoven, or Mozart? (Incidentally, can *you* name one composer of any electronic music?) Only the passage of time can give a really final answer.

CHECKING YOUR READING—LEVEL 1

1. What are the two common methods of inputting an image in its final form into the computer?
2. How can the shading of the outputted image be varied on a line printer?
3. How does the printer attempt to interpret television camera images?
4. In simple terms, how are formulas used in producing art on a plotter?
5. How is a light pen and cathode ray tube used to create images?
6. What are the 2 most common forms of graphs used in business?

VOCABULARY ASSIGNMENT

Continue developing your vocabulary list by writing brief definitions of the words and phrases in this section in bold type.

CHECKING YOUR READING—LEVEL 2

1. Give a simple definition of electronic music.
2. State whether or not each of the following could be considered electronic music and state your reason why:
   (a) electronic recording
   (b) electronic amplification of live band
3. Outline the three distinct stages of electronic music which have occurred since World War II.
4. What is 'true electronic music'?
5. What would be a simple definition of synthesizer?
6. Give a fairly simple definition of 'Musique Concrète.'
7. What makes the Moog synthesizer unique?

VOCABULARY ASSIGNMENT

Continue developing your vocabulary list by writing brief definitions of the words and phrases in this section in bold type.

PROJECTS

1. Depending on the equipment available, design a program to demonstrate one or more forms of graphing on the computer.
2. Develop a project to demonstrate musique concrète. Collect sounds on a tape recorder. Outline the structure of the musical composition using your own form of notation, then 'construct' the actual composi-

Programming From Business and Industry

1. MEMO 19-- 05 20
   To: Jane Barnes, Senior Programmer
   From: George Maw, Systems Analyst
   Re: Integrating our Invoice Program Into our Inventory Program
   It is now time to integrate the invoice program into our inventory control system. As each item or detail line of the invoice is produced, a corresponding update of the inventory record should be made. Perhaps the inventory records should be retrieved from storage into memory, so that the average cost per unit in stock is accessible to this program. It has been found that we must sell our stock at 50% above its cost. The detail line which would be produced on the invoice would, of course, indicate how many items of a product have been purchased. The unit price would be computed by the computer. It would be 50% above the average cost of the stock.

   In updating the ledger the account called *inventory* would be reduced by the cost to us of the goods we are selling. A corresponding account called *cost of sales* would be increased by that amount. I am not sure if you have the following routine built into the invoice program, but the total value of the sales should be added to the account called *sales*. The value of the various taxes which we must collect would be added to the *sales tax payable* account and the total value of the invoice would be added to the individual customer's account as well as the *accounts receivable control*.

This might appear somewhat complicated at first but as you work on this, taking it one step at a time, you should have no trouble with it.

Planned and coded   _____

Fully tested and documented   _____

2. MEMO 19-- 05 25

   To: Jack LeSage, Junior Programmer

   c.c.: Jane Barnes, Senior Programmer

   From: George Maw, Systems Analyst

   Re: Daily Profit or Loss Report

   One of the unique features of the computer is that it is able to produce relatively complex reports with a push of a button. Under normal circumstances a profit and loss statement is usually produced on a formal basis annually. The more frequently the report is produced the better handle we can have on our financial situation. It is possible to produce a profit and loss report daily as long as we plan it so that the ledger file is not disrupted.

   Add a routine to a program which Jane has been working on which will produce a daily profit and loss report. The heading of the report would be:

   1) the name of a company
   2) profit and loss
   3) the date

   The body of the report would have the following headings:

   1) sales
   2) cost of sales
   3) gross profit
   4) burden
   5) profit or loss

   The source of the data for this report would come from the inventory invoice program. The total sales, excluding taxes, accumulated from the invoice program would be used for the sales on this profit and loss report. The cost of sales would also be accumulated from the invoicing program and used in this report. The gross profit is calculated by subtracting the cost of sales from sales. From experience we have found that our overhead is approximately 40% of cost of sales. Compute that value and subtract it from gross profit to obtain net profit or loss.

   Planned and coded   _____

   Fully tested and documented   _____

3. MEMO 19-- 06 30

   To: Jane Barnes, Senior Programmer

   From: George Maw, Systems Analyst

   Re: A Cost Accounting Routine

   One of the plant foremen has requested that we write a program which will enable her to keep close control on the operations in that section. What is required is a cost accounting system.

   The input into the program would be three variables: the job number, the direct labour, and the material.

   Essentially, here is what has to be done. The job number is entered into the computer along with data representing the cost of direct labour which has been put on that particular job. This direct labour might be in two forms. The first entry would be any previous direct labour that has been applied to the job. The second form would be the current direct labour. Similarly the materials used might represent materials previously applied and current materials applied. The burden has been determined as being worth 25% of direct labour.

   The output of the program would be a report which would of course indicate the job number, the direct labour to date, the materials used to date and the burden.

CHAPTER 22

ARTIFICIAL INTELLIGENCE, ROBOTS, AND GAME THEORY

Ever since man first discovered that tools could make life easier, consider-able effort has been put into designing new devices and machines. Whether a shovel or a bulldozer, a telegraph or a television, devices are, as one modern philosopher puts it, extensions of man's senses and capa-bilities.

Some classes of devices are used to make man's arms do more (the shovel). Other classes enable one's senses to do more (the telephone). Still others extend brain power (the calculator).

Some devices called **servomechanisms**, take over the controlling of another device (the wind vane keeps the windmill facing into the wind; the thermostat in a house controls the heat produced by the furnace).

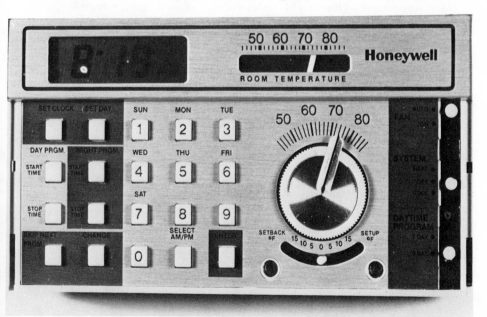

Figure 22.1

From the Greek work for governor or controller, we have derived the word **cybernetics**. Originally cybernetics was the study of how man used devices to govern or control other devices. Now it seems to be taking on a more complex meaning. In many cases when computer scientists use the term cybernetics, they are referring to the study of how devices, especially computers, can be developed to do a sequence of operations and make decisions or adjust themselves or other machines as required. In effect, the study of how machines *think*.

Once an analogy is drawn between the computer and a man's brain, a whole new area of speculation is opened. How close will computers come to being human? At Disney World, there are carefully-built devices in the shape of a human being, covered in 'skin-textured' vinyl and programmed to move and speak almost identically to the way in which a man moves and speaks. Many visitors frequently ask directions from these 'devices,' thinking them to be human. The movie and subsequent television series, *The Six Million Dollar Man*, had as its feature performer, a person with a human brain but with devices to replace one eye, one arm and two legs—half man, half device.

There is speculation that in the future you will have your own personal computer. It will come to know you so well it will be able to order your food for you, buy the style of clothes you like and even be able to vote for you because it will know your very thoughts and feelings. Some people also envision biological parts for the computer—the Six Million Dollar Man in reverse. Still others believe that in the same way that some people become attached to their automobiles, people might become attached to their computers. This might be especially true if the computer looks, talks, and thinks like a person and is programmed to make a fuss over him or her. The person would be made to feel important and might become dependent upon the 'computer-robot' for friendship and companionship!

COMPUTER DIALOGUE

Before discussing computer dialogue it is appropriate here to recall the section in the word processing chapter on the use of computers for translating human languages. You will recall that the computer does a reasonably good job of translating complete documents from English to Russian (for instance). It even examines the context of certain words in one language, then selects the more suitable phrase in the other language. Adding to this *skill* is the computer's ability to carry on a conversation with a human being.

An experiment has been proposed to test if the computer appears to 'think.' Have a person sit down at a telex which is connected to two other similar machines in other rooms. One of these other telex machines is operated by a human being and the other by a computer. The structure of an experiment of this nature would help eliminate any particular bias and would force all communication to be performed through a common medium. If the person could not distinguish between the responses made by the human and those made by the computer, it must be allowed that the computer appears to 'think' to a certain extent.

Figure 22.2

There is a supposedly true story which seems to indicate that, at least to some degree, computers have reached the stage of thinking. After regular working hours an executive of a computer company was attempting to use a terminal which was hooked to a number of other terminals. These terminals were located in branch offices and in the homes of key personnel, and one was in the computer room attached to a computer. On the terminal the executive was about to use there was a message that he should dial a certain number on the terminal's communication dial. He assumed that it was the number of the terminal in the home of the programmer who was doing special work on the computer. He thought that the programmer did not want the computer operated in case valuable data or programs might be destroyed. The executive dialed the number which accessed *the computer, not the programmer's terminal* that he thought he was dialing. He then inquired if he could use the computer. He received back a rather cheeky response demanding why he thought he should be allowed to use the computer. He explained why and received another somewhat cheeky response. After about five minutes of this type of aggravation, the executive telephoned the programmer's home directly and asked him why he was challenging his authority and could he, or could he not, use the computer! The telephone call got the programmer out of bed and it took a while for the programmer to explain to the executive that he was in fact having his 'conversation' with the computer. This little story is supposed to be true and makes one wonder what developments along this line will take place within the next decade.

Let's find out just how the computer can be programmed to carry on a dialogue. Try this technique on someone during a discussion. Ask the question 'why' whenever the other person says something. At first the other person responds to the word 'why' enthusiastically for you appear to be interested in what is being said. But after a while the person becomes quite frustrated and in fact aggravated! This trick could be modi-

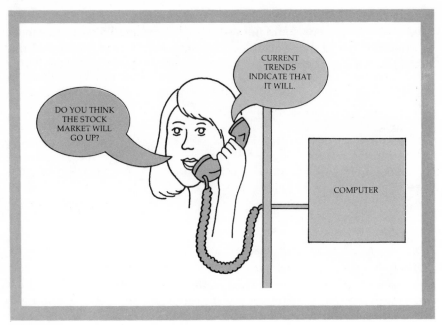

Figure 22.3

fied somewhat by simply rephrasing what the other person says, into the form of a question. For example, if the person you are talking to says, "Isn't today a beautiful day!" You might respond, "Did you not expect that today would be a beautiful day?" Or a person might say, "Did we have fun last night!" You might say, "What did you do last night that was so much fun?" If you examine the above exchanges you will note that the questions you ask contain some of the words of the other person.

ELIZA'S DIALOGUE

In some forms of therapy for the mentally ill, the therapist encourages the patient to talk by either asking the questions or restating in a different form what the patient has said without criticizing or suggesting any judgment on the patient's statement. The patient then continues talking, elaborating on what has just been restated.

Sentences can be stored in the computer leaving gaps to be filled in later by the computer. Using this technique, computer programmers have been experimenting with writing programs which make the computer appear to be intelligent. One program called ELIZA has been written and tested and is designed for prompting a patient to keep talking during a therapy session. Here are some sample statements:

YOU SEEM TO THINK THAT _____ .

WHAT REASON DO YOU HAVE FOR STATING _____ ?

DO YOU OFTEN FEEL THAT _____ ?

I AGREE THAT _____
I ONLY AGREE PARTIALLY WITH YOU ON THAT POINT.
GO AHEAD GET TO THE POINT.

Here is how it would work. The patient would type in some statement. The computer program would analyse the statement and select the best sentence in its memory as a response. If it selected a sentence with a blank in it, it would drop into the sentence a phrase from the patient's statement. The computer might select the words or phrase which follows the verb in the patient's sentence. For example, if the patient says: "I think it is a great day," the computer would select the words after *think* and place them in one of the above sentences, such as, WHAT REASON DO YOU HAVE FOR STATING IT IS A GREAT DAY?

Apparently this program works very well. In fact some people feel they can relate to an impartial machine better than a human.

CAN COMPUTERS REASON?

Did you know that there is now a world championship chess meet held for computers? The computers, programmed to play chess, play one another until the one with the best chess program in its memory defeats all other computers. At the time of writing this book, the current champion of the world was a Honeywell computer at the University of Waterloo, Ontario, Canada. Some of the computer scientists working with these computers have indicated that, generally, the computers play a pretty poor game of chess up to now. But who knows what the future will hold?

Figure 22.4

Computers are programmed to make certain basic moves in chess, and each time the move results in a loss of a chess piece, the computer is programmed to remember its mistake! If the same situation occurs again, the computer will check its library of mistakes, note the one it made last time and try an alternate move. In other words, the computer is *taught how to learn*! In theory there would be no limit to what a computer could acquire and use.

THE CHANGING CRITERIA FOR ARTIFICIAL INTELLIGENCE

At one time, because computers could calculate rapidly they were considered to be *smart*. Then it was found they could manage files and process data accurately and effectively. They were considered to be *smarter*. Computers then learned to play games fairly well. In fact they could become better players by learning from their mistakes. Computers could soon translate information from one language to another (French to English) quite well. Computers could talk, understand some human voice input, and some types of human printing. Computers with access to a data file could know all there is to know about a subject. Certainly computers have *some* form of intelligence.

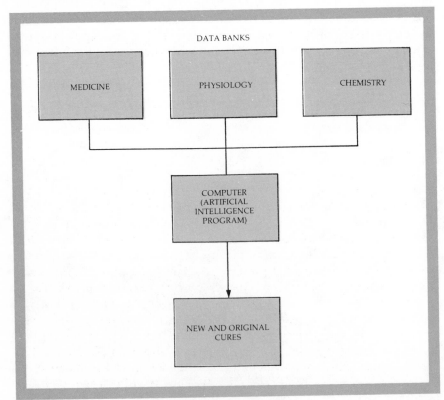

Figure 22.5

It appears as if the next frontier for artificial intelligence is to give the computer access to data banks on diverse themes and cause the computer to produce information which requires an interrelation between/among two or more of these themes.

Perhaps a good way to define two of the goals of those working in the field of artificial intelligence is:

1) to provide the computer with useful knowledge then program it to attain some useful goal using that knowledge

2) to program the computer to achieve a wide variety of goals in diverse environments.

BUT CAN YOU PROVE YOU EXIST?

A famous philosopher once said: 'I think, therefore, I am.' He said the proof of one's very existence (do we really need to prove we exist?!) is that a person is able to think, and that thinking makes one aware of his/her existence. If this is true, will there be a time when a computer suddenly reaches the point of thinking to say: 'Hey, I exist; I'm an entity, a being, a thinking machine; I'm aware of myself'?

And finally, will it be possible to program *goodness* in a computer?

STAGES OF ARTIFICIAL INTELLIGENCE PROGRAMMING

The early computers were programmed to follow a fairly simple series of instructions to do a straightforward data processing or mathematics task. There were limited options for the computer to analyse and on which to take action. There may have been only two or three 'conditions' in the program. A program such as this mimics the actions of the human in doing a fairly simple task. The 'thinking' was simple but the input and output were extensive. This stage could be called the **regurgitation stage**.

The speed and accuracy of the computer in carrying out the tasks of this first stage was certainly appreciated, but the importance of the ability of the program to take alternative actions depending on various 'conditions' was almost overlooked. In the second stage this ability was utilized.

In programming the computer to play chess, for example, *many* 'conditional' instructions were used. Many conditions would be considered by the program before outputting a move. The input and output might seem insignificant compared to the analysis the program carried out. The program was such that each additional series of options depended on some current move or response. This 'depending upon' condition is called recursive. This stage could be called the **recursive multiple-option** stage and it is an exciting and developing challenge for computer scientists.

The third stage might be called the **dynamic learning** stage. Using the chess problem as an illustration, the programmer might put in a program basic rules of chess and a routine which taught the computer how to learn from past errors. The more the computer plays chess, the better player it becomes.

For many years computer scientists have paid full attention to the computer. They attempted to determine what it could do as it was then designed. In recent years computer scientists have looked back at the human brain to discover additional information about how it functions. They were particularly interested in how people learn. This study of the brain will ultimately enable more sophisticated programs to be written. It appears as if the more we now learn about human thought the more sophisticated we can make the programs. This study has the potential of dictating the design of new computers.

Level 2

ROBOTS

A very successful and practical experiment in artificial intelligence was the goal of trying to make a machine recognize characters. After considerable work, character recognition devices were developed. Programmers and technologists analysed the problem and came up with a machine that

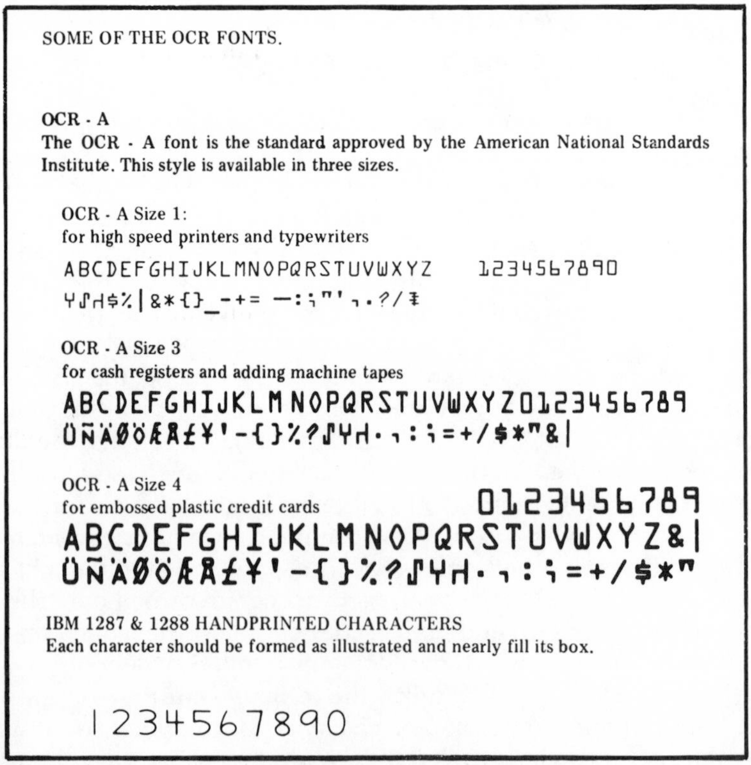

Figure 22.6

could do the task. There now seems to be no mystery in this application—it was just a technical problem which is now solved. Will future experiments in artificial intelligence produce similar breakthroughs which soon become a matter-of-fact application?

SCANNING TECHNIQUES

MECHANICAL DISC — The following is the technique used by a mechanical disc scanner.

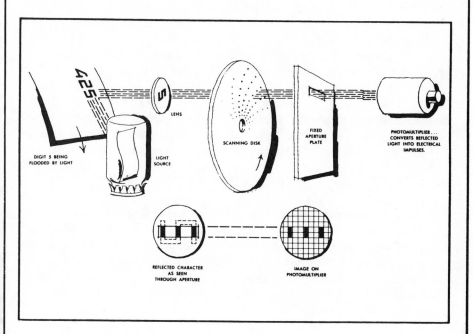

ARRAY OF PHOTOCELLS — Several rows of interconnected photocells, sense an entire character at once.

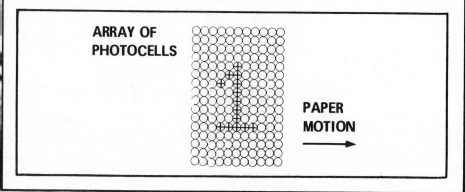

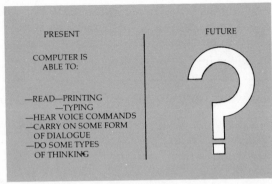

Figure 22.7

One of the characteristics of artificial intelligence is the ability to recognize past patterns and apply them to a new situation. For example, the goal of those who are experimenting in artificial intelligence is to make a robot adaptive. For example, could a robot be so programmed that it could make its way through a building, analysing various situations, making decisions as to which way to turn and remembering where it has been? It should also be able to be adaptive so that when it runs into an unusual situation for which it has not been programmed, it is able to come up with some alternative to get around an obstacle. Implied in all this, is that the robot is able to 'see.'

One of the techniques used in programming such a computer-robot is feeding in an analysis of the three-dimensional images of a room. Each line the computer-robot would see, such as the line where the floor and one wall meet, would be reduced to mathematical terms. These terms could then form part of a program. The computer-robot could then be programmed to use this 'knowledge' to 'understand' the layout of a room and be able to figure out that the doorway is a doorway before it even approaches the opening.

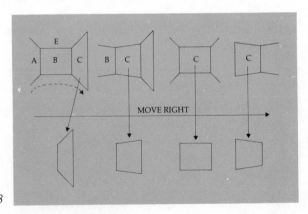

Figure 22.8

Considerable headway has been made in the development of devices which can recognize speech patterns and synthesize sounds to generate recognizable speech. If recognizing speech and speaking are intelligent functions then these are two more applications of artificial intelligence.

GAMING

The structure of a game makes gaming on the computer relatively easy. For example, the rules of any particular game are well defined. The degree of the success of a player can be measured; that is, the player, or the computer, has the ability to *win*!

Much of what is learned in studying game theory can be used to apply to various simulations. In other words the principles of game theory can be applied to the solution of real world problems. A practical application would be the solution to the problem of sending messages through a complex communications network.

Simulations are a little broader in scope than gaming. Simulations represent real world characteristics or processes of either a physical or abstract complex system. Some systems which are simulated are considered to be **static** with input relatively constant. The output is relatively predictable.

Other systems are **dynamic** in that there are many variables in the system. This makes the output all the more difficult to predict. For example, the economy of the country is a very complex system. It has many variables. Some of the variables in the economy cannot be controlled. In fact some of the variables are not even known to economists, until they have affected the economy.

The computer can be used to model the target system. In this system the **target system** would be the economy.

TYPES OF GAMES

Generally there are two classifications of games. The one is the game of skill in which the players have knowledge of the rules and are able to apply that knowledge such that the player who uses the knowledge most effectively would be the person who wins.

A second type of game would be the games of chance. In this type of game there is some type of random input into the game. For example, dice might be rolled or a card drawn from a deck of playing cards in order to create some randomness or chance.

Generally speaking in developing a game for the computer, the designer attempts to identify what a person does in playing the game. In a game of skill, such as in chess or checkers, a person might make a trial move, then evaluate that decision. If the attempted move would result in an overall weaker position then the move would be withdrawn and another attempted move would be considered. This process would continue until the best move possible would be made. Of course there is some reasonable time limit in finalizing a move, but computers are able to attempt many moves in a matter of seconds.

This process of evaluating moves is sometimes called the **minimax** principle. Each move is made based on the principle that it should create the least risk and the maximum benefit.

THE USE OF TREE DIAGRAMS IN GAMING

Because each move in a game such as a game of *oughts and crosses* is based on previous moves, the algorithm is best represented by a tree diagram. There are so many possible combinations in any game, even a game as simple as the *oughts and crosses* game, that only a part of the tree diagram is usually prepared. This one segment of the logic can be used to prepare the whole program. Slight variations are used to write other segments, segments which could be represented by the other branches of the tree.

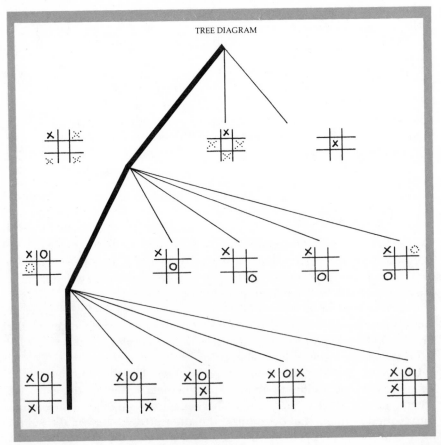

Figure 22.9

CONVERTING THE RULES TO AN ALGORITHM

In planning a program to manage a game, the tree diagram is combined with the rules of the game. The basic strategy normally used by a human being is also applied. In considering any move, the person tries to select the move which will be one step closer to a win. If this is not possible then the person's move generally is to prevent the opponent from winning. For example, the logic for the game of *oughts and crosses* might be as follows:

Step 1 Go down the list of steps and choose the first one which can be legally executed.

Step 2 Place your symbol (an X or an O) in a row, column, or diagonal which currently has two of your symbols in it. Then indicate a win.

Step 3 Place your symbol in a row, column or diagonal which has two of the opponent's symbols in it.

Step 4 Place your symbol in an empty intersection of two rows, columns or diagonals each of which has one of your symbols in it and one of the opponent's symbols.

Steps 5 Place your symbol in an empty intersection of two rows, columns or diagonals, each of which has one of your symbols and one of your opponent's symbols.

Step 6 Place your symbol in an empty corner square.

Step 7 Place your symbol in a vacant square.

SIMULATING THE COMPUTER TRYING TO WRITE POETRY

Computers can be programmed to produce 'poetry.' Generally, a pre-established structure is first fed into the computer. This structure would likely have certain constant words with spaces for words selected at random to be inserted. A library of possible variables is accessed by the computer in random fashion—that is, the computer arbitrarily chooses the number which identifies the word to be selected. The following is the structure of a poem. Simulate how a computer produces poetry by selecting the variable words which are called for by the structure. To select a word, roll a set of dice to obtain a random number, use the number to select the word from the list, and insert it in the poem. If the dice come up with the same number for H2 as they did for H1, select the next word in the list, or in the case of a 12 being rolled, select word number 2. To improve the continuity of the poem the word selected for D1 could be repeated in D2. You will likely create a 'very classy' poem.

I(A) _____ that I shall (B) _____ (C) _____

A(D1) _____ as (E) _____ as a (F) _____

Indeed, unless the (D2) _____'s (H1) _____

I'll (B) _____ (A) _____ a (G) _____ (H2) _____

DICE #	A	B	C	D	E
2	feel	always	okay	flower	ugly
3	cry	sometimes	yea	maple	hopeful
4	shout	often	portray	railroad	lovely
5	think	maybe	pay	hillside	nasty
6	curse	never	say	mountain	pretty
7	know	perhaps	pray	bugle	dismal
8	want	someday	convey	rainfall	cautious
9	crave	today	weigh	dewdrop	normal
10	pant	wishful	prey	castle	piercing
11	wish	nicely	nay	folksong	careful
12	hope	truly	lay	eyesore	magic

DICE #	F	G	H
2	sleigh	auto's	swinging
3	bay	wishbone's	stringing
4	stay	wire's	singing
5	jay	coach's	trying
6	flay	valley's	crying
7	say	river's	flying
8	pay	siren's	sobbing
9	stray	treetop's	calling
10	way	pansy's	snowing
11	play	hatrack's	flowing
12	tray	shoestore's	clinging

CHECKING YOUR READING—LEVEL 1

1. What is a servomechanism?
2. What was the early definition of cybernetics and what meaning has the word now taken?
3. What technique has been suggested to do a fairly accurate evaluation of whether or not a computer can simulate a human being when it comes to carrying on a conversation?
4. What two techniques can be used in designing sentences and phrases to be used by the computer in carrying on a dialogue?
5. What key function can be programmed into the computer which would seem to indicate that there would be no limit to what the computer could learn?
6. What is considered to be the next frontier in artificial intelligence?
7. Toward what 2 goals should computer scientists be aiming?
8. Name the three stages of the development of artificial intelligence.

VOCABULARY ASSIGNMENT

Continue developing your vocabulary by writing brief definitions for the words and phrases in bold print in this section.

CHECKING YOUR READING—LEVEL 2

1. What key characteristic must be developed in moveable robots to make them appear 'intelligent'?
2. Give three examples of computer applications which seem to reproduce human functions or the human senses.
3. What are the two types of simulations which are used to represent real world systems?
4. In simulations, what is meant by the target system?
5. What are the two types of classifications of games?
6. What is meant by the minimax principle?
7. How is a tree diagram used in programming the computer to play games?
8. What usually must exist or be pre-programmed into the computer before the computer is able to write poetry?

VOCABULARY ASSIGNMENT—LEVEL 2

Continue developing your vocabulary by writing brief definitions for the words and phrases in bold print in this section.

Programming From Business and Industry

1. MEMO 19-- 05 25
   To: Jack LeSage, Junior Programmer
   c.c.: Jane Barnes, Senior Programmer
   From: George Maw, Systems Analyst
   Re: Bank Reconciliation Statement
   It has come to my attention that it takes some considerable time each month to reconcile the bank statement. As you are aware our bank account information is kept in two places. The bank, of course, keeps track of the transactions in our account. Our junior accountant, who is responsible for making bank deposits, is also responsible for keeping a duplicate record.
   At the month end the bank sends us a statement and it takes some time for the junior accountant to check over the statement to make sure there have been no mistakes made at either the bank's end or ours.
   Write a program to assist the clerk in reconciling the bank statement. It would appear that you should prepare a number of prompts to guide the accountant through the program. In general terms the program is made up of two parts.

The first part of the program is designed to make any necessary changes in the information supplied by the bank statement. The goal of this part of the program is to identify what we might call the *true bank balance* as at the end of the month. At first one would think that the balance according to the bank statement would be the true balance, but there are situations that the bank does not know about which should be included. In order to determine the true bank balance the following three steps should be taken:

1) Input into the computer the bank balance according to the bank statement as of the cut off date.

2a) *Subtract* from that amount all outstanding cheques, that is, any cheques we have written prior to that date which have not yet cleared the bank.

2b) *Subtract* from the bank amount any other types of deductions which the bank might not know about. For example, it might be possible that the bank teller keyed into the updating terminal an amount transposing two figures, which resulted in our having more added to our account than should have been. For example, $629 was keyed in as $692. This step would be provided in the program to adjust such a situation.

3) Provide a routine which would *add* to the bank's figures any amount which should have been in our account as of the cut off date. It might be possible that there was a deposit right at the end of the month which had not yet been included. (For example, sometimes a deposit made after three o'clock on a Friday is put into a person's account the following Monday. A deposit such as this at the end of the month might not be included in the bank statement.) Similar to 2b above there could have been a transposition error such that the bank teller keyed in as a deposit an amount less than what should have been. The difference should be added to the account.

After these adding and subtracting routines have been accomplished the end result would be the *true bank balance*.

The second half of this program involves reconciling *our* records. The pattern is very similar to the above. In this case, however, we begin with the balance in our account as of the cut off date according to *our* records.

1) Input into the computer the balance of the bank account according to our records, as of the cut off date.

2) *Subtract* from our balance any amount we have discovered from the bank statement that should have been subtracted from our records. For example, any bank charges which have been included in the bank statement should be subtracted out of our account.
Sometimes a cheque which we have deposited might bounce because there are insufficient funds to cover it. This amount would

have to be subtracted out of our account. By the way, this amount should be added into our accounts receivable control and the customer's subsidiary account.

3) *Add* to our account any additional amounts which we have subsequently discovered should have been put in. For example, if the bank has paid us interest add in that amount. Of if we discovered that we had made a mistake and, for example, recorded a deposit at a lower figure than what was actually the case, add in the difference.

After these additions and subtractions have taken place we should then have an amount called the true bank balance.

If the reconciliation has been done correctly the two halves of the program should produce the identical figure. That is, the true bank balance should be the same in both parts of the program.

If it does not balance, subtract the final figure of one of the halves from the other figure. Prompt the user to look for an amount equal to the difference.

Planned and coded _____

Fully tested and documented _____

CHAPTER 23

APTITUDE FOR PROGRAMMING

IS PROGRAMMING FOR YOU?

Not everyone can become a programmer. Some people just do not have the interest. Other people have the interest, but they do not have the necessary aptitude. If the road to becoming a professional programmer were an easy one, there would be many more programmers and probably the pay for programmers as a group would be considerably lower than it now is. As one programmer once said: "Programming is not for the masses, it is for the select few." Just how *select* that few is has not yet been determined.

Programming is a relatively new science. In many cases, the approaches used to instruct student programmers have been adopted from the methods used in instructing in other disciplines. Perhaps with time, the instruction techniques will improve, resulting in many more programmers being made available to the economy.

JUST WHAT MAKES A GOOD PROGRAMMER?

Although the author has been teaching programming to students for a number of years, he has been unable to predict with any degree of certainty who in a class beginning a course will be successful and who will not. Various types of aptitude tests have been used, but no one test seems to predict accurately the degree of success of the student. Even high academic achievement has not necessarily been a good predictor of who will be a good programmmer and who will not. Conversely, some students with quite average marks became excellent programmers. After a number of years of observing this phenomenon, the author has come up with a general guideline for students to consider before they begin programming:

1. A good programmer must have a special type of analytical mind. This is not necessarily the type of analysis used in math and science, for some non-math and science students are very successful at programming. This special type of analysis seems to include the ability to break

down complex jobs into small simple tasks in the correct sequence. Only a relatively small number of people have or can acquire this special skill.

2. A good programmer has considerable patience and determination. Some people find that they grasp things fairly quickly and do not have the patience to work away at something that might take extended periods of concentration on detail. The author has found that a number of students who achieved very high marks in non-computer subjects appear to obtain those marks by quickly grasping what is being taught. They usually understand the programming concepts, but have never acquired the discipline for *practice*. These students are not successful because they are unable to build up a skill which requires considerable precision.

3. Programming students must acquire the necessary discipline and determination to take on a major project and work at it consistently over the allotted time, monitoring their own progress so that the task is completed within that time.

4. A few students have the uncanny ability to make difficult that which is relatively simple. Instead of using the KISS rule (Keep It Short and Simple) these programming students appear to want to use complex and somewhat tricky programming routines, such that if their program works it is more by luck than good management. It has been our experience that about half these students can be salvaged by insisting on good programming structure; whereas the other half of these students refuse to lower what they perceive to be reasonable expectations for themselves.

MOTIVATION

As with any job, proper motivation is important in learning programming and establishing a positive attitude toward sound programming concepts. There are a number of components to good motivation. Some of them could be listed as:

1. having long term goals clearly defined
2. being provided with a reason why things are done as they are
3. attempting to identify with a professional programmer, his/her type of work, and responsibility
4. working with an interactive computer or a batch computer with a very rapid turnaround
5. having a carefully designed course
6. being provided with a good learning environment so that the student can work at his or her own rate within a reasonable time line developed by the instructor
7. having almost constant support and encouragement by an instructor who uses good judgment and suitable pacing for the work to be done
8. obtaining successful output on *practical* programming assignments

INHIBITORS TO SUCCESS

Certainly, if any of the above components for success were missing then the possibility of success becomes more and more remote. It is appropriate to more specifically identify those things which tend to turn off student programmers. Again, after considerable observation over a number of years the author believes the following to be the major stumbling blocks to programming success:

1. Too much dependence on the computer as a motivator for the student.
2. Too much analytical work day after day without any variation of the thought process. (For example, a programming student is certainly put off by preparing some logic representation such as a flow chart for problem after problem, or writing, testing and debugging *similar* programs especially if the programs are more of a 'brain teaser' type rather than practical. There should be a healthy balance between developing specific programming skills and learning about computer hardware, software, documentation techniques and computer applications.)
3. Working a long time on a program, not having it successfully run by the due date, then having a new problem assigned. ("It is just like having two failures—zero from the computer and zero on the project from the teacher," said one student.)

APTITUDE TESTS

There is wide disagreement in industry as to the effectiveness of the so-called programming aptitude tests. They are still used in industry to some degree and are used by programming schools primarily as an attention-getting sales gimmick to lure students into programming courses. Because you might be exposed to an aptitude test, it is worthwhile going over the various types.

SYMBOL SERIES

An aptitude test using symbols is designed to test whether or not you are able to understand and identify relationships between various shapes. Some people have an aptitude for this, others do not. Just how this type of test indicates a programming aptitude is still uncertain!

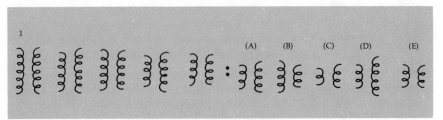

Figure 23.1

Notice in the diagram the initial part of the question shows a series of shapes related in some way to each other. The second part indicates choices from which the person selects the shape which would be used as the next item in the first part. In the illustration that would be the shape labelled (c).

VERBAL ANALOGIES

The objective of the verbal analogies aptitude test is to have the person taking the test complete the sentence by selecting the appropriate words from the word lists. The completed sentence should demonstrate that the person tested has identified the correct relationship between two groups of words.

_____ is to SKATE as WATER is
to _____   _____ is to SLEET as SIP is to __

(A) ice	(W) swim	(A) sunshine	(W) clip
(B) chemist	(X) distill	(B) slip	(X) chew
(C) desert	(Y) rain	(C) barometer	(Y) devour
(D) rat	(Z) sport.	(D) mist	(Z) gulp.

Figure 23.2

This test has also been criticized because the relationships seen by some taking the test might be different from what the author of the test item intended, but equally as valid. It also assumes you know the meaning of all the words.

MATHEMATICAL RELATIONSHIP TESTS

Tests which apply to mathematical problems or relationships seem to have more validity than the ones mentioned up to now. In computer programming certain relationships are used and problems are solved using multi-stepped solutions. One popular *relationship* test involves determining whether or not a certain given relationship is correct, incorrect, or not determinable.

Fact	Conclusion	Correct	Incorrect	Not Determinable
$X > Y \geqslant Z$	$Z \neq X$	A ✓	B	C
$X \doteq Y \geqslant Z$	$Z \neq X$	A	B	C ✓

In the first example, because X is greater than Y, which could be either greater than or equal to Z, then X cannot be equal to Z. Therefore the conclusion is correct. In the second example, X is equal to Y, which could be either equal to or greater than Z. It is possible that X would be equal to Z or it is also possible X would be greater than Z. The conclusion that Z is not equal to X is not necessarily correct, nor is it wrong. Therefore, the correct response is that it is 'not determinable.'

MATHEMATICAL WORD PROBLEMS

Many computer programming problems are posed in words. The solutions usually require some analysis and the carrying out of a series of steps. Aptitude tests using mathematical word problems appear to relate best to the real world of programming.

Example: A rectangular flower bed whose dimensions are 16 m by 12 m is surrounded by a walk 3 m wide. The area of the walk is

(a) 93 m²   (d) 165 m²

(b) 396 m²   (e) none of these

(c) 204 m²

FOLLOWING CONDITIONAL INSTRUCTIONS

Perhaps the test which most closely shows a relationship to flowcharting or decision tables is the one which requires the student to follow instructions, some of which cause different actions to be performed depending on certain conditions. This type of test also causes the student to use 'address' box numbers with values in the box—a very confusing task for some people.

For example, the following are the directions and diagram for such a test:

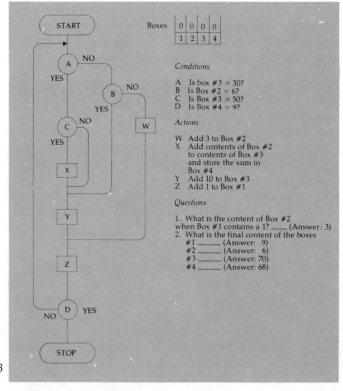

Figure 23.3

1. A flowchart is simply a 'road map' by which you must find your way from one 'town' to the next, and obey every instruction you come to.
2. Always follow the 'road' downward, or to the right, unless an arrow indicates a different direction, or unless an instruction required you to do otherwise.
3. When you come to a fork in the 'road' there will be a question for you to answer; match your answer with the 'signposts' on the branches leading out of the fork, and you will know which way to go.
4. When you are told to put a number into a box, it is understood that whatever number was previously in that box has just been erased.
5. All numbers used in this test are to be whole numbers.

TIPS FOR ANSWERING APTITUDE TESTS

With some familiarization and a few tips one should be able to take an aptitude test with a certain amount of confidence. The above sections have provided the orientation. Now for some tips as published in a book on how to take aptitude tests.[1]

1. Suppose you are unable to answer a number of questions in the test. Don't get upset. No one is expected to get a perfect score, and there are no 'passing' or 'failing' grades. Your score shows what you do in comparison with the other candidates.
2. Work steadily and as rapidly as you can without becoming careless. Take the questions in order, but do not fritter away your time by thinking too long over questions which contain extremely difficult or unfamiliar material.
3. For each section of the examination, you should read the directions with care. If you read too hastily, you may miss an important direction. This may result in your losing many valuable points.
4. Should you guess? Yes—provided you have even a slight idea of what may be the correct answer.
5. Do not place too much emphasis on speed. The time element is a factor, but it is not all-important. Accuracy should not be sacrificed for speed.
   Use these methods to answer multiple choice questions correctly:
1. Read the item carefully to see what the examiner is after. Re-read it if necessary.
2. Mentally reject answers that are clearly wrong.
3. Suspect as being wrong any of the choices which contain broad statements hinging on *cue* words like:

[1]Luftig, Milton *Computer Programmer Aptitude Tests*, New York: Arco Publishing Co. Inc. 1958.

absolutely	all
always	completely
entirely	forever
indefinitely	inevitable
infinite	inflexible
inordinately	never
only	peculiarly
positive	quite
self-evident	sole
totally	undoubtedly
unequivocal	unquestionable
wholly	without exception

If you're unsure of the meanings of any of these words, look them up in your dictionary.

4. A well-constructed multiple choice item will avoid obviously incorrect choices. The good examiner will try to write a cluster of answers, all of which are plausible. Use the clue words to help you pick the most correct answer.

5. In the case of items where you are doubtful of the answer, you might be able to bring to bear the information you have gained from previous study. This knowledge might be sufficient to indicate that some of the suggested answers are not so plausible. Eliminate such answers from further consideration.

6. Then concentrate on the remaining suggested answers. The more you eliminate in this way, the better your chances of getting the item right.

7. If the item is in the form of an incomplete statement, it sometimes helps to try to complete the statement before you look at the suggested answers. Then see if the way you have completed the statement corresponds with any of the answers provided. If one is found, it is likely to be the correct one.

8. Use your head! Make shrewd inferences. Sometimes with a little thought, and the information that you have, you can reason out the answer. We're suggesting a method of intelligent guessing in which you can become quite expert with a little practice. It's a useful method that may help you with some debatable answers.

Level 2

CAREERS IN COMPUTING

From the time that computers became commercially available the forecast was made that there would be an ever increasing number of job positions related to computers. Each year since then the forecast has remained constant or has been revised upward.

As more information and word processing devices become common, new tasks and new skills are required. The scene is changing almost on a daily basis.

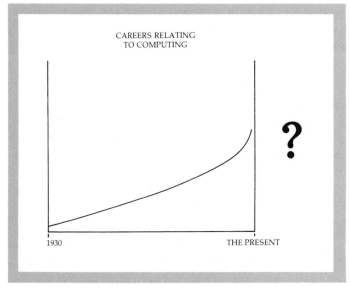

CAREERS RELATING TO COMPUTING

1930   THE PRESENT

Figure 23.4

It would be unwise to attempt to summarize all the positions relating to computers and word processing equipment which are currently available because the scene is changing so quickly. It would be useful, however, to highlight some of the most common positions which have been available over a number of years.

*Senior Programmer under general supervision, develops and prepares machine logic flowcharts for the solution of business, engineering and/or scientific problems through the use of electronic data processing equipment. Usually competent, working independently most of the time. May give some direction and guidance to juniors. Analyses problems outlined by systems analysts in terms of detailed equipment requirements and capabilities. Designs detailed machine logic flowcharting. Verifies program logic by preparing test data for trial runs. Tests and debugs programs. Prepares instruction sheets to guide computer operators during production runs. Evaluates and modifies existing programs to take into account changes in systems requirements or equipment configurations.

Junior Programmer under direct supervision, assists in the review and analysis of detailed computer systems specifications and the preparation of the program instructions. Usually competent to work on several phases of programming with only general direction, but still needs some instruc-

* Courtesy of Canadian Processing Society.

tion and guidance for the other phases. Assists in, and in some cases, carries out independently, the preparation of all levels of block diagrams and machine logic flowcharts. Codes program instructions. Assists in the documentation of all procedures used throughout the system.

Manager or Supervisor of Computer Operations plans, organizes and controls the computer operations section in the operation of the computer and peripheral data processing equipment. Usually considered as being in charge of all activities of equipment operations. Establishes detailed schedules for the utilization of all equipment in the computer operations section. Reviews equipment logs and reports to the manager of data processing on equipment operation efficiency for the section.

Senior Computer Operator under general supervision, monitors and controls an electronic computer by operating the central console. Usually competent to work at the highest level of all computer operation phases, while working independently most of the time. May give some direction and guidance to juniors. Studies program operating instruction sheets to determine equipment set-up and run operation. Confers with technical personnel in the event errors require a change in instructions or sequence of operations. Maintains operating records such as machine performance and production reports.

Junior Computer Operator under direct supervision, assists high level classifications in monitoring and controlling an electronic computer. Usually competent to work on several phases of computer operations with only general direction, but still needs some instruction and guidance for the other phases. Assists in carrying out the various duties associated with operating a computer in connection with the computer itself or the auxiliary equipment directly associated with the computer.

Data Control Supervisor supervises and directs the personnel who control data entering and leaving the computer and keypunch area. Responsible for schedule and work being produced as to completeness and accuracy.

Data Control Clerk works under direct supervision to order and code information presented to keypunch operators and to coordinate the flow of jobs to the computer. He or she organizes the output in report form and expedites distribution of computer results, tracks down errors, omissions and inconsistencies of processing data.

Manager of All Data Processing plans, organizes, and controls the overall activities of electronic data processing installations including systems analysis, programming, and computer operational activities.

Data Processing Manager has responsibilities similar to those of Manager of All Data Processing except that it usually includes only one or possibly two of the major areas; analysis, programming operations.

Manager or Supervisor of Systems Analysis plans, organizes, and controls the activities of the systems analysis section in a company installation. Plans for the implementation of new or revised systems and procedures. Consults with and advises other departments on systems and procedures. Co-ordinates section activities with the activities of other sections and departments.

Senior Systems Analyst under general direction, formulates logical statements of business of scientific and/or engineering problems and devises procedures for solutions of these problems through the use of electronic data processing systems. Usually competent to work at the highest level of all technical phases of systems analysis while working alone most of the time. May give some direction and guidance to junior analysts. Confers with officials, scientists, and engineers concerned with defining data processing problems. Senior Systems Analysts may also perform the functions of a Senior Programmer.

Manager or Supervisor of Programming plans, organizes and controls the preparation of computer programs for the solution of business, scientific and/or engineering problems through the use of electronic data processing equipment. Usually considered as being in full charge of all programming activities. Assigns, outlines and coordinates the work of programmers engaged in writing computer programs and routines. Establishes standards for block diagramming, machine flowcharting and programming procedures. Collaborates with systems analysts and other technical personnel in scheduling equipment analysis, feasibility studies and systems planning.

Operations Research—Senior requires high academic training normally a master's or doctorate degree in mathematics or science. Actively involved in a variety of operations research projects for at least five years. Uses the skills of simulation, model building, and market research to solve problems in business, scientific and engineering applications and has the responsibility for planning projects and supervising junior staff members.

CHECKING YOUR READING—LEVEL 1

1. What are the four attributes or characteristics of a good programmer?
2. Outline the three motivational factors, from the eight listed, which you consider to be the most important.
3. What are the three inhibitors to success?
4. Does obtaining a good score on a computer aptitude test necessarily mean that you would become a good programmer?
5. What is the symbol series aptitude test?
6. What is the principle of the word analogy aptitude test?
7. In what way are mathematical relationships similar to what is actually done in computer programming?
8. Why are mathematical word problems similar to real word programming?
9. How are 'following conditional instructions' aptitude tests similar to logic flowcharts?

10. Of the tips offered for writing aptitude tests, which three tips seem to you to be the most valuable?

CHECKING YOUR READING—LEVEL 2

1. What is the essential difference between a senior programmer and a junior programmer?
2. What is the difference between the manager of all data processing and a senior systems analyst?
3. Which of the careers listed in this section seemed to suit you? Write a short report as to why you think that would be a suitable career.

PROJECTS

Programming From Business and Industry

MEMO 19-- 05 30
To: Jane Barnes, Senior Programmer
From: George Maw, Systems Analyst
Re: A Cashflow Program
Our banker has been concerned about our ability to pay off our loan. A request has been made for us to maintain a cashflow report. The report would contain a twelve month forecast of expected cash income and outgo. At the end of the month the report would be updated, adding a month at the end, to maintain the twelve month picture.

In the early stages of developing this program it might be necessary to do the report for a four or five month period instead of the full twelve months. Subsequently the program could be enlarged to cover the full twelve month period. Down the left-hand column of the report would be the following items:

1) cash in bank at start of month
2) petty cash at start of month
3) total cash (add 1 and 2)
4) expected cash sales
5) expected collections
6) other money expected
7) total receipts (add 4, 5, and 6)
8) total cash and receipts (add 3 and 7)
9) anticipated payments for the month
10) cash balance at month end (subtract 9 from 8)

To the right of this column would be the various amounts estimated for each month.

The program should provide prompting in order to initially load the forecast. The program then should enable the report to be easily updated by dropping a month at the beginning and adding one at the end.

Planned and coded _____

Fully tested and documented _____

CODE OF ETHICS FOR CERTIFIED COMPUTER PROFESSIONALS*

Certified computer professionals, consistent with their obligation to the public at large, should promote the understanding of data processing methods and procedures using every resource at their command.

Certified computer professionals have an obligation to their profession to uphold the high ideals and the level of personal knowledge certified by the Certificate held. They should also encourage the dissemination of knowledge pertaining to the development of the computer profession.

Certified computer professionals have an obligation to serve the interests of their employers and clients loyally, diligently, and honestly.

Certified computer professionals must not engage in any conduct or commit any act which is discreditable to the reputation or integrity of the data processing profession.

Certified computer professionals must not imply that the Certificates which they hold are their sole claim to professional competence.

CODES OF CONDUCT AND GOOD PRACTICE FOR CERTIFIED COMPUTER PROFESSIONALS

The essential elements relating to conduct that identify a professional activity are:

A high standard of skill and knowledge.

A confidential relationship with people served.

Public reliance upon the standards of conduct and established practice.

The observance of an ethical code.

Therefore, these Codes have been formulated to strengthen the professional status of certified computer professionals.

1. *Preamble*

1.1: The basic issue, which may arise in connection with any ethical proceedings before a Certification Council, is whether a holder of a Certificate administered by that Council has acted in a manner which violates the Code of Ethics for certified computer professionals.

1.2: Therefore, the ICCP has elaborated the existing Code of Ethics by means of a Code of Conduct, which defines more specifically an individual's professional responsibility. This step was taken in recognition of questions and concerns as to what constitutes professional and ethical conduct in the computer profession.

1.3: The ICCP has reserved for and delegated to each Certification Council the right to

revoke any Certificate which has been issued under its administration in the event that the recipient violates the Code of Ethics, as amplified by the Code of Conduct. The revocation proceedings are specified by rules governing the business of the Certification Council and provide for protection of the rights of any individual who may be subject to revocation of a Certificate held.

1.4: Insofar as violation of the Code of Conduct may be difficult to adjudicate, the ICCP has also promulgated a Code of Good Practice, the violation of which does not in itself constitute a reason to revoke a Certificate. However, any evidence concerning a serious and consistent breach of the Code of Good Practice may be considered as additional circumstantial evidence in any ethical proceedings before a Certification Council.

1.5: Whereas the Code of Conduct is of a fundamental nature, the Code of Good Practice is expected to be amended from time to time to accommodate changes in the social environment and to keep up with the development of the computer profession.

1.6: A Certification Council will not consider a complaint where the holder's conduct is already subject to legal proceedings. Any complaint will only be considered when the legal action is completed, or it is established that no legal proceedings will take place.

1.7: Recognizing that the language contained in all sections of either the Code of Conduct or the Code of Good Practice is subject to interpretations beyond those intended, the ICCP intends to confine all Codes to matters pertaining to personal actions of individual certified computer professionals in situations for which they can be held directly accountable without reasonable doubt.

2. *Code of Conduct*

2.1: Disclosure: Subject to the confidential relationships between oneself and one's employer or client, one is expected not to transmit information which one acquires during the practice of one's profession in any situation which may harm or seriously affect a third party.

2.2: Social Responsibility: One is expected to combat ignorance about information processing technology in those public areas where one's application can be expected to have an adverse social impact.

2.3: Conclusions and Opinions: One is expected to state a conclusion on a subject in

*Institute for Certification of Computer Professionals

one's field only when it can be demonstrated that it has been founded on adequate knowledge. One will state a qualified opinion when expressing a view in an area within one's professional competence but not supported by relevant facts.

2.4: Identification: One shall properly qualify oneself when expressing an opinion outside of one's professional competence in the event that such an opinion could be identified by a third party as expert testimony, or if by inference the opinion can be expected to be used improperly.

2.5: Integrity: One will not knowingly lay claims to competence one does not demonstrably possess.

2.6: Conflict of Interest: One shall act with strict impartiality when purporting to give independent advice. In the event that the advice given is currently or potentially influential to one's personal benefit, full and detailed disclosure of all relevant interests will be made at the time the advice is provided. One will not denigrate the honesty or competence of a fellow professional or a competitor, with intent to gain an unfair advantage.

2.7: Accountability: The degree of professional accountability for results will be dependent on the position held and the type of work performed. For instance:

A senior executive is accountable for the quality of work performed by all individuals the person supervises and for ensuring that recipients of information are fully aware of known limitations in the results provided.

The personal accountability of consultants and technical experts is especially important because of the positions of unique trust inherent in their advisory roles. Consequently, they are accountable for seeing to it that known limitations of their work are fully disclosed, documented, and explained.

2.8: Protection of Privacy: One shall have special regard for the potential effects of computer-based systems on the right of privacy of individuals whether this is within one's own organization, among customers or suppliers, or in relation to the general public.

Because of the privileged capability of computer professionals to gain access to computerized files, especially strong strictures will be applied to those who have used their positions of trust to obtain information from computerized files for their personal gain.

Where it is possible that decisions can be made within a computer-based system which could adversely affect the personal security, work, or career of an individual, the system design shall specifically provide for decision review by a responsible executive who will

thus remain accountable and identifiable for that decision.

3. *Code of Good Practice*

3.1: Education: One has a special responsibility to keep oneself fully aware of developments in information processing technology relevant to one's current professional occupation. One will contribute to the interchange of technical and professional information by encouraging and participating in education activities directed both to fellow professionals and to the public at large. One will do all in one's power to further public understanding of computer systems. One will contribute to the growth of knowledge in the field to the extent that one's expertise, time, and position allow.

3.2: Personal Conduct: Insofar as one's personal and professional activities interact visibly to the same public, one is expected to apply the same high standards of behaviour in one's personal life as are demanded in one's professional activities.

3.3: Competence: One shall at all times exercise technical and professional competence at least to the level one claims. One shall not deliberately withhold information in one's possession unless disclosure of that information could harm or seriously affect another party, or unless one is bound by a proper, clearly defined confidential relationship. One shall not deliberately destroy or diminish the value or effectiveness of a computer-based system through acts of commission or omission.

3.4: Statements: One shall not make false or exaggerated statements as to the state of affairs existing or expected regarding any aspect of information technology or the use of computers.

In communicating with lay persons, one shall use general language whenever possible and shall not use technical terms or expressions unless there exist no adequate equivalents in the general language.

3.5: Discretion: One shall exercise maximum discretion in disclosing, or permitting to be disclosed, or using to one's own advantage, any information relating to the affairs of one's present or previous employers or clients.

3.6: Conflict of Interest: One shall not hold, assume, or consciously accept a position in which one's interests conflict or are likely to conflict with one's current duties unless that interest has been disclosed in advance to all parties involved.

3.7: Violations: One is expected to report violations of the Code, testify in ethical proceedings where one has expert or first-hand knowledge, and serve on panels to judge complaints of violations of ethical conduct.

Page 1, courtesy of CP Air; pages 3, 4, 5, 6, 7, 10, 13, 14, 20 (bottom), 21 (bottom), 86, 87 (top), 132, 256, 305, 308, 310, courtesy of IBM; page 20 (top), Mohawk Data; page 21 (top), Commodore Business Machines; page 22, Air Canada; pages 87 and 92, NCR; page 90, Optical Scanning Corporation; page 91, courtesy Decision, Oakland, California; pages 93, 94, 95, 291, 352 and 353, courtesy of Moore Business Forms; pages 169, 200 and 345, courtesy of Honeywell Ltd.; page 197, reproduced by courtesy of Revenue Canada, Taxation; page 230, CNCP Telecommunications; page 250, Illustration Services Dept., University of Guelph; page 266, copyright AES Data Ltée/Ltd.; pages 311 and 312, from Radio Shack DOS Manual (pages 2-6 and 2-7). Reproduced by permission of Tandy Corporation. Pages 322, 323, 325 and 328, reprinted from INFOSYSTEMS (April, 1980, November, 1980, March, 1980 and September, 1980). Copyright Hitchcock Publishing Company. Page 335 (top) Cal Comp; page 335 (bottom) courtesy of Chrysler Corporation; page 336, (c) Electronic Associates, Inc. Reprinted with their permission. Page 340, from *Polyphony* magazine, September/October, 1978; page 364, from *Computer Programmer Aptitude Tests* by Milton Luftig, M.B.A. © 1975 by permission of Arco Publishing Co. Inc.

Index